GENERATION *TEXT*

GENERATION *TEXT*

Raising Well-Adjusted Kids in an Age of Instant Everything

Dr. Michael Osit

AMACOM

American Management Association

New York • Atlanta • Brussels • Chicago • Mexico City • San Francisco
Shanghai • Tokyo • Toronto • Washington, D.C.

Library of Congress Cataloging-in-Publication Data

Osit, Michael M.
    Generation text : raising well-adjusted kids in an age of instant everything /
Michael Osit.
        p.   cm.
    Includes bibliographical references and index.
    ISBN-13: 978-0-8144-0932-9
    ISBN-10: 0-8144-0932-6
    1. Child rearing.   2. Technology and children.   I. Title.
HQ769.O854   2008
649'.7—dc22

                                                                    2008013544

Printing Number

10   9   8   7   6   5   4   3   2   1

To my wife, Terri,

*Who has given me access to a wonderful life
and an excess of love*

Contents

....

Acknowledgments

···

EVEN THOUGH IT WAS ME WHO SAT WITH MY LAPTOP FOR COUNTLESS hours, there were many people behind the scenes whose help and support made writing this book possible. I am privileged and proud to be able to acknowledge their assistance.

First, I would like to thank all of my patients and their families for sharing a piece of their lives so that others can benefit. The privilege of working with all of you teaches me something new every 50 minutes.

It was very gracious of Jeffrey Coles, Ph.D., of the University of Southern California Annenberg School Center for the Digital Future, to provide me with his extensive and insightful research, *The 2007 Digital Future Report: Surveying The Digital Future-Year Six.*

My concerns about how difficult it is to grow up in today's world was among countless interesting discussions with Rosalie Greenberg, M.D., author of a must-read book, *Bipolar Kids.* As usual, Dr. Greenberg went above and beyond when she took it upon herself to pitch my ideas to her literary agent. This book became a reality due to her efforts.

It is a blessing to be surrounded by professionals who know their business. My respect, appreciation, and gratitude to Joelle Delbourgo, for having the insight and vision to give a first-time author and a worthy topic an opportunity to be heard. My literary agent, Molly Lyons, has been completely supportive and helpful every step of this process. Thank you for taking me by the hand and introducing me to the amazing world of publishing. I also want to thank Molly for introducing me to Christina Baker-Kline and Alys Yablon-Wylen, who not only provided fantastic suggestions, but were able to make my words sing—even when they were tone deaf.

I have the utmost respect and gratitude for Jacquie Flynn, my editor at AMACOM. Jacquie has uncanny understanding and insight, always providing just the right amount of guidance to help me crystallize my ideas and communicate them clearly.

I am extremely fortunate to have the support of wonderful friends. My discussions and exchange of ideas with the Linda Lane crew have contributed enormously, providing me with perspective and ideas. It also helped to have Neurvana on Long Beach Island supplying the sounds of gulls and surf as tranquil inspiration.

I want to thank Margot Kotler for offering me a wonderful essay that hit the nail on the head. I am quite certain that Margot will be writing her own acknowledgments one day.

Michael Rosen, who happens to be my brother-in-law, friend, and resident computer mechanic, is always on call for a computer crisis. He generously gives his time and expertise, performing magic inside the world of CPUs.

I come from a large, loving family with supportive parents who attended every baseball game (Cleo and all), school play, and academic milestone. I know that I have learned valuable lessons about being a parent from my parents. Without realizing it, your collection of stray animals and less fortunate people provided me with the desire to help others.

Finding the words to convey my ideas in this book was easy. But there are no words that adequately express the endless love I feel for my wife, Terri, and my children, Daniel, Nicole, and Matthew. Terri, your tolerance for my absence this past summer is just the tip of the iceberg, exemplifying how you enable me to pursue my career. Your caring, sensitivity, thoughtfulness, and ability to keep on giving makes everyone around you better. My children call me "The Terminator," but the secret truth is that I derive all of my strength and stamina from your love. Daniel, Nicole, and Matthew are the children I could only dream about having. I am the luckiest father in the world to have all of you (and you too, Bailey). I know that you will continue to make me proud.

GENERATION *TEXT*

CHAPTER 1

The World at Their Feet—
and Fingertips

·····································

Unfazed and Unimpressed

A SIXTEEN-YEAR-OLD GIRL ENTERS MY OFFICE, PROUDLY FLAUNTING her new cell phone—probably the fourth or fifth new phone she's had since she started seeing me several years ago. She obviously wants me to notice the phone, so I congratulate her and ask what new features it has.

She gives me a perplexed look. "What do you mean?"

Trying to ask the question in a different way, I say, "What does it allow you to do?"

She shrugs. "Everything."

The fact of the matter is that the cell phone probably has three or four more features than her previous phone had. Beyond that, it has about thirty features she could have listed in answer to my question. But she has become so accustomed to the technology that she is unfazed by the color screen, caller ID, Web access, memory dial, still camera, video camera, and other features available to her on this tiny device. She takes these things for granted, automatically upgrading her phone whenever technology advances a half-step forward, whether she "needs" the new features or not.

The seemingly constant stream of upgrades for cell phones and other high-tech devices certainly does not overwhelm kids living in the millennium. The problem is that as they are taking these changes in stride, their parents are left in the dust. As a result, a huge cultural divide is being created between parents and kids.

Darwin's theory of evolution purports that as the environment changes animals create adaptations. This change process occurs over the course of thousands of years. Remarkably, kids today are regularly adapting to what I refer to as the Technological Evolution over short periods of mere months, while we as parents often remain confused, unsure of what our kids now know, and sometimes intimidated or resistant to the changing technology. Common tasks and activities routinely performed by our kids are alien to us. The ease with which our kids can communicate with each other, as well as with perfect strangers, enables them to maintain a private world that escapes parental awareness.

The cell phone is a prime example of how easily kids adapt to the frequent changes in technology, how they use technology to suit their needs and desires, and, in turn, how technology is shaping their attitudes, behaviors, and values.

In some ways cell phones and other technology devices facilitate friendships for the technologically astute child, but in other ways they hinder social-skill development. Kids have access to each other and the larger world to a much greater extent than they ever did before, but less effort is required for them to communicate. Cell phones, the Internet, e-mail, and instant messaging reduce human contact and yet, paradoxically, make people constantly available and endlessly distractible.

As another teenage patient tells me, when a high school student wants to talk to a friend sitting on the other side of the school cafeteria, he may be more inclined to call or text the friend on his cell phone than to walk across the room. If he were to walk across the cafeteria to speak to his friend, he may encounter a teacher or another kid he doesn't want to talk to. When he approaches the friend, he may have to wait to speak with him so as not to interrupt a conversation. He then must establish eye contact, read nonverbal cues in the conversation, and react to body language.

All of these rudimentary social skills are acquired with practice. In the past, social skills were practiced in the natural course of peer interactions. Today it's not uncommon for kids to spend more time relating to machines than to each other, making social skills more difficult to attain.

Because electronic gadgets are present in the majority of American households, they invade every aspect of our kids' lives, from the moment they wake up in the morning until they fall asleep to their favorite tunes on an iPod at night. High-tech, digitally driven machines are so much a part of our culture that kids can't escape their impact and influence on their psychological development, even if they wanted to. The pervasive impact our high-tech age has on kids creates unique challenges for their parents. The following chapters will help parents cope with, and eventually overcome, the challenges presented by children who belong to what I call Generation Text.

SHOULD WE BE WORRIED?

In the field of psychology, it is commonly accepted that a baby is born with personality traits and general behavior patterns determined by the neurobiological workings of his brain. Those neurobiological traits are rooted in the baby's family gene pool. The combination of one's biological heritage and customized brain wiring presents itself as one's temperament.

Once that baby begins to interact with family members and social environments, his biologically based personality traits and behaviors are shaped to varying degrees. Some features of his personality and behavior patterns are mitigated and others are accentuated, depending on how his parents and others respond to him.

Every person throughout history has had to negotiate positive and negative experiences in the social environment. The unique challenge facing Generation Text is the ease with which these kids interact with a much more powerful and complex social environment, one with far-reaching implications. Furthermore, because their parents are often shielded from the social environment that shapes their personality and behavior, Generation Text kids often have to navigate these psychological waters on their own.

Let's examine just a few of the areas in which Generation Text faces special challenges:

> ▶ *Aggressive Personality Traits.* An infant may be born with the biologically determined temperament of "aggressiveness." If, over the years, this child repeatedly experiences negative consequences for his behavior, doled out by parents employing firm limits, it is highly possible that the child's aggressive impulses will be controlled. On the other hand, if the child grows up in a family that provides positive reinforcement for aggressive behav-

ior, he will enter adulthood with an aggressive aspect to his personality.

But for Generation Text, the possibility of becoming an aggressive adult is not completely mitigated by his home environment. Exposure to violence in television shows, movies, and video games is universal. Although a child's parents might ban those violent shows and games from the family living room, kids know where to find them online, on wireless devices, and certainly outside the home as well.

► *Impulse Control.* Other variables, such as impulse control, evolve developmentally. I have an immature twelve-year-old patient who talks online with classmates and frequently gets into arguments because he writes before he thinks. Young children's neurological systems prevent them from having adequate impulse control. They often act before thinking. They are incapable of fathoming the potential consequences of their actions until their neurological systems are mature enough. When parents are overly indulgent, the development of impulse control can be severely impaired. If children do not experience negative consequences for impulsive acts, they will keep doing them. Of course, if parents are unaware of what their children are doing, they cannot help them develop a healthy impulse control.

► *Social Skills.* In addition to biology, family, and social influences, technology plays an increasingly large role in shaping the personality traits and behaviors of Generation Text, because of the nature of the interaction between the child and the machine. From voice mail to text messaging to instant messaging (IMing) to e-mail to Internet shopping, technologically driven communication limits or even eliminates human interaction. These "intermachine" interactions are not necessarily detrimental; the challenge for parents is to figure out how to use them to facilitate healthiness in our kids.

Technology has changed the nature of communication so dramatically that it is having a tremendous impact on the social-skill development of children. Social skills have traditionally been synonymous with "interpersonal" skills, meaning face-to-face interactions between two or more people. With communication increasingly synonymous with technology, a new means of developing social skills has arisen. Technology impinges on the amount of human contact our kids have, which can impede their ability to read other people's nonverbal cues in the real world. At the same time, it affords them the opportunity to interact with many people in a way that can, if parents succeed in setting proper guidelines and limits, minimize social awkwardness and facilitate positive relationships.

Growing up in a technological culture affects children's development in a way that is characteristically different from the way their parents grew up. Sure, this happens in every generation, but today's kids have tremendous and unprecedented access to the world. At the same time, technology affords them information and material goods in incredible excess. The magnitude of your kids' exposure to attitudes, values, and behavior that compete with your notion of what is appropriate and healthy for them is a far greater force than any other generation has experienced. Access and excess create real disruptions in their development, affecting it in a number of negative ways.

There is no question that technology is the conduit to access and excess issues influencing our children's development. The question is, how? And even more important: How can parents mitigate the negative impact of technology and capitalize on its positive influences?

INSTANT ACCESS TO EVERYTHING

Forty years ago, of course, the world was a different place. Unquestionably, it was fraught with its own obstacles and difficulties for children and families. But it was inconceivable to teenagers in the 1960s that their own children might one day communicate with friends and strangers at all hours of the day and night, without their parents' knowledge. In the 1960s, parents had to keep tabs on their kids' whereabouts around town. Today, kids can go anywhere in the world without leaving their bedrooms. How many parents and grandparents, when they were teenagers, could call their friends while walking down the street? How many could cook a pizza in a minute and a half? How many could conduct extensive research for a history paper without going to the library? Keep track of breaking news as it happened, minute-by-minute? Get free music and movies (often inappropriate for their age) without going to a store? Watch their favorite cartoons at 3 A.M. or whenever they wanted?

Technological advances have made many tasks so easy to accomplish, and part of this is truly wonderful. But like most things available to kids, if they go unchecked, unsupervised, or without proper education, these life tools can turn into weapons of self-destruction.

The amount of information available to children is mind-boggling. More than 2,500 satellites currently orbit the Earth, providing instantaneous global information. One example could be seen during the first days of the Iraqi conflict in 2003. The press reported live, via satellite, during actual battles. The images were immediate and graphic, and a number of the children who came to my office were terrified after seeing them. Children do not have an accurate sense of geographic distance, and they are egocentric by nature. They were watching a war, in real time, on their television sets, and it instilled a belief in some of my patients that the Iraqi army would soon bomb their houses. Because the stories and pictures could be accessed twenty-four hours a day on TV and the Internet, the conflict felt close to home. As a result, my patients' anxiety levels increased significantly.

Satellite technology is only one of the ways children access the world. According to the Cellular Telecommunications and Internet Association, cell phone use has skyrocketed from 4.3 million users in the United States in 1990 to 254 million by February 2008, while the average monthly cell phone bill decreased from $83.94 in 1990 to $49.94 in 2007. Children and adolescents represent a rapidly growing sector of that market. Internet subscriptions have increased 300% from 18 million subscribers in the mid-1990s to 66.2 million in 2007, with Internet access for almost nine out of every ten children living in a household with a computer and with 30 percent to 40 percent yearly increases in Internet subscribers.*

Access to the larger world is a double-edged sword. Vast amounts of valuable information can be found in seconds online, an unprecedented resource for developing minds. Teenagers can hone their social skills with casual peer interaction via e-mail, text messaging, and instant messaging. But as I have witnessed in my

---

*Enid Burns, "High Speed Internet Subscribers Revved in 2004," *The ClickZ Network*, July 8, 2005, www.Clickz.com.

practice, without proper monitoring and supervision, this kind of access can also cause serious psychological and developmental damage, affecting kids' relationships with their parents as well as their peers.

Generation Text experiences constant exposure to negative influences online—both actively pursued and inadvertently encountered. Hate messages posted on social networking sites like Facebook and MySpace, as well as personal websites, have had devastating results beyond the expected damage to self-esteem. Free websites promote drug usage and help kids learn techniques to use specific drugs. A seventeen-year-old patient showed me a picture he obtained online illustrating the proper way to grow marijuana plants indoors. He told me in detail how to create the proper climate, what nutrients the crop needed to flourish, and how to process the flower so that it transformed into potent cannabis. The site also offered special lights for sale and outlined an optimal lighting schedule. Is this something kids need to have access to? I don't think so. These examples barely scratch the surface of what Generation Text kids are getting involved with online.

TOO MANY CHOICES

Your kids are growing up in a culture that is fundamentally different from the one you knew as a child. It is markedly more complex, offering a multitude of options and opportunities—a world in which people, places, and things are accessible with the touch of a button. Frustration and confusion often accompany the numerous options that complexity offers. At the same time, we provide our kids with an excess of material possessions. They are bombarded with product placement in all forms of media and on the Internet. Our culture breeds an "I want the latest and best, and I want it now" attitude, and our kids are at the front of the line, taking for granted that they will have access to a technologically sophisticated world with an excess of material goods and options.

The scope and variety of choices available to consumers has increased significantly through the decades. On the surface, it is wonderful to have so much to choose from. But the options can also be overwhelming—for parents and kids alike.

A simple trip to the store for orange juice provides a perfect illustration of how our society has become more complex, specialized, and excessive. Walk down the breakfast cereal aisle and you may marvel at the many brands and types of cereal available, noting in particular the dizzying array of brightly colored, sugar-filled boxes on the shelves at a child's eye level.

After wandering the floor-plan maze, cleverly designed to slow the customer's progress and maximize exposure to the many goods for sale, you finally find the orange juice in its brightly lit refrigerator case. It is available in plastic jugs, glass bottles, cardboard cartons, child-size juice boxes or pouches, as well as that outmoded frozen concentrate in a can, in a range of sizes.

But that's not all. You can now select from so many types of orange juice in the fresh beverages section of your colossal supermarket that the choice may be bewildering. Unbelievably I counted twenty-nine different kinds of orange juice on my trip to the store. Really.

1.	Concentrate	16.	Tangy Orange
2.	Fresh-Squeezed	17.	Tangerine Orange
3.	Premium	18.	Banana Orange
4.	"Grovestand"	19.	Pineapple Orange
5.	"Homestyle"	20.	Strawberry Orange
6.	Vitamin-D Fortified	21.	Orange-Grapefruit
7.	Vitamin-C Enhanced	22.	Reduced Acid
8.	With Calcium	23.	Heart-Wise
9.	Calcium Pulp-Free	24.	"Healthy Kids"
10.	Calcium and Vitamin-D Enhanced	25.	"Immunity Defense"
11.	With Pulp	26.	Light 'n Healthy
12.	No Pulp	27.	Organic
13.	Some Pulp	28.	Fair-Trade
14.	Lots of Pulp	29.	Low Acid
15.	Extra Pulp		

Obviously, deciding what to buy was much easier when there were only one or two options available. Technology seems to have invaded even orange juice production, providing the ability to alter the product's consistency, add nutritional supplements, fortify the juice, and package it in a variety of ways.

Orange juice is just one example of how the age we live in has become vastly more complicated. The decision-making skills required to make this one purchase are mind-boggling. Just think about how many choices we—and our children—must make every day. These decision-making skills need to be honed more than ever so that we can cope with both trivial and life-altering choices. And kids are both the targets and recipients of most consumer-oriented technology.

THEN AND NOW

If many of us can remember an age with only one or two types of orange juice available, we can certainly recall a time when computers, the Internet, and cell phones did not yet exist. Our children have never known such a world. Over the past forty years, technology has changed so rapidly that by now kids are blasé about its wonders. The unimaginable for us has become their norm.

To illustrate how fundamentally society has changed in the past half-century, let us begin by considering a morning in the life of two teenagers—one who lived in the 1960s, and the other who is growing up today.

Bobby's Morning

Fourteen-year-old Bobby wakes up on a school day in 1968. He squints at his alarm clock, then turns on his brand-new transistor radio with fifteen AM stations—a birthday present. He tunes in to WABC to hear the latest rock 'n' roll tunes, then gets up, goes to the bathroom, takes a shower, and brushes his teeth. Back in his bedroom, he slips on a clean pair of Levi's (his other pair is in the wash) and a BVD T-shirt. He chooses the navy BVD because it is at the top of the drawer where the seven other BVD T-shirts, in assorted solid colors, are stacked in a pile. Bobby notices that the green one is on top now; he'll wear that one tomorrow.

The analog alarm clock is ticking away, edging toward the time that the bus will pick him up. He puts on his white canvas Converse high-tops and rushes downstairs for a quick breakfast. His mother is dishing out scrambled eggs, placing toast from the toaster onto his plate, pouring orange juice into an eight-ounce glass, and plucking bacon from the frying pan.

At the table, Bobby's father and little sister join him for breakfast. He chats with his mom and dad for a minute or two as he finishes eating, then goes out the front door to catch the yellow school bus. On the bus he talks to his friends about sports, music, the big science test during third period, and last night's episode of *Bonanza*.

Jake's Morning

When Jake wakes up in 2008, his CD digital alarm clock is blasting a high-pitched voice shouting M-rated ("Mature Audiences") lyrics. The volume is so high that it causes the walls to vibrate, which prompts a parental shout to lower the volume. After three more requests, a groggy, fourteen-year-old Jake turns off the alarm. Why is he so groggy? Three nights ago, he was up until three in the morning watching a marathon of "Friday the 13th" movies on one of the 327 digital satellite high-definition television stations to which he subscribes. Two nights ago, he went to sleep at 2 A.M. after surfing the Net and instant messaging some of the 489 friends on his AIM Buddy List. Last night he played the hottest new "kill 'em, steal it, and wreck it" video game until 4 A.M.

Still under his blanket, he gropes for a remote control and turns on his private nineteen-inch flat-screen TV, tuning in to rock videos and sending punk rock blaring through the house on the 1,000-watt home theater system, with its 100-watt subwoofer connected through not only his television, but his DVD player and seven-component stereo system. This summons Jake's mother to the bedroom, yelling over the music to "lower it and get up!" She is busy getting ready for a court appearance, in which she is representing one of the firm's most important clients. She leaves her son's room cursing her ex-husband for not being there to help.

Jake finally gets up and makes a beeline for his computer, awakening it from "sleep" mode. He instant messages two friends, then checks the weather and his e-mail. Jake heads for the bathroom and absentmindedly applies toothpaste to his electric toothbrush. Next, it's gel in the hair to emulate his favorite musician. His cell phone rings, and he talks in short, one-word sentences that communicate entire thoughts.

Opening his walk-in closet, Jake chooses an outfit and rips the tags off, dropping them on the floor. The fleeting impulse to pick up the trash is quickly replaced by relief that Maria, the cleaning lady, is coming today. He changes twice more before finally deciding on an outfit for the day. Then he goes down to the empty kitchen for breakfast—heats a Pop Tart in the microwave for thirty seconds and opens a twelve-ounce can of Dr. Pepper. His mother has already left for the office, and his father has come by to take his little sister to school. Jake chooses between three pairs of sneakers— $200 Nike Air Jordan Specials with cushion action, pumps, and turbo, Reebok Iversons, and Nike IDs with his surname on the side and his favorite number on the back. He then grabs his iPod, backpack, and heads out the garage door, a Pop Tart in one hand and a Dr. Pepper in the other.

◄ ►

The contrast between Bobby's 1968 world and Jake's environment in 2008 is striking. Though ostensibly both boys go through the same process of getting ready for school, their experiences are completely different. This difference can be attributed primarily to the cultural changes that have occurred in the last generation— largely due to the pervasive presence of technology.

In 1968, the mood of the morning is calmer, with more interaction between family members. Bobby is faced with one or two clothing decisions and briefly interacts with one electronic device, the alarm clock. He is focused on the single task at hand—getting ready for school—with relatively few distractions.

Jake, on the other hand, experiences the omnipresent pressures of scheduling, peer contact, and parental tug, not to mention numerous distractions in the form of gadgets and clothing choices. The tempo of his morning is chaotic and rushed. His day starts with a negative, even adversarial, communication with his mother. Other than his "nagging" mother, he has little family interaction. The parents are divorced and the family is less cohesive; his father and mother attend to their own independent schedules, as does Jake. In fact, the teenager interacts primarily with machines—though his mother doesn't realize it. She has no idea to whom her son is talking, no idea that he is even communicating with others, and certainly no idea what they are saying to each other. Because of the iPod in his ears and the use of instant messaging, e-mail, and text messaging, his person-to-person interaction is limited in general.

The negative tone begins with Jake's arousal from sleep. He is

slow and grouchy because of his late-night socializing and technological entertainment. Jake's distractions interfere with his efficiency, so he feels time pressures. There is a disconnected feeling
among family members due to the fast-paced tempo, the nature of
his family structure, and the need for speed in order to compensate
for the distraction delays.

THE TIMES THEY ARE A-CHANGIN'

As a clinical psychologist, I have had the privilege to enter the daily
lives of thousands of young children and adolescents like Jake, and
their families. In addition to my clinical work, I have conducted
dozens of interactive seminars and presentations with parents,
which have given me another window into the variety and scope of
issues families encounter. Several years ago, I began to notice that
the conflicts between the parents and children with whom I worked
were changing.

Parents began complaining about their kids flitting from one
screen to another. These kids were no longer accepting and appre-
ciative of what they had—they were always wanting more and relentlessly pressing their parents to get it for them. Respect for
authority figures, including parents and teachers, were deteriorat-
ing. I see a change in the family climate with parents catering to
their kids more frequently than is warranted and far too often placing their kids' needs above their own. As I repeatedly addressed
these issues, I discovered that more often than not, the culprit at
the core of the conflict was some technological device.

Because of technological advances, kids have unprecedented access to people, places, and things beyond their doorstep. Almost
anything they could want is accessible with a mere touch of a button. Take Cheryl, for example, a mother who comes to my practice
for weekly therapy sessions. Even before we've settled into our
chairs, she starts to complain about her eleven-year-old son.
"Would you believe that Justin called me on my cell phone last
night at 10:15 while my husband and I were out to dinner with a
client? He told me to give him my credit card number so he could
buy a new lacrosse stick online. But he just got a new lacrosse stick
three weeks ago!" she says with exasperation. I ask Cheryl how she
responded to her son. "I wanted to know what happened to the

one we just bought. He told me it wasn't good enough. So I gave him the credit card number and told him that this was the *last* time."

This brief interaction between Justin and his mother highlights a number of related issues that come up frequently in my practice. Here is Justin, shopping on the Internet on a school night. His parents are both out of the house, working late. Justin not only has immediate access to a new lacrosse stick, he has immediate access to his mother via cell phone. He doesn't ask for the credit card—he demands it. His mother gives in, perhaps due to guilt feelings about not being at home, or wanting an easy way to avoid a confrontation, even though she knows he doesn't need a new stick. Justin is able to order it with a few short keystrokes; the stick will be delivered to his front door, priority mail, two days later.

It is easy to relate to Justin's mother. We have all been there. When faced with mitigating circumstances, it is often easier to say "yes" to our kids when we should be saying "no." The point is that Justin—most like your child—has the ability to present these situations with frequency and intensity, wearing you down and affecting your otherwise sound decision-making abilities.

A recent session with Nicole, a conscientious eighth-grader, illustrates another aspect of what it means to grow up in this high-tech age. Nicole described working at home the night before on a short paper assigned by her social studies teacher. As she researched her topic on the Internet, instant messages kept popping up on the screen.

"I really wanted to get that paper done so I could watch *American Idol*," she told me. "But I just couldn't stop talking to my friends. My dad kept coming into the room and yelling at me to get back to work. I should have closed down AIM and put up an away message, but I couldn't; I was drawn to it. I missed my show because it took so long for me to finish. Not only that—my dad got so mad that he ended up grounding me for the weekend."

Nicole desperately wanted to complete her assignment. Apparently, she had enough self-discipline to write the paper before watching TV, but she was unable to thwart the immediate and persistent access to her friends.

To successfully enter adulthood, adolescents must accomplish two psychological "tasks": crystallizing their identities and "individuation." Individuation, the transfer of identity needs from the

family to the peer group, is when kids start to become more susceptible to outside influence.

The strong need for social acceptance, intensified by kids' ability
to "one-up" their peers, means that the issue of excess is particularly acute. The cumulative effects of our children's access to the
world through technological advances, and the excess of "things"
and privileges offered to them, can pose as a significant deterrent
in raising healthy kids. Kids like Justin and Nicole run the risk of
developing a distorted self-image, a poor work ethic, a sense of
entitlement, and weak social skills.

I have become alarmed about the potentially negative path our
youth may be taking. As a father and a clinical psychologist who has
worked with children and adolescents for four decades, I have
drawn upon my own professional and personal experiences to identify the impact of technology and contemporary culture on Generation Text. Unprecedented access to the world, and tremendous
excess, in terms of possessions and privileges, shapes the values, attitudes, and behavior of Gen Text kids in a way that is fundamentally
different from previous generations—and provides unique challenges for parents today. People usually talk about the "generation
gap" that exists between parents and children. The difference between kids growing up today from the world in which their parents
grew up is so expansive that a better description of the gap would
be "generation crater."

As both parenting and growing up have become more challenging, parental attitudes and styles have changed markedly. Several
years ago, I began to notice striking changes in the issues and problems I am called on to address as a clinical psychologist. These
changes were evident both in my patients and in the issues and
questions posed to me during parent training seminars.

Observing behavioral and attitudinal patterns among children
from diverse family types,* I became aware of a common thread in

---

*Issues of access and excess are not, of course, restricted to upper-middle and
upper-class families. In my work with children from less affluent backgrounds, I
see a similar phenomenon, with slight variations. Kids in less advantaged families
also get cell phones, iPods, computers with Internet access, and expensive sneakers; in fact, there seems to be a status subculture among more impoverished kids
related to clothing labels and the sophistication of their cell phones. The distinction between which gadgets rich and poor kids choose is largely cultural—different
styles and models are considered desirable, but the need to have them remains the
same.

the specific parent–child conflicts presented almost daily in my office. More often than not, at the root of the problem lies a conflict about technology—the Internet, computers, cell phones, and satellite communications. In a study published in 2005, a survey of 1,500 clinicians produced an inventory of eleven types of problematic Internet experiences reported by youth and adult clients. The eleven problems were identified as:

- ▶ Overuse
- ▶ Pornography
- ▶ Infidelity
- ▶ Sexual exploitation and abuse
- ▶ Gaming, gambling, and role-playing
- ▶ Harassment
- ▶ Isolative, socially avoidant use
- ▶ Fraud, stealing, and deception
- ▶ Failed online relationships
- ▶ Harmful influence websites
- ▶ Generally risky or inappropriate use

In my office, I have seen how all of these problems have both direct and indirect impact on the children and families I treat.

THE CHALLENGE FOR PARENTS

As society has become more complex, evolving into an age of specialization and options, adults have become more career-minded and competitive. Parenting styles are often dictated by this competitive culture; parents who feel guilty for being less available tend to buy their kids more things and say "yes" more often. Economic prosperity sometimes prevails at the expense of good parenting. In addition, changes in the family structure have resulted in many children who spend extended periods of time with surrogate caregivers or unsupervised.

The following chapters will discuss how parents can develop critical skills through education, early intervention, communication, monitoring, and finding a balance between parental values and cultural norms, but for now let's lay out the two basic challenges that you face as parents: parental guilt and "modeling down."

Parental Guilt

Ray is a seventeen-year-old patient with two cars and two cell phones. He has had three iPods in the past year, each one better and more expensive than the last. Ray's parents feel guilty about their demanding work schedules, so they provide him with excessive and elaborate toys. Meanwhile, Ray is in therapy with me because he has trouble controlling his anger when he doesn't get what he wants.

On the surface, it appears as if Ray is simply spoiled and indulged because of his guilt-ridden, hardworking parents. The fact is, if you take a step back—a very big step back—and examine all of the stuff your child has accumulated, you can see how normal it is for kids to have plenty of everything.

Do we all spoil our kids? I think not. It is just that we have become gradually desensitized to our culture of plenty. We give things to our kids because we are used to giving things to them. Our competitive, complex culture encourages us to provide our children with the latest and greatest gadgets, toys, clothing, and activities so they can maintain their edge with peers. Can you imagine your home without a computer and Internet access? How badly would you feel if your child's academic and social life were compromised because you didn't buy her a computer? It would be unreasonable and detrimental if we didn't provide our kids with these essentials.

The problem is, we don't stop there. We get them a better computer, their own laptop, and software galore. By nature, kids ask for things. Of course, sometimes parents deny their requests, but it has become acceptable and normal to give them many things beyond what is necessary. For Ray, the excessiveness caused a significant problem obvious enough for his parents to seek psychological treatment. For your kids, the impact of excessiveness may be subtler, but nonetheless a problem that affects their moral character, relationships, and work ethic.

Modeling Down

Over the past ten years, I have observed children being given privileges and material possessions at younger and younger ages.

This is known as "modeling down." In my own family, I have three children. My oldest son, now twenty-six, got his first cell phone when he was seventeen, my middle daughter got hers when she was sixteen, and my youngest child received his when he was just twelve—and he was one of the last of his friends to get one. There seems to be no end to this trend. I can just imagine toddlers programming their speed-dial numbers into big, shiny cell phones, calling each other to complain about how their parents don't understand them!

Let's consider sushi as a relatively innocuous example of how modeling down works and how it can be detrimental to kids. How often did you eat sushi when you were a child? Even though my family dined out frequently, I never even heard of sushi when I was a child. Chances are that unless you are Asian, you never did, either. Today, sushi is a regular offering in many elementary school cafeterias. Preteens and teens go out for sushi together.

Sushi is the kind of exotic, sophisticated delicacy that used to be reserved for adults. Here's the problem: If kids are eating sushi at age ten, what will they be asking for at fifteen or twenty-five? One of the problems with modeling down is that when kids get things and privileges at younger and younger ages, the bar is raised as they get older. Will kids who eat sushi for lunch in elementary school ask for lobster when they are in high school? And how will they cope if they don't get it? What will happen when they are adults and they may not be able to afford costly exotic foods? If kids reach adulthood and feel as if they are going backward in terms of possessions and privileges, they will feel angry, disappointed, and inadequate. It is easy to see how receiving things at younger and younger ages can lead to low self-esteem in adulthood.

The second problem with modeling down has to do with readiness. No teacher would attempt to broach the subject of algebra in the first grade, because first-graders simply lack the intellectual skills to master algebraic concepts. The course of a child's social and emotional development is no different from developing academic skills—they must be approached slowly, over time. First of all, it is difficult for kids to take full advantage of privileges and use them to benefit themselves when they are developmentally unprepared. Even more alarming is the high potential for such privileges to become emotionally or even physically harmful.

While eating sushi may not have a long-term impact on your

children, allowing seven-year-olds to attend concerts, giving nine-year-olds cell phones, allowing eleven-year-olds to watch R-rated movies with sex, strong language, and nudity, and giving your four-teen-year-old the go-ahead to have coed sleepovers almost certainly will.

The Good News

With smart parental guidance, the opportunities and information available to your kids today can broaden their minds and critical thinking skills. Privileges and possessions can enhance self-esteem; social connections can be fostered in even the most withdrawn child. Technology offers an educationally rich environment for children who are taught to make good decisions and judgments. With high-speed Internet access, sophisticated search engines, and instant connections to people and information across the globe, Generation Text is poised to become the best informed, most literate, and most international generation ever. They have the opportunity to take advantage of all the world has to offer. But this opportunity is largely contingent on their parents' ability to understand and monitor a myriad of influences.

Let me use a simple example to illustrate this complicated issue. The hammer is a rudimentary tool. If you place a real hammer in the hands of a five-year-old, you can expect to have holes in your walls. Give him a foam toy hammer, however, and he can have fun while learning the appropriate use of the tool. With instruction and monitoring, the hammer becomes constructive rather than destructive.

The Internet is also a tool. For a seven-year-old, it can reinforce and expand upon basic skills introduced in the classroom. But it can also expose that child to violent or frightening material that is inappropriate for his age.

How do we provide guidance and limits for our kids, especially when their knowledge of technology far exceeds ours? By now, many of you have developed basic computer and Internet literacy either leisurely or through your job. Your kids are still miles ahead of you in their sophistication and ability to go places online you don't even know exist. How can parents help their children navigate through this world so that they develop into happy, healthy adults with solid morals and values? In short, how do we raise our children in a time that is so different from the one in which we grew up?

Parents need to understand how access to the world serves as our competition, contributing to the attitudes, values, and behaviors of our children. The impact of our children's ability to easily obtain material objects and privileges in excess also needs to be understood. If we are armed with sensible and effective strategies, the advantages of technology and the options available to our kids will become opportunities instead of problems.

While some challenges facing parents are the same regardless of a child's age, specific issues are associated with each developmental stage. With this in mind, I will address the unique needs of younger children (ages twelve and under) separately from the needs of adolescents (aged thirteen and up). There are two critical tenets to keep in mind: First, intervening when the child is very young establishes a strong foundation for parent–child interactions; and second, parents of teenagers need to learn how to use access and excess to facilitate a healthy adolescence as a precursor to adulthood.

The good news is that pragmatic and reasonable strategies are available, and you can learn about them in this book. Your kids will grow up with healthier self-esteem, as well as a stronger work ethic and value system, when you become equipped with the knowledge and skills you need to address the issues they face today.

CHAPTER 2

Who Am I and How Did I Get Here?

....

Identity Formation

"After I am finished playing for my college team, I know I'll be playing soccer either in Europe or for MLS. I can play with anyone."—Josh, age 19

"The kids love my cartoon characters. They all stand around my desk when I draw them."—Hope, age 9

"I used to be smart, but now I'm not."—Randall, age 13

JOSH, HOPE, AND RANDALL ARE FORMING OPINIONS ABOUT THEM-selves based on the feedback they receive from their social environment. Their sense of who they are is based on this feedback. Generation Text kids in particular run the risk of forming a negative or unhealthy identity due to the unique culture of access and excess in which they grow up.

Throughout their lives, children hear many messages regarding their abilities. Sometimes they get positive reinforcement, encouraging them to succeed. At other times, they may be discouraged, haunted by negative criticism. Whether these messages are positive or negative, the fact remains that children are inundated with constant feedback—from their parents, teachers, peers, coaches, and increasingly from the media. Over time, children integrate all of these messages and organize them into a consistent idea of how they view themselves. This is called a "schema," the scientific term for what is best described as an internal self-portrait.

The schema is comprised of the child's diverse cluster of beliefs about himself, be they positive or negative, healthy or unhealthy, rational or irrational. Developing a schema is largely a cognitive (thought) process that determines the child's self-esteem, his sense of self-worth. If he believes that he is inadequate, we would describe him as having low self-esteem. But when a child believes she is competent, we would describe her as having high self-esteem. A child's schema involves more than her sense of adequacy. Values and attitudes are also part of how a child views herself.

The formation of this internal self-portrait begins in infancy and continues to evolve throughout one's lifespan. Infants begin to experience self-awareness the instant they start affecting their world. Babies are enticed by the colorful, attractive mobiles dangling over them in their cribs. They reach up to touch them, causing the mobile to move and make noise. As a result, they have effected a change in their environment. This is the very beginning of a sense of competence. In the coming months and years, that child will repeatedly perform actions that affect his environment. When babies "perform," their parents provide them with positive feedback that gradually translates into an early sense of efficacy, or self-worth. Eventually, the baby begins to differentiate himself from the environment, which is the beginning of his individual identity. As childhood and adolescence progress, massive identity changes occur as the youngster begins to interact more extensively with the environment.

In elementary school classrooms, for example, kids quickly become aware of the level of their reading group. Even first-graders tell me who they think the smartest kids in the classroom are. By the time they are teenagers, kids are bombarded with media and peer influences that impact their identity. Since one of their primary missions in life is to crystallize their identity, they easily emulate the attitude, behavior, and clothing of rock stars, athletes, and peers. As your children develop, new social feedback alters their view of themselves. In that sense, their schemas are in a constant state of flux over time. In a young child, the sense of self is highly fluid and malleable. Messages shaping identity easily permeate and alter the schema of young children who are insecure and highly impressionable to outside influences.

Psychologists have known for generations that cultural and social influences sculpt a child's identity. What is new, however, is that today's children are faced with a unique set of challenges in our access and excess society. Because of peer pressure overload, it is easy for Generation Text kids to develop low self-esteem and a generally unhealthy identity. As a result, these kids face the potential for abusive relationships, underachievement, oppositional or rebellious behavior, nonconformity to social norms, depression, and suicide.

GROUPTHINK AND NORMALIZATION

Something interesting happens to children and adults when they engage in unfamiliar group situations. Given enough time and repeated exposure, we begin to adopt the norms, behaviors, attitudes, and even the lingo of the group as if we identified with them all our lives. A good example of this phenomenon is what I myself experienced when a good friend of mine was soon to be married. Although he was a traditional guy, he made it clear to us that he did not want a "traditional" bachelor party. Accordingly, a weekend of good, clean fun was arranged for twenty of his closest friends—all of us college-educated professionals. The majority of the men in the group had been raised in well-educated, middle-class to upper-middle-class families with liberal-minded parents. None of us had ever served in the armed forces, hunted, or even shot a gun. So when we arrived at the paintball facility, we were all undoubtedly out of our element. We rented paintball guns and army fatigues and began the day with much the same attitude as we had the day we went white-water rafting—open to the new experience and just hoping to have fun.

At the beginning of the day, we were saying things like, "I need to get more paintballs," "I crept up behind him," and "That's okay, you go first." By the end of the day, we were yelling: "I need more ammo," "I ambushed him," and "You take point." Our group of novice soldiers quickly began to adopt a military identity, and in a matter of a few hours we were speaking the jargon. This phenomenon, called "groupthink," is the process by which we begin to manifest the sentiments of those around us after a certain amount of exposure.

The same process that transformed our thinking on the paintball field is happening to your kids on a daily basis. Something uncanny occurs when there is repeated exposure to a new behavior set. Initially, behaviors may seem strange and uncomfortable. As the frequency and repetition increases, however, people become desensitized to the newness, and what was once unfamiliar eventually becomes familiar and comfortable. Unfamiliar stimuli are then integrated into the person's schema and value system. When people adopt these behaviors and attitudes as their own, it becomes normal for them. This process is known as "normalization."

As we know from simply turning on the television or flipping through a popular magazine, kids are exposed to massive doses of sex, violence, manipulative behavior, alternative living choices, illegal activities, self-destructive behavior, inappropriate language, and on and on and on. Clearly, these behaviors and messages are inappropriate for their age. And they are everywhere—racy billboards, television shows, movies, video games, Internet sites, magazines, and advertisements. They are inescapable. So we all become desensitized to them, and they become normalized for us. In the same way that we have accepted and grown used to aspects of our culture that were once new and shocking, your kids' constant exposure to moral and value systems that are antithetical to yours can easily sway them to adopt those new values as part of their schema.

Video games are perhaps the most easily accessible example of the phenomenon of normalization. By playing violent games such as *Destroy All Humans, Killzone, Heavenly Sword, Assassin's Creed, First to Fight, Mortal Kombat,* and *Halo* for countless hours, kids become indoctrinated to the violent subculture that the games promote. If you were to spend just fifteen minutes listening to two or three twelve-year-olds play an FPS (first person shooting) game, you would be sure to hear them say things like: "Kill him!" "Shoot him!" "Look at the blood!" "Use your sniper rifle, he won't know what hit him." "How many head shots do you have?" "This guy takes about twenty shots before he dies." It is important to note that I am not suggesting that when children play violent video games they will automatically become violent themselves (although there are current research studies looking into that correlation). What I am suggesting is that by introducing a child to an aggressive behavior set through fantasy play for hours on end, we allow him to become desensitized to violence, which in turn becomes incorporated into his schema.

As I experienced with my friends on the paintball field, and as I have observed with children who play violent video games, the process of normalization is commonly demonstrated by the way we speak. We emulate speech patterns and cultural phraseology from role models. For our bachelor party crowd, we reverted to war stories and movies. For today's kids, language comes from contemporary television, music, and of course the Internet. In addition to the violent vernacular, inherently obscene words like *sucks, butt, bitch, ass, screwed, pissed of,* and *friggin* soon become acceptable when they are expressed in the company of adults, on television and radio, in movies, and in peer group conversation. Normalization occurs on a grandiose scale in a generation of kids who adopt negative attitudes, unintelligent conversational vocabulary, and inappropriate behavior. Two examples of normalization include how kids learn to link their self-worth with body image and net worth.

Body Image

Bailey, a six-year-old girl with social problems, was clearly upset during our therapy session. Apparently, the movie *Charlie's Angels* had just aired on television and several of the girls in her first-grade class formed a Charlie's Angels club, excluding Bailey. Compassionately, I reflected her all-too-familiar feelings of hurt and peer rejection. To my surprise, Bailey corrected me: "I'm not upset about Donna and the girls not letting me into the club. I'm upset about not being pretty!"

Even though her focus in therapy was her problematic social style, Bailey was more distressed over being considered unattractive than being socially ostracized. As a novice in my earlier years as a therapist, I would have missed this very important issue in my efforts to help Bailey. After all, my initial reaction was to focus on her peer rejection, an overriding issue for many children during their formative years. It is just as easy for a parent to make the same mistake, focusing on social rejection while overlooking the strong connection between self-worth and physical attractiveness in our society. Bailey heard a clear message at a very early age—she wasn't worth much if she wasn't one of the pretty girls.

Unfortunately, children—especially girls—will only experience feelings like this with increasing intensity as they get older. If a six-year-old is distressed about not being considered pretty enough for her friends, how will that translate into her preteen years, when she begins to want to impress the boys? Because physical attraction is so inherently linked with body image, and body image so intertwines with sexuality, it sets off a veritable cacophony of alarm bells. Will Bailey soon succumb to eating disorders? Will she propel herself into sexual activity before she is emotionally prepared to handle those experiences? Will she choose clothing and makeup that she feels will "make up" for her external flaws?

Today's children are acutely aware of body image, sex, sexual overtones, and sexual innuendo. How can they not be when they are literally surrounded by it in the mass media? Professional models, entertainers, and athletes exude sexuality in their physical appearance, their attire, and their behavior. The late basketball great Wilt Chamberlain boasted of having sex with 20,000 women in his life, as if this was something to which all men aspired. Today's sports stars need not make such bold statements. Their sexual escapades are readily publicized by the media, and our children are exposed to such stories from a very early age. Advertisements appearing in magazines, on television, in movie trailers, and on highway billboards express blatant sexuality, and they often include partial nudity and other sexual content, innuendo, and direct references. Ads for every product, from clothing to bubble gum to alcohol to automobiles, transmit sexual messages about normalcy and what is "in."

Inevitably, kids emulate the clothing and physical attributes of these psychological models and products. Even young children unwittingly express identity with sexual overtones through their physical appearance. Consequently, sexuality becomes part of their identity prematurely. On the bright side, a combination of superb sex education and the fear of contracting sexually transmitted diseases is believed to have reduced the incidence of teenage pregnancy these days. However, there are indications that continual exposure to sexual content in any form, including sex talk, touching, inferred sexual situations, and even listening to expert advice, leads to younger initiation of sexual activity, including kissing, oral sex, and intercourse.* In effect, twelve-year-olds with high exposure to sexual material tend to act the way fourteen- to sixteen-year-olds with minimal exposure used to act.

---

*Rebecca L. Collins, et al., "Watching Sex on Television Predicts Adolescent Initiation of Sexual Behavior," *Pediatrics* 114, no. 3 (September 2004).

Finally, sex is commonly depicted as a casual activity. Sex without love, marriage, or even an emotionally intimate relationship is portrayed as something to strive for in relationships, especially in popular television shows such as *Gossip Girls, Grey's Anatomy, Scrubs,* and *Friends.* The quest for sex is the entire plot of the 2005 film, *The 40-Year-Old Virgin.* The message of all of this is clear: Sex and sexuality are associated with attractiveness, social status, and self-esteem. Sexuality has become a part of our children's everyday lives—it is both familiar and normal to them.

Turning our attention back to six-year-old Bailey, I am concerned about what she faces during her formative years. If one Charlie's Angels Club experience makes her feel unattractive and unworthy, how will hundreds or thousands of media and social messages make her feel? Bailey, and most children, end up equating physical appearance with personal desirability. The fact is that Donna—the self-proclaimed president of the Charlie's Angels Club—was mean and insensitive to Bailey. Yet Donna is the popular girl at school because she is considered pretty. In turn, Bailey is at risk of thinking that being cruel makes you popular. Fortunately for Bailey, she has astute parents and is receptive to therapeutic intervention.

Self-Worth = Net Worth

Like Bailey, who believes that she is only as good as she looks, kids today also tend to equate self-worth with money and possessions. The number of new, state-of-the-art "things" a child possesses has become immensely important. As increasingly significant symbols of social status and power, money and physical possessions like computers, phones, and cars, not to mention clothing and jewelry, have become integral to the Generation Text child.

Sally, a teenage patient, talks about her best friend: "Amy has a BMW and gets whatever she wants. She is so popular—I love her and I hate her." Jordan, a twelve-year-old patient, recently returned from a weekend visit with a friend he met at an overnight camp the previous summer. In his discussion of the weekend with his new friend, Jordan almost exclusively emphasized the huge size of the friend's house, how many garages it had, how many video game systems his friend had, the pool, and the basement filled with arcade-like sports games. Very little was mentioned about the actual friend, or his parents, or how much fun he had and how great it was to see his friend for the first time in several months.

How have kids come to care so much about material things? One answer is that advertising in the media has incredulous power in determining what children want and how they should act. Product marketing messages express direct and subliminal messages about what is "cool" and what is "out" of fashion. Many advertisers specifically target children and adolescents, appealing to their need for peer acceptance. When athletes and entertainers endorse kid-oriented products, and when advertisers use rap and other contemporary music in their ads and depict the actors as being popular and "cool" if they own the product, kids automatically "need" those products. All this is happening while our children passively observe, integrate, and assimilate the social messages associated with the advertised product into their own schema—from the comfort of the family-room couch.

The onslaught of kid-directed media and advertising capitalizes on the fluidity of the developing child's schema. Fads are created and re-created, and Generation Text sucks them up like sponges. The mentality is that "everybody has it" or "everybody is doing it," and this thinking doesn't just apply to the latest gadgets and fashions. Studies show that one of the main reasons children become sexually active before they are emotionally ready is because they believe everyone else is doing it. Whether this belief is based in reality or fantasy is irrelevant. The fact is that kids want to do and have the same things as other kids. Their need to comply with social and materialistic fads stems from their natural inclination toward environmental influence in their quest for identity.

As a parent, stressing uniqueness as a positive and attractive trait is a way to diminish the impact of these trends. If children are taught that being different is valuable, they will be less likely to answer "How high?" when the media says, "Jump." Furthermore, teaching your kids from a young age that the true meaning of friendship is based on caring and companionship, rather than having the latest purse or iPod, can go a long way as they grow up. A good way to do this is to compare yourself to a friend of yours who is part of a different socioeconomic sector. Have confidence in the goodness of your children by asking them questions about how they react to others, such as, "Do you think I should stop being

Mary's friend because she doesn't wear designer jeans?" Kids respond to concrete examples based on their realities more effectively than they do to abstract value concepts. Based on that logic, it stands to reason that kids will respond more effectively to their parents than to advertising executives, as long as their parents begin to exert their positive influence while their children are still at a very early age.

Modeling a desirable attitude toward money and possessions is another way parents can dispel the "self-worth equals net worth" concept. Be careful about how you discuss money and status symbols with your spouse. Work to convey the notion that you are not defined by what you earn or own. The manner in which you handle your own finances can also communicate the value of who you are, not what you have. I don't think it is appropriate to discuss your financial situation with your kids. However, it is prudent to let them know how you scrutinize and justify certain purchases. They should know that you are buying things that are consistent with your needs and values—not because having those things will impress the neighbors. Similarly, let your kids in on your thinking when you decide *not* to purchase something. To them, being able to afford something means having enough money in the bank to cover it. Explain that big purchases also affect the possibility of future purchases and long-term financial security. Our kids are living in an age of excess, and they are inundated with the message that materialism is ideal. Growing up with that notion will cause kids to judge people superficially based on their possessions and appearance rather than the way they treat others and respect themselves. We must work to teach them that the opposite is true, and we must use as much enthusiasm and drive as those advertising executives use to push their opposing agendas.

SOCIAL REFERENCING AND MEDIA

In the 1950s and 1960s, when I grew up, we watched movies like *Godzilla,* in which a giant dinosaur-like monster lifted an ocean liner that looked like a plastic toy boat out of the sea. The poor-quality fabrication in movies of those days allowed the audience to experience psychological detachment from the scene. Consciously or subconsciously, we knew that there was no such thing as a larger-than-life monster that could pick up enormous boats with two fingers. It was absurd, but it still kept us entertained.

Today, technology has become so advanced that special effects in movies can easily trick the observer into identifying with the visual images on the screen. Gone are the days of *King Kong* and *Godzilla*. This is the age of *Spider-Man* and *Jurassic Park*. As if the borderline reality of movies and television wasn't enough, video games take this phenomenon of false reality to a different level altogether, bringing the child directly into the scene with first-person interactive games.

In some Xbox games, the player can design a character, or avatar, that physically looks like himself, and proceed to make decisions that influence the course of the game at every interval. What appears as a very realistic scene becomes real indeed, especially to an easily influenced and impressionable child. To further flood the market, popular video game and movie "heroes" appear everywhere, on clothing and cereal boxes and in the form of action figures, cartoons, coloring book characters, Happy Meal insertions, and anything else advertisers can think of to put into the hands of kids.

Two problems can result from this hype. First, the recurrent presence of these characters in the child's life increases the chance of that child identifying with such characters and all the features that go along with them, positive or negative. The second issue is that when normalization inevitably occurs, every kid develops a "need" to have one.

Furthermore, a social sense of belonging is created as a function of having this "in" stuff. When children observe their social environment, they acquire important information that becomes part of their schema. One aspect of this acquisition is called *social referencing*, the process by which children interpret and adopt emotional styles when they are exposed to novel situations, when they experience various real-life events, and when they observe how others respond emotionally. In these ways, children formulate ideas regarding appropriate reactions to social situations, incorporating actions and feelings using the social environment as a reference. For example, if a child witnesses her mother accidentally bump into another adult, she has the opportunity to observe the feeling of remorse as well as the expression of it. If the mother reacts to her mishaps by saying, "Oh, I'm so sorry, are you alright?" she helps her child acquire these same behavior sets. This is the classic parenting tool of "setting a good example."

Social referencing has taken on a new meaning as a result of the media explosion in the past forty years. Technology-enabled access has vastly broadened the scope of the child's ability to witness the social environment well beyond live models. Broadcast media contributes to pervasive cultural changes in America by providing live feeds and extensive programming. Between excessive contact with child- and teen-targeted advertisements, television, movies, radio, music videos, magazines, and video games, and the messages and role models found in all these media, Generation Text is exposed to more lifestyle options than ever before. The "I want to be like Mike (Michael Jordan)" idolization and idealization of personalities in professional sports and entertainment provide children with attitudinal and behavioral options. Some are consistent with your values and others are antagonistic to the way you want your child to act and think of himself.

Television, too, has dramatically changed from the days of *Ozzie and Harriet*. Shows geared to children, tweens, and teens, such as *SpongeBob SquarePants, Seventh Heaven,* and *Friends,* routinely include sex scenes, violence, abusive relationships, divorce, blended families, questionable moral behavior, and drug and alcohol use. The good news is that if you are aware of what your kids are watching, and you engage them in a discussion about the subjects presented, none of these issues need to be detrimental to your kids. The bad news is that if you are not aware, you may be making an erroneous assumption that your kids are watching age-appropriate programming of which you approve, when in fact they are being exposed to more adult programming.

Other contemporary television shows, such as *Tak and the Power of JuJu, Gilmore Girls, 8 Simple Rules,* and *Sabrina the Teenage Witch,* attempt to communicate moralistic plots, admonishing inappropriate behaviors related to relationships, drugs, and criminal activity. But unfortunately, it is usually the intrigue of such clandestine behaviors that becomes indelibly imprinted in kids' memories, rather than the healthy messages these shows attempt to convey about those activities. My patients will often ask me if I saw a specific movie or television show. I respond by asking them to tell me what it was about. More often than not, they summarize the plot by describing the raucous behavior it depicts, such as: "It was about these two guys who rob a bank," or "It was about this girl on drugs," or "It was about these two boys who were mean to a new kid," or "It was about a boy who was not good in basketball," or "It was about this family that was divorced." The exact same story could be described with moralistic messages: "It was about how crime doesn't pay." "It was about the bad things that could happen to you when you take drugs." "It was about how you should treat someone when they feel left out." "It was about how even if you are not good in one thing, you probably have other strengths that are important." "It was about a family that went through a hard time but still loved each other in the end." Even when I press children to evaluate the moral message of a show or movie, they quickly return to the negative (intriguing) aspects of the show. This tendency to dwell on the negative was much less prominent in my practice a decade ago.

As parents, we need to initiate open conversations with our kids about how to find the ultimate moral or value expressed in the programs they watch. Beyond that, your kids also need to be directed to appropriate movies, television programming, and Internet sites in the first place.

Popular movies can also be used to help teach your child important moral lessons. For one of my fifteen-year-old patients, watching *Mean Girls* with her parents, and discussing the themes and social issues it brought up for her, helped to assuage her own fears. In the movie, a naïve fifteen-year-old character named Cady (played by Lindsay Lohan) moves to America from South Africa and attends a public high school. There, she encounters social stratification with girls on the A-list and the not-so-popular nerdy group of girls. The A-list girls, referred to as the Plastics, are superficial, manipulative, materialistic, catty, and elitist. The nerds, or the Out Crowd, are considered sweet, caring, geeky, unpopular, and uncool. Cady is immediately accepted by the Out Crowd but desperately wishes to be part of the Plastics. She is able to obtain friends in both groups, but to maintain her status she is forced to engage in deceitful, scheming, betraying, and untrustworthy behavior. Eventually, Cady realizes the value of true friendship.

Social referencing occurs every time your child watches a movie. That is not to say that kids immediately adopt and copy every message a movie communicates. It is a gradual, repetitive process, but if left unchecked the negative messages can become part of how a child acts or treats people—an expression of his or her identity. Close monitoring is one way to facilitate healthy discussion so that your child will be able to understand the proper socially oriented, cause-and-effect relationships.

Naturally, parents try to teach their kids a set of behaviors, attitudes, and values that are consistent with their own. Some of the more common values parents try to instill in their children are "Mind your manners," "Don't hit people," "Treat others the way you would like to be treated," "Get a good education," "Use appropriate language," "Family is important," "Respect authority," and "Respect the bodies and feelings of others." These social codes are critical teachings to help your child formulate a healthy identity. So why do children and adolescents seem destined to stray from those core values?

During infancy and early childhood, parents have almost total control over their child's exposure to culturally based values and attitudes. Parents attempt to develop a healthy behavior set in their children through modeling and reinforcement. Modeling is the set of behaviors you exhibit in front of your kids. Your behavior needs to match your words if you want your child to emulate your values. I once saw a mother in a parking lot hitting her son while she was yelling at him, "Don't ever hit your brother again. We don't hit in this family!" Obviously, this mother missed the modeling mark. Reinforcement is the reward or punishment that follows a behavior. Taking your daughter to the movies because she was very brave when she got her immunizations is a reward, or positive reinforcement. Taking away television for a day after she fails to clean her room is a punishment, or negative reinforcement.

School is the first formal opportunity children have to recognize different behaviors, attitudes, and values in relation to their own schema. It is at this point that parents begin to compete with outside influences on their children. As children grow up, they are increasingly exposed to the models and values of other families. Soon enough, parental supervision is not needed when kids get together for play dates and birthday parties. When they reach what we psychologists call the latency age (six to eleven years old), kids start going to sleepovers and more elaborate birthday parties; they have longer play dates and stay for dinner at their friends' houses. Next, in adolescence (the teenage years), kids go with each other to the movies, attend concerts, hang out at the mall, and go to restaurants, experiencing greater and greater autonomy. Soon, parents are not even needed to drive their kids from one social engagement to the next, since the children have driver's licenses and can get places on their own.

As this process of maturation continues, external influences increasingly compete with parental guidance. Parents begin to experience a sense of loss of control. What parent has not heard at least one of the following statements from their child: "All of my friends are allowed to see R-rated movies!" "Mary has a television in her room, why can't I?" "John's parents let him watch TV during dinner!" "Nick can play video games whenever he wants!" Many of these declarations are followed by stinging statements like, "It's not fair!" or "I hate you!"

When your son or daughter compares his or her life to those of a friend, or to the world at large, your child is using a sophisticated form of "social referencing." Social referencing gains powerful momentum in identity formation during latency and adolescence because self-concept is so malleable during these years. Children inculcate the behaviors, values, and attitudes of role models and peers into their schema because doing so seems to aid their need for social belonging—and wanting to fit in with the other kids is powerful motivation. Their sense of self is an ongoing comparison between who they are and what is socially revered.

THE RACE TO ADULTHOOD

When kids engage in activities that are not age-appropriate, they are ill equipped to handle them emotionally. As a result, there are often negative consequences that can disrupt a healthy identity formation. The most obvious circumstance would be premature sexual activity creating negative self-esteem or humiliation.

It is a commonplace feeling that kids grow up too fast. Before you know it, your little babies are getting married and having families of their own. This has always been a challenge for parents. But for today's parents, the truism takes on an exaggerated element. Generation Text is privy to sex, nudity, and other adult world privileges well before they (or we!) are ready. Growing up in a technologically fast-paced society, they are used to adapting to rapid and widespread change and advancement.

Just as their understanding of technology has reached a level once thought beyond their years, Generation Text kids try to *look* physically older. They go for manicures and pedicures, color their hair, and wear provocative clothing. All of these things send visual queues that mistakenly transmit the idea that they are ready for a certain level of adulthood. Teens who are given the luxuries of limos for birthday parties, spa days, coed sleepovers, hotel parties, and parent-sponsored credit cards in their name receive the message that they are in fact ready for those premature privileges and responsibilities. Kids, who naturally idealize adulthood, are drawn to these socially accelerated activities. As a result, Generation Text has become more likely to engage in sexual activity and alcohol consumption. Today's fifteen- to twenty-year-olds are more sexually experienced than teens were in the early 1970s.* Although underage drinking decreased in the 1980s (largely due to Nancy Reagan's "Just Say No!" television ad campaign), it has soared to new heights in the 1990s and the present decade.†

How do kids catch on so fast to what their peers are doing? How do they become attracted to these activities in the first place? The answers, once again, lie in their ability to access each other using mobile phones, text messaging, instant messaging, and e-mail. News of who's done what and who owns what spreads faster than a wildfire. At the same time, cable TV stations such as VH1 and MTV, featuring provocative role models, are available twenty-four hours a day.

Technology and the media, however, are not the only ones to blame. The acceleration of our children's maturation is largely our own doing. Academic expectations and pressure are imposed on our children at a very early age. Preschool children are routinely introduced to readiness skills and reading and math concepts that were previously introduced in kindergarten and first grade. Recently, a five-year-old kindergarten child told me that he had to study for a science test! The new social need to teach a child to read before entering kindergarten has created much anxiety and pressure for both the child and the parent. When we put such unnatural

---

*Sandra L. Caron and Eilean G. Moskey, "Changes Over Time in Teenage Sexual Relationships: Comparing the High School Class of 1950, 1975, and 2000," *Adolescence* (Fall 2002).
†Barbara K. Hecht and Frederick Hecht, "Teens Drinking Too Much in U.S." MedicineNet.com (September 16, 2004).

pressures on our young children, their self-esteem is often compromised. After all, even the brightest children can have trouble meeting an advanced preschool curriculum because they are simply not ready to function at that level. This is a pattern that only continues from grade to grade, in a nation that insists on introducing age-specific educational concepts earlier and earlier every year.

Academic acceleration is one piece of the puzzle. Social acceleration in children and adolescents is another, more dangerous piece. Drinking, drug use, and sexual experiences are reported at increasingly younger ages every year. The twelve- and thirteen-year-olds who come to my office talk to me about oral sex and drinking at parties. Most parents would be astonished at the sophisticated sexual knowledge their kids have at such young ages.

In 1991, I had my own rude awakening when Magic Johnson, the once-premier basketball player for the Los Angeles Lakers, announced that he was HIV-positive. The announcement received a tremendous amount of press. My wife and I were driving in the car with our kids, who were six and eight at the time. Both children were quietly sitting in the backseat. Out of nowhere, breaking the silence, my daughter asked, "What's a condom?" My wife hesitated and looked at me with an expression that said she would gladly acquiesce to the child psychology expert in the family. I returned the look, trying not to laugh, both astonished and nervous, and hesitated as well. In that relatively brief moment of awkward silence, my eight-year-old son interjected, "It's what Magic Johnson should have used but didn't." Imagine my surprise. We had no idea where either child had accessed that knowledge or awareness.

But aware they are. Although we like to think of our children as little boys and girls for as long as possible, our kids have another agenda. Not only do they glean incredible amounts of age-inappropriate information from sources over which we have little control, but they are anxious to prove that they are grown up enough to handle and assimilate this information. The main ways that Gen Text kids try to attain this adult status is by trying to look the part. Clothing, makeup, jewelry, and gadgets like phones, computers, and iPods are all pawns in this race-to-adulthood game.

The way in which children dress has become more adultlike over time, and only becomes more so with each passing year. Little girls used to wear gingham jumpers and little boys wore overalls and T-shirts. Today, Baby Gap sells bikinis for girls and chinos for boys.

It is entirely possible for parents and children to wear matching ensembles. By the time they become preteens, girls are tempted to wear provocative clothes—tight tops, short skirts, and shorts—trying to look like their favorite pop stars. As Britney Spears donned a naval piercing and wore midriff-baring tops, so did thousands of adolescent fans. Boys began wearing impossibly baggy pants and oversize shirts to mimic rappers and rock stars. Boys and girls alike began to pierce everything from ears to tongues, and tattoos became increasingly popular. Girls bring makeup to school in their book bags and put it on after they arrive on campus, so that even if their parents don't "allow" it, they end up wearing the makeup anyway.

In my day, high school students used to hang out in malls, eat in diners, go bowling or to the movies, and have reasonable curfews. Now, they have much later curfews or no curfews at all. They have coed sleepovers in groups. With parental consent, boyfriends and girlfriends spend the night together. Even if these "slumber parties" are completely innocent, the bottom line is that kids are introduced to the concept of sleeping with the opposite sex at an early age. This is yet another way in which a concept once held sacred becomes familiar before a child is emotionally prepared for the consequences. The race to adulthood accelerates as normalization begins.

Finally, material objects have come to signify the rite of passage for children. Acquisition acceleration enables children and adolescents to receive various privileges and "things" that are usually associated with attaining a specific age. They get their first two-wheeled bicycle when they turn six; they get a computer and cell phone at nine, a TV in their room when they are ten, permission to go to the mall alone at twelve, and of course they can obtain a driver's license and car to drive as a young teen. These are just some of the milestone events that signify to the child and the world around her that she is growing up.

While some of these privileges are linked to specific ages due to developmental ability and legalities—such as the two-wheeled bicycle and the driver's license—the others are subject to parental judgment alone. Generation Text kids receive these symbols of adulthood at increasingly younger ages. For example, when cell phones were first invented, no child was expected to have his own phone. As time went on and the phones became more commonplace, parents began to purchase cell phones for their teenagers around the time that they received their driver's license, largely as a safety precaution. Soon, fifteen-year-olds wanted their own cell phones too, because once one teenager in a group has something, the others feel the need to have one. Before long, children in sixth and seventh grade had their own cell phones. This age has now become the new norm or standard by which parents gauge the timeliness of such an adult-oriented privilege.

A nine-year-old girl started her session by telling me how excited she was for her birthday the following week. "Why are you so excited?" I asked. She answered, "Because I'm finally getting a cell phone." Children will often request a cell phone long before they are ready to handle the responsibility of learning how to use, and making sure not to lose, such an expensive item. It is important to understand, however, that just because they ask and their friends have them, it does not mean that you have to say yes. The race to adulthood may sometimes seem inevitable. You may feel helpless in the face of its seeming universality. But you can slow down this race. Remember, your child's identity is shaped by the feedback he receives from his social environment. If children are engaged in social acceleration, acquisition acceleration, or academic acceleration, they will think of themselves as older, which can be a formula for precocious sexual and substance abuse behavior. For the rest of this chapter, let's focus on how parents can help their children remain kids for a while longer, and how they can ensure that when those kids do take their inevitable steps toward adulthood, they are more effectively prepared with a positive identity.

DOING YOUR PART

What happens when children sway from the values you tried to instill in them from the time they were old enough to understand? You become frustrated with them, and they become frustrated with you, and in time, communication begins to break down. The good news is it doesn't have to be this way.

As with most things in life, effective change begins from within. It is easy to lose sight of your parental expectations because you, too, succumb to familiarity and normalization. Don't you find yourself using some of the words you wish your child wouldn't use?

You can help your children change if you start correcting your own "loose language," sending the message that a different level of speech is expected around adults. Since you are potentially the most powerful role model for your children, you must practice what you preach. If you have a double standard, one for your own language and another for your children, they will more than likely speak the way you do—not as you want them to.

Generation Text kids tend to express their identity through vernacular. The way your child uses jargon, chooses vocabulary, and articulates his ideas can be representative of the type of person he is. His verbal communication will in turn be one of the factors people consider when making judgments about his intelligence, family life, and personality. As a young, first-year graduate student in a vocational psychology course, I once interviewed a man named George. George was born and bred in Brooklyn and spoke with a stereotypical accent. One of the first things he told me was, "Yeah, I live ova on tirty tird street, around da cawna frum de olt Rialto Teater." My initial impression of his intelligence, level of education, and even the quality of his culinary abilities was immediately tainted by that dialect. Once he started discussing his work as a *chef de sauciér* in a top French restaurant in Manhattan, however, he eloquently described French sauces and delicacies, as well as any Parisian might have. I left the interview with a completely different impression of George. Encouraging your children to express themselves intelligently will decrease their chances of being unfairly prejudged in situations like this one.

Whether we admit it or not, we are all prone to judging people based on appearances and first impressions. As we have already discussed, Generation Text has an acute awareness of clothing as an expression of identity. Parents need to allow their children to express themselves using clothing while setting limits when clothing is inappropriate for their age or the social situation. You should provide and demand appropriate attire and grooming at family functions, religious engagements, and school and social events with adults in attendance. Clothing alluding to sex, drugs, and alcohol should be banned and discarded. Help your kids discriminate between the projection of a healthy identity and one in which they may be judged (albeit unfairly) negatively. Ask them to consider how differently they act when they wear jeans and when they wear formal suits or dresses. Just as George's verbal communication shifted when he spoke about his profession, your children's behavior will change when their attire does.

When it comes to clothing decisions (one of the many difficulties in raising Generation Text kids), the lines of appropriateness are often blurred. I once treated a fifteen-year-old boy whose appearance was as bizarre as possible. Other patients, kids and adults alike, would often take one look at him and ask me about his drug use, low intelligence, and loser identity. In reality, this young man adamantly rejected drugs and alcohol, was a gifted student, and felt passionately about animal rights. As to his clothing, he researched clothing manufacturers and refused to purchase any article from a company that engaged in animal abuse or child labor. Despite all this, he was often misjudged based on his appearance. It was obvious to me, and his astute parents, that this young man's off-center appearance was extremely important to his own identity formation. We consciously decided to accept and respect his appearance by not challenging it. Instead, we acknowledged and praised his positive personality traits such as his fortitude and strong conviction to his values. Sometimes, stepping back and looking at the whole picture helps you decide on the best course of action for your children.

Simply put, constant exposure to a moral and value system that is incompatible with yours can be combated with counter exposure. These suggestions may appear to be basic and simplistic, and in actuality, they are. However, many parents are either not noticing the language or attire due to the normalcy phenomenon, or they are electing not to implement the strategies. To illustrate how familiarity creeps into family life overtaking family values, let's take a look at the Landesang family.

THE LANDESANG FAMILY: A CASE STUDY

The Landesang family was referred to me by their family physician following an emergency room episode in which sixteen-year-old Courtney was treated for alcohol poisoning. Courtney's fourteen-year-old sister, Jaime, attended the same party. Jaime was also drinking alcohol and was intoxicated but not treated in the hospital. Rich and Sarah had caught Courtney drinking once before but did not suspect that Jaime was following suit.

For the initial session, I met with the parents alone. Their marital relationship seemed to be intact, and they generally presented a unified front to their children. Rich and Sarah had similar backgrounds and until now, they had the usual battles with their teenage daughters over curfews, too much socializing, and insufficient attention to academics, but nothing more serious.

At our first full family meeting, both girls appeared to be cooperative and affable. They were contrite and remorseful when discussing their recent alcohol escapade. As sessions progressed, I made several subtle observations. The girls almost always wore jeans and a casual top—the typical teenage uniform. At times, they would show up with T-shirts featuring the Coors Light logo, a rock band known for drug and alcohol abuse, and a comical anti-authority slogan. Courtney came to one session in a low-cut tank top, and one time Jaime wore a tube top that looked to be a size too small. Both girls sat in their chairs slumped over with poor posture. They generally listened and participated in the conversation, but if it wasn't directly related to them, they would look down or away. Once, Courtney skipped a session because she went away for the weekend with her best friend's family.

As for Rich and Sarah, they made their own contributions to the problematic family dynamic. Rich periodically said things like, "Get your butt out of bed," "Your ass is in trouble," and "Clean your damn room." When the discussion became heated, Courtney would immediately use a sarcastic and annoyed tone of voice. Sarah responded to Courtney's comments while ignoring her tone of voice. Jaime was also disrespectful at times, using sarcastic phrases such as, "Whatever!" "Who cares?" and "Right, Mom." Since both girls were decent students, rarely was homework discussed or checked by their parents. Rules for lights out and screens off on school nights were initially established and enforced, but they disintegrated when homework demands increased and the girls tended to keep late hours regardless. Over time, the solid rule structure the parents had established years ago gradually slipped away. Although they could all remember the initial family rules about language, clothing, homework habits, and tone of voice, no one could explain what had happened to those rules. Sarah reflected and realized that at some point the girls started resisting and challenging the rules. This became very tiresome, and eventually the girls' tenacity outlasted the parents' ability to stand firm. Concessions to the kids began in small parcels. Unfortunately, the parents' flexibility did not satisfy either Courtney or Jaime. Once they were given the proverbial inch, the girls took a foot. Consequently, the original standards went by the wayside and the new standards became the norm without anyone's conscious awareness. Furthermore, by not addressing the issues, Sarah and Rich gave tacit approval for both girls to continue acting in the same manner.

I am not suggesting that the gradual erosion of the parental standards and values indigenous to Generation Text caused either girl to experiment with alcohol. However, the general climate in the family, which is commonplace in Generation Text families, was conducive to a lack of respect for authority, rules, socially acceptable behavior, and self-respect. Without realizing it, this transformed into familiar and normative behavior, becoming incorporated into the girls' identities. They talked, dressed, and acted the part that is all too familiar to Generation Text parents.

The task at hand was to reinstitute the standards that were initially important to Rich and Sarah. First, I asked the parents to be careful about the language, tone of voice, and behavior they displayed in view of their daughters. Next, every time the girls expressed a hint of sarcasm or disrespectful tone of voice, I softly intervened. "Could you say that differently?" I'd ask, before the parent could respond, and I instructed the parents to get in the habit of doing the same. The messages their clothing communicated became a topic of discussion. The girls sifted through their wardrobes and removed clothing Sarah, their mother, deemed inappropriate. This was somewhat of a battle, but I calmly explained to the teenagers how it negatively portrayed them in a manner in which I knew they did not want to be known.

I asked both girls to express how they felt about family counseling. Courtney had a negative feeling but was willing to try it, and Jaime saw the possible benefits. I explained to the girls how their posture during sessions communicated indifference and a poor attitude, and that if they sat that way in class, their teachers would receive the same message. Because neither girl wanted to send negative messages about themselves, they were able to listen to and accept this criticism. Other renewed expectations had to do with required family participation and homework. The fact that Courtney missed a family session for a social engagement proved where the family landed on her priority list. There are times when attendance at family and extended family functions is mandatory. That means giving up or rescheduling social events to reinforce the importance of family. Additionally, the parents reaffirmed wearing proper attire to match the occasion. Homework rules were reestablished and the parents began asking about homework and periodically checking over the assignments.

In time, Rich and Sarah reminded each other of the rules if one parent started to slip. Courtney and Jaime began to comply, and there seemed to be less stress for all. The parents no longer had a feeling of "walking on eggshells." There was less arguing, less combativeness, and the parents began to see an improvement in the girls' self-esteem and academic performance. The girls began to take pride in their appearance and became more motivated to do their schoolwork. It took persistence but the Landesangs found a new (old) norm for family interactions that translated into positive identities for their daughters.

The Landesang girls fell into a behavior pattern that is characteristic of Generation Text kids. The process of normalization in their family, coupled with their ability to push the limits and get more of what they want, created grave consequences. The gradual shift to compromised family functioning occurred over time. It took some time to regain positive family functioning, which coincided with the teenagers' shift to a more positive self-identity. The increase in self-esteem and respect for their parents' rules translated into better decision making regarding alcohol use and other teenage temptations. For the most part, Courtney and Jaime steered clear of alcohol-involved parties. By reaffirming the family values and expectations for appropriate behavior, the Landesangs were able to challenge the strong influence of the Generation Text culture.

BEING A GOOD ROLE MODEL

Kids tend to imitate the role models with whom they have the most contact, and to whom they are closest emotionally. Fortunately, this person is probably you. But parents are not the only role models for Generation Text. Beyond parents or guardians and other adults living in the home, kids are affected by extended family members, teachers, coaches, peers (and their parents), professional athletes, musicians, actors, politicians, and even fictional characters from movies, video games, Internet sites, and television shows. We know by now that our instant access, 24/7 culture provides Generation Text with constant exposure to attractive, high-status figures from the worlds of music, movies, television, and sports. Kids can read about these role models online, play video games in which they are key characters, and even chat with them (or their representatives) on fan club websites. Of course, the potency of a role model is not only related to morals and values, but to the perceived attractiveness and social status of the model. Frighteningly, our society's emphasis on beauty and wealth can make role models even out of people who portray themselves as vacant as someone like Paris Hilton. As children engage in social referencing and exposure to these role models, they internalize alternate values and attitudes, and the parent's role is increasingly compromised.

One reason children may choose to replicate the behavior of a fictional character or a movie star over and above their flesh-and-blood parents is because those parents are not as interesting or engaging as the stars seem to be. But remember, kids tend to watch and copy everything you say and do, so be careful what you model for them. Do you talk about other people in front of them? Do you gossip about friends and other families with your kids? Do you treat shopping as a need or a social activity? Do you keep your eyes peeled to the football game on television as your child speaks to you? What are the messages communicated if you do? Remember, role models providing emotional closeness will have the most sustained influence on children. Appropriate modeling is one of the most instrumental weapons in a parent's arsenal to combat undesirable influence. Being a positive role model for your children means:

- ▶ Treating others with consideration and in a caring manner
- ▶ Showing respect for bodies, feelings, time, and possessions of others
- ▶ Displaying a positive work ethic
- ▶ Showing that you are human and can make mistakes
- ▶ Maintaining strong convictions in spite of their unpopularity
- ▶ Being flexible and understanding
- ▶ Managing responsibilities
- ▶ Respecting the rules of society
- ▶ Knowing when to handle things independently and when to ask for help

Famous personalities splashed all over the Internet, television, and athletic fields perpetuate a self-centered and reckless lifestyle that can seem very attractive to your kids. To combat these narcissistic messages of self-indulgence, consider participating in community-minded groups, donating time and money and seeking leadership roles within the community. The way in which you conduct your own life serves as a powerful model for your kids. It would be prudent to closely examine how you may be contributing to their views of materialism, respect or disrespect for others, treatment of feelings and bodies, and other values that comprise self-worth and identity.

Countless parents complain to me about their kids' tight-fitting or revealing clothes, visible thong underwear, body piercings, and tattoos. What I always ask them is, "Who is buying all this stuff?" To fix a problem, you must first realize that you are part of the problem, as well as part of the solution.

Take, for example, eight-year-old Samantha. Samantha was engaged in "play therapy" with her toy cell phone in my office. She called the spa on her cell phone and made an appointment for a manicure, pedicure, and massage. How does an eight-year-old know about such pampering? Obviously, she "learned" it somewhere.

Parents need to have a clear understanding of the personality traits they want to emphasize in facilitating a positive schema in their kids. There is a degree of subjectivity in choosing these values, but how kids treat themselves and others are universal qualities for healthy kids. How do you treat yourself and others?

A surefire way to confuse a child is to send mixed messages. Be very careful to avoid sending mixed messages. Are you teaching kids about "correct" morals, while acting in a contrary manner? Ryan, a teenager with whom I work, insists his teachers pick on him. Whenever a teacher disciplines him, he focuses on the unfair treatment or the inappropriate way the teacher handled the situation. His parents, while imposing their own punishment for Ryan's bad behavior, openly criticize the teachers' actions as well. But this is confusing for Ryan, who needs to understand that although his parents are allowed to challenge a teacher's authority, he is not. Ryan will never benefit from discipline until he learns to accept the possibility that he has misbehaved.

Children learn how to treat others by imitating your attitudes toward relationships. If you make it a lifelong goal to climb the social ladder in your community, you are sending a clear message about social identity. Shunning those who do not have the social status to help your social climb promotes unequal treatment of others based on their value to you. Your attitude and treatment of cultural, religious, ethnic, racial, and other differences and diversity also demonstrates your respect or lack thereof for others. Here is where it can get tricky. You don't want your kids to confuse acceptance of a morality and lifestyle that is alien to yours with the feeling that it is okay to adopt it as their own. There is a delicate balance between maintaining respect for another person's morality and value system while communicating that it does not fit your lifestyle. Modeling the virtue of a "live and let live" attitude (i.e., accepting others, not judging or condemning others based on their appearances) is another way to instill a positive schema in your kids. It will reinforce the message that it is okay to be unique without worrying about the pressures of fitting in or being judged.

PARENTS AS LANDSCAPE ARCHITECTS

If you were a landscape architect developing a raw piece of land, you would use your knowledge and experience, the materials available, and the advice of selected experts to mold the project into what you envisioned. The parcel of land may have inherent limitations, some of which you have to accept and some of which you can change. In much the same way, cultivating your child's positive self-image—enabling a sense of security, competence, and self-confidence—is one of the most important goals of parenting. But how can this be accomplished, knowing that you have to battle the competition of powerfully invasive external cultural forces? You want your child to reap the benefits of today's rich culture while tempering the negative effects it can have on their self-image and sense of who they are. There are several approaches you can use to facilitate positive self-image, which is an integral part of your child's identity.

1. *Understand your child's wiring.* As discussed in Chapter 1, your child is wired with a predisposition for specific traits and abilities known as temperaments. The first step in facilitating a positive

self-image is to understand those innate temperaments. Once you understand your child's wiring, you want to try to control his environment to increase the likelihood of success. In other words, you want to manipulate or control your child's social environment whenever possible so that there is a "goodness of fit."

Let's use the temperament trait of "distractibility" as an example. If you know that your child has difficulty sustaining attention and is easily distracted, you should organize her space (e.g., bedroom, bathroom, play areas) so that there is order and organization. This kind of child cannot do her homework with a computer, a handheld video game, and a television in view, even if those items are turned off. Have you ever taken your toddler out to dinner and found yourself constantly reprimanding him because he doesn't stay in his chair, plays with his silverware, or spills his milk? In this case, the child's high activity level is not being acknowledged; instead, your reprimands send negative messages that chip away at his positive self-image. Instead of reprimanding, try providing him with crayons and a coloring book or some other object of interest to channel his high physical energy. Matching your child's temperament with what you can control in his environment will maximize successful experiences.

2. *Build character.* A person's character is comprised of morals, values, and behavior patterns that are developed both passively (through daily interactions) and actively (through direct instruction). As parents, you should be actively involved in helping your kids adopt a set of morals, values, and behaviors that facilitate a comfortable and healthy identity. You need to actively teach your children the features of a positive character in order to combat the plethora of competing negative messages.

Active teaching comes in many forms. By simply listening to and observing your child's interactions with siblings, peers, cashiers, and others, you can verbally reinforce or instruct them on how to treat others. By asking them to hold the door for the next person entering a room, you teach them common courtesy. By instructing them to express cordialities by saying "Please," "Thank you," and "Excuse me," you help bolster their social skills. By pointing out the immoral and negative interactions of some people and clearly identifying the positive morals, values, and behaviors of others, you help them distinguish between right and wrong. By taking advantage of these day-to-day experiences, you can help your children build solid characters. Once equipped with such character, a child's self-image and identity can withstand and reject negative messages from peers, the media, and beyond.

3. *Accentuate strengths and accept weaknesses.* Having a positive self-image doesn't only mean being able to recognize one's assets and strengths. To be secure with oneself and present an identity of self-assuredness, people need to be able to accept their limitations and weaknesses as well. Part of your job as a parent is to actively help your child cultivate strengths while also coping with weaknesses.

Most parents recognize the importance of praise and reinforcement when their child gets an A on a test, hits a home run, performs well onstage, or creates a beautiful drawing. But children will truly learn to recognize what they are good at by being praised frequently for the numerous, small, daily actions they perform, and not just for their obvious accomplishments. A good rule of thumb is to express ten praises for every one criticism, which means that on a daily basis you should make it a point to reinforce as many behaviors as possible, even if they seem to be things generally taken for granted. Just because something comes easily or is natural for them to do, doesn't mean that it isn't special. Challenge yourself to find ten things every day to praise, for example:

Child's Accomplishment	Positive Statement
Sharing	"I really like the way you are sharing with your brother."
Organization	"You really know how to organize your desk so that homework can be done easily."
Loyalty	"You are a good friend to stick by John like that."
Good Behavior	"This was a long car ride and you guys really behaved well."
Effort and Work Ethic	"Whatever grade you get on your test tomorrow, you know you've done your best because you are so good at putting your best effort into studying."

Recognizing your child's weaknesses and getting him to accept them is just as important as focusing on his strengths. While it may not seem natural to point out a child's weakness in the interest of building his positive self-image, think of it this way: If he realizes that a certain weakness can be improved, it will no longer be a weakness. Recognizing and accepting a weakness also means that a child is better able to avoid situations or activities that accentuate it, and that the child will not be defensive or act inappropriately when that weakness is revealed.

Talking about your children's weaknesses in a gingerly manner is the best way to help them identify and accept their weaknesses. Avoid using statements like, "You are not a good drawer." This statement defines the child, inferring that the specific skill deficit is part of his identity. Instead, say, "Drawing is something that you aren't that good at and that's okay. There are other things you do well—like math." This statement simply identifies and isolates one skill—one small piece of the child—as a weakness and balances it with a strength. It is also helpful to ask your child to identify a strength that she recognizes in herself. Another helpful tactic is to help your child realize that many people share the same weaknesses, and that people are not expected to be good at everything. Finally, be prepared to counterbalance the weaknesses with a list of strengths. Sharing your own personal list of strengths and weaknesses also helps to normalize the weakness.

Though kids have always needed to be recognized for their strengths, Generation Text kids need it more than ever. Passive parenting will ultimately lose out to the powerful influences of access and excess. As with any work in progress, you must remain flexible and be prepared to make adjustments as needed. With your knowledge of how groupthink and normalization, global access, and role models affect identity formation and self-image, you can capitalize on the advantages they offer.

4. *Encourage social activities.* The technological evolution has helped create a specialized culture, one that breaks down tasks and activities performed by people and machines into smaller, more manageable components. Remember the orange juice example from Chapter 1? That same specialized culture affords a multitude of options for kids to experiment with different interests in the form of structured, formal social groups. Social interactions in both formal and informal groups help shape self-image in kids. For Genera-

tion Text kids, there is a heightened awareness of social interaction that intensifies the impact on identity formation.

Without overscheduling, parents should offer their children a variety of activities to expand their interests and perhaps even create lifelong passions. In this way, your child's potential to discover a sense of competence is increased. Formal, organized social activities provide an opportunity for your child to discover things about herself with adult supervision. Additionally, exposing your child to an interest or activity may turn into something that shapes his identity in the long run. For example, taking a gymnastics class at the age of seven can lead to a lifelong interest in the sport and a self-definition as "gymnast."

Informal play (play dates and impromptu peer interactions) are also important to encourage, but the frequency and duration of such play should not be excessive. Excessive informal play should be individually assessed based on what the child verbalizes, his overall energy level, changes in mood (mainly irritability), and changes in academic performance. I have seen patients who are used to having scheduled activities or play dates every day. This kind of overscheduled day places far too much value on having friends, diminishing the importance of being with the family and saving time for relaxing activities. Informal play dates usually need to be orchestrated with younger children. For older kids and teens, it is enough to suggest and encourage those social interactions, ensuring that even children who may not pursue those interactions on their own will still experience and benefit from them.

5. *Establish a sense of family.* Children obtain part of their self-image and identity through the groups in which they belong. It stands to reason that establishing a strong sense of family will facilitate a positive self-image in your children. We sometimes take the family unit for granted, but it should be understood that children do not automatically feel a strong connection to the family as a group member, but rather need that concept to be reinforced continually. Regardless of your busy schedule, you should make sure that for at least two or three nights every week, all family members are present for a proper family dinner. These dinners should include conversations about accomplishments, local and world events, personal daily events, and feelings. Dinnertime should absolutely exclude telephone calls, reading material, television, and all other electronics.

Scheduling family outings (something as simple as going to a baseball game or as elaborate as a weeklong vacation) on a regular basis is another way to maintain a strong sense of family belonging. It is also important to require siblings to attend each other's plays, dance recitals, sporting events, and other activities. The goal of all of this is to establish a strong family presence to mitigate the impact of your child's excessive access to the world. The effects of familiarity and normalization of competing values can be balanced by establishing and maintaining a strong sense of your own family values.

In my family, from day one, my wife and I insisted on our children's participation as described above. As a result, friends of my twenty-six-year-old son, who tell him they have trouble spending ten minutes with their families, don't understand why he comes home to visit so often. As independent as he is, Dan still has a strong connection to his family.

6. *Engage in cultural activities.* A well-rounded child helps round off self-image. Exposure to a variety of foods, lifestyles, sports, music, art, religions, and other cultural diversities at home and abroad can expand and enhance your child's developing identity. Seeing options and diversity in the world under your watchful eye is yet another way your child can use the wealth of information television and the Internet provide as a frame of reference. For example, using the Internet, you can visit a Third World country and see the poverty, difficult living conditions, and lack of education and possessions your child undoubtedly takes for granted. Such a visit can reinforce a feeling of gratefulness for all that one has.

TEACHABLE MOMENTS

Six-year-old Sheila executed an Internet search with the keyword "fairies." Among the expected fantasy pictures of the Tinker Bell variety, a confused Sheila came across a picture of a gay rights protest and brought it to her father. Fourteen-year-old Max was researching nuclear weapons for a homework assignment and accidentally Googled the word "nake" instead of "nuke." A variety of nude photos appeared on his screen. This kind of mishap is inevitable in the age of the Internet. Recent studies indicate that 70 percent of fifteen- to seventeen-year-olds will accidentally encounter pornographic websites. With the push of a button, kids are privy to a world of influence beyond parental knowledge, consent, or control.

Because there is no way to stop this from happening, it is important that you use these inevitable events to your advantage. When your children present you with something they have learned either through social or technological access, utilize it as a "teachable moment."

- ▶ Take the time to talk with them about what they have found, discussing the implications of the information.
- ▶ Ask your children to make their own judgments about how healthy or appropriate the behavior is. Try to impart, without being too judgmental, the lesson that is consistent with your family values.

Sheila's father may have very well dismissed the discovery of the gay rights poster and sent her on her merry way. Instead, he sat her down and explained that the picture was of a group of people who were standing up for what they believed in. Of course, that wasn't enough information for the curious six-year-old.

"What do they believe in, Daddy?" she asked.

Not riled in the least, her father explained, "They have a different type of family than us. Instead of a mommy and a daddy, they either have two mommies or two daddies, not one of each. Some people don't think that kind of family is right to have. So they are marching in the street to let people know that their type of family is okay. Just because their family is different from ours, it doesn't make them bad people. Do you have any other questions?"

"Why do they call them fairies?"

"It is actually not a nice name and they don't want to be called fairies. The people who don't agree with their type of family are mean to them and call them names. Would you like to be called names just because you believe in something different from, say, the kids in your class? How would you feel if you and your friend Karen liked to straighten your teacher's desk and all the other kids called you teacher's pets?"

Sheila's father took an incidental Internet picture and transformed it into a teachable moment. It became an opportunity to help Sheila learn about standing up for what you believe in, alternative lifestyles, judgment, diversity, and sensitivity.

We all realize that it is impossible to insulate the Generation Text child from improper messages. Even your awareness and active involvement cannot prevent your child from integrating unhealthy beliefs into his schema. However, once it is evident that your children are gravitating toward a negative social element, visiting inappropriate websites, or engaging in behaviors that are contrary to your values, you need to dispel the beliefs associated with them by:

- ▶ Using the techniques listed above
- ▶ Having reasonable, objective discussions
- ▶ Showing them attractive alternatives to their poor choices
- ▶ Pointing out the possible negative consequences that they never considered

COGNITIVE RESTRUCTURING

Over the past decade I have seen a marked increase in verbal aggression, verbal abuse, and physical violence directed at parents and teachers by the youngsters with whom I work. Not only has it been reported to me by parents and teachers, I witness it regularly and directly in my office. It is common for five-year-olds to call their parents "stupid," "jerk," "asshole," "bitch," "shit head," and worse. Violence against parents comes in the form of hitting, pushing, and throwing objects at them or in their general direction. Granted, the children I work with are generally less stable emotionally than the average child, and they often have limited internal controls. Even so, I see a cross-section of children ranging from the mentally healthy to the mentally ill in my practice, and from one end of the spectrum to the other, I have noticed that Generation Text children have repeatedly transmitted a negative attitude toward authority. In the late 1960s and 1970s, young people were involved in an anti-establishment movement, "the establishment" being an abstract entity that included the government as a body, government officials, corporations, and large businesses. Today's "anti-authority" movement, however, seems to be directed closer to home. The police, teachers, and parents are often depicted as the "bad guys" in music and on film. Consider these examples:

- ▶ Rapper Chamillionaire sings a song about riding in a car to escape the police, too coy to get caught.

▶ Eminem writes lyrics about slicing his girlfriend's mother's throat and dumping her in the ocean so they can be together.

▶ In the movie *Riding in Cars with Boys,* a teenage girl rebels against her parents and makes bad choices, sneaking out of the house, attending a party with older teenagers, and having sex, resulting in pregnancy.

▶ In the movie *Thirteen,* two out-of-control thirteen-year-olds deviously shun their parents and societal rules by buying sexy clothing, doing drugs, shoplifting, associating with inappropriate boys, and piercing their bodies.

▶ Although released in the mid-1980s, *Ferris Bueller's Day Off,* a comedy about a teenager duping his parents and school principal, is still popular among today's kids.

▶ *Accepted* is about a group of college students who delude their parents and ridicule college administrators.

▶ Comedies such as *Super Troopers* and *The Naked Gun* mock the intelligence and authority of law enforcement personnel.

▶ Super athletes such as Terrell Owens, Tiki Barber, and Alex Rodriguez denigrate their coaches' authority in press conferences. Numerous other professional athletes, politicians, and entertainers have flouted authority and laws when arrested for drug possession, driving while intoxicated (repeatedly), murder, tax evasion, domestic violence, assault, possession of an illegal weapon, and the list goes on.

The indoctrination has been overt and subtle, but consistent and undeniable. Parents need to dispute the belief that it is acceptable for kids to act disrespectfully toward adults. We need to challenge the belief that all people in positions of authority are "bad." The way to accomplish this is with a strategy called *cognitive restructuring,* which entails confronting unhealthy beliefs and replacing them with realistic, rational healthy beliefs. Whenever you hear an unwarranted comment about an authority figure, point out true statements about their credibility, positive motivations, and the need to respect them (assuming the person is acting responsibly). For example, if your son complains about a police officer abusing his power when he pulled his friend over and gave him a speeding ticket, you must combat the negative belief about the officer by pointing out the fact that the friend was breaking the law; by serving a violation, the police officer is ensuring that the friend and others will be safer.

To understand how you can use cognitive restructuring in your own family, keep in mind the following examples:

- ► Your child comes home from school and says he hates his teacher. Consider responding, "I realize that your teacher seems unfair at times, but his job is to teach you math and your job is to learn it."
- ► The woman who watches your kids for a few hours after school tells you that your kids are saying things to her like, "We don't have to listen to you," and "My mom doesn't make us eat a healthy snack after school." Address their insolence by telling your kids that even though Mrs. Smith is not mom or dad, she is an adult that you've put in charge and therefore they need to follow her rules and speak to her respectfully.
- ► Your twelve-year-old comes home from his baseball game, throws his glove down, and calls his coach a jerk and an idiot. After learning the reason for the display of anger, you respond, "I understand that you wanted to get more playing time. I'm sure Mr. Stengal wants you to play as much as possible because you are a great player. He is just giving other kids a chance. Being angry doesn't give you the right to call an adult names."

When your child presents you with a teachable moment, use cognitive restructuring to gradually dismantle negative beliefs about authority figures. Finding appropriate ways to challenge authority, without being disrespectful, will become incorporated into your child's overall identity.

WHEN YOUR CHILD DOES NOT COOPERATE

By employing some or all of the suggestions discussed thus far, you will begin to regain the power you may feel you are losing to access and excess. Unfortunately, the very nature of Generation Text is to be actively or passively overwhelmed with alternative behavior sets—both positive and negative. So when the negative behavior seeps through, you have to either present other ways to think about it, be firm with limits, or go with the flow to allow a natural learning process to occur, crossing your fingers that your kids will eventually make good decisions.

How many of you secretly want your child to be different so that she can conform more to what *you* had in mind for her? Perhaps you would prefer her to be a better athlete or student, to be more popular or ambitious, a more competitive ice skater, or simply a more giving person? Charlie's parents—both hardworking professionals—were not shy about expressing their dismay when their sixteen-year-old son told them he wanted to be a rap artist. Charlie attended an upper-middle-class suburban high school with a student population that was predominantly white, with a small percentage of Asian Americans and no African Americans. The majority of students at Charlie's school pursued post–high school education, and his parents certainly expected him to join his older sister at a competitive college. But Charlie, who had significant learning disabilities and was the only "rapper" in the school, didn't feel as if he fit in at home or at school. Charlie was at heart a quiet, kind kid, a Caucasian teenager who dressed on the preppy side.

As Charlie's story unfolded during therapy, it quickly became apparent to me that my goal was to find a way to encourage Charlie to pursue his own identity—not to make him become something he had no desire to be. And Charlie was sure of what he wanted—to write and perform rap music. One summer, while on vacation, he met three teenagers who shared the same interest. They all lived hours away from one another, but they were Charlie's lifeline, peers with the same taste in music. While his parents relentlessly pushed him to apply to colleges and drop the idea of a music career, Charlie defiantly stopped applying himself academically. He simply wanted something else altogether.

Sometimes, it is better to join a resistant youngster rather than fight him. In many cases, what the child ultimately craves is his parents' support, and once that support is given, he tends either to give up the struggle or to end up where his parents wanted him to be all along. As for Charlie, he was uninterested in college, too small to pursue sports, and had poor mechanical ability. I explained this to Charlie's parents and we started exploring ways to help encourage him to pursue his rapper identity. I coached his parents to do so while imposing limits as a way to prevent disaster for their impressionable son.

We found a computer program that mixed music. Charlie and his three group members would write lyrics, compose music, and perform it from the comfort of their own homes. The work was sent via Internet to Charlie, who put all the pieces together and compiled them into songs. Technology allowed them to form a rap group, write music, mix it, and burn CDs to be sent to various record labels—all done long distance. All the while, Charlie agreed to his parents' limitations regarding the language and content of the lyrics, and he also agreed to begin applying himself in high school.

One week, I asked Charlie to bring in a CD so that I could hear his work. The quality and depth of his lyrics and performance shocked me—he was genuinely talented. Charlie was able to pursue his identity as a rap musician despite a family and school environment that was overtly dissuading him from doing so. I eventually had to modify my therapeutic goals to help Charlie get his parents' acceptance and to encourage him to crystallize his dreams. As disappointed as his parents were in him (and probably in me, too), Charlie was able to strike a compromise in which he would attend a community college part time while pursuing his music career. Interestingly, during his first semester at County College, Charlie discovered that he actually liked college courses. He announced to me that he was applying to a four-year college away from home. His music is still important to him, but it has taken a backseat to his newly found academic interest.

Sometimes, the best thing parents can do is to accept who their children are, accentuate their strengths, and allow the pursuit of identity. Doing otherwise will often result in an endless battle in which no one wins. In this case, Charlie's parents finally accepted his goal of becoming a rap musician, but insisted on a college education so that he would have something to fall back on should his career in music not work out.

I have compared parents to landscape architects, people who start with raw material and impose their idea of how to make it more beautiful. They design what they believe to be a creative scheme, inserting trees, flowers, walkways, berms, and lighting. Since the land is susceptible to environmental conditions such as flooding, wind damage, and extreme temperatures, they try to protect the design by attending to these invasive elements. Landscape architects consult with other professionals such as engineers, surveyors, and architects to help them sculpt the land. No matter how careful they design and plan, or what their expectations are to make the land beautiful, they must contend with and accept the limitations of the land and the fact that some environmental elements may challenge the integrity of the design.

Parents, like landscape architects, try to create their idea of what makes a beautiful child. They impose their values, try to protect them from bad elements, and consult with professionals to help sculpt a positive identity. No matter how careful they design or plan, or what their expectations are to shape their child's schema, they must contend with and accept the limitations of the child's capabilities and passions. Unlike landscape architects whose job is complete once the design is on paper, parents have the ability to continually shape and influence their child's identity.

CHAPTER 3

I Want It Now!

··

Immediate Gratification

IDENTITY FORMATION IS CRUCIAL FOR YOUR CHILD'S OVERALL WELL-
being. But your kids are primarily on the receiving end of that process. As they interact with their environment through the normal
course of each day, they internalize specific encounters.

But what happens when kids set their sights on something they
want and actively seek it out? As parents know all too well, that is
where a child's passivity ends. When kids encounter something they
want, they don't hesitate to ask for it—in fact, they often demand
it.

This active process is what we call seeking *need gratification*. It
is the way in which a child tries to get what he wants or needs. As
all parents know, this process begins the moment a child is born.
Infants cry in order to express their needs. At first, these needs are
limited to food, sleep, and comfort. Naturally, parents strive to satisfy these basic needs. This is one of nature's devious ways of setting
you up for one of parenting's biggest challenges. After you become
conditioned to satisfy your infant's basic needs, he begins to grow
up, and you are faced with requests for things he "wants" as well
as those things he really needs, and you may have difficulty distinguishing between the two.

As children get older, they move beyond wanting one kind of
food over another, or wanting to stay up past bedtime. For children, "wanting" and "needing" are often confused, experienced as
one and the same. A child might say, "I need a new iPod" with the
same intensity as she says, "I need to eat now." One of your main
goals as a parent is to teach your child how to tell the difference

between wanting and needing. To do this, *you* must be clear on the difference.

It is always up to you to provide or deny things that are truly optional. While gratification is a concept and feeling that every human being should be able to experience, and one you should aim to give to your child, too much gratification leads to spoiled children. Feeling satisfaction, be it from something you receive or something you experience, is an important part of developing a sense of worthiness and empowerment, two key components of positive self-esteem. But if a child consistently gets everything she asks for, she will not learn how to effectively cope with not getting what she wants. A well-adjusted child is one who can both wait to get what he wants, and accept that he may not get everything he asks for without pitching a fit or repeatedly asking for it. It is our job as parents to train our children to temper their reactions and cope with the delay or denial of their wants.

Of course, the issue here goes beyond avoiding the pitfalls of raising a "spoiled" child. When kids become accustomed to getting what they want unconditionally, they face significant social problems in the future. What happens when they ask to play with a friend's toy and the friend says no? How will they react when a teacher denies their request for an extension on an assignment? How will they handle it when their girlfriend or boyfriend does not want to engage in a specific sexual activity? If your kids are conditioned from early childhood to expect to get whatever they want, they will be confused and disillusioned when the rest of the world does not follow suit. As adults, these children face significant problems with anger management, professionalism, and personal relationships. If an individual doesn't learn effective coping mechanisms regarding need and want gratification in childhood, that person runs the risk of developing a number of immature and inappropriate behaviors as an adult and can subsequently suffer from depression and anxiety later in life.

Generation Text kids in particular have significant problems learning how to cope with not getting what they want, and even with a slight delay in gratification. Even if they know that they will eventually receive something they want, their "I want it, and I want it *right now*!" attitude prevents them from accepting the delay gracefully. I am quite concerned about how these tendencies will affect a whole generation of children and their values, attitudes, and treatment of others in the long term.

Averting the "spoiled child" syndrome is nothing new. What is new, however, is how the issue of need and want gratification is intensely magnified in Generation Text children due to specific cultural and technological factors impinging upon their ability to cope and your ability to help them as parents. This chapter will provide you with the three components you need to facilitate your children's ability to effectively cope with want gratification. First, you need to develop an understanding of how gratification issues develop in children. Second, you must become aware of the unique cultural and technological factors that place your kids at greater risk. Finally, specific strategies are presented to help you mitigate these factors and develop healthy ways for your children to cope with want gratification.

THE GRATIFICATION MUSCLE

Imagine that you have never exercised in your life. You decide to get into shape, join a gym, and start weight lifting. Do your biceps become toned and shaped after the first workout? Of course not. Instead, the muscle becomes toned through repetitive exercise. In the beginning, those muscles ache after every workout, but you soon notice less pain and the beginning of definition. Then once you reach your initial goal of getting in shape, it becomes easier to maintain the muscle tone you've gained.

The results of working out are visible and tangible. Your body looks different, and you can actually feel the muscle tissue. Unlike a well-toned muscle, gratification awareness is an abstract concept in child development that cannot be seen or touched. Despite this major difference, I want you to think of the *process* of developing gratification awareness in your child as similar to the process of developing muscle tissue. Both processes include specific steps: In one case, the steps involve shaping a flaccid muscle into a well-toned one over time. In the other case, you take steps to shape your child's need for immediate gratification into the ability to calmly accept denial of gratification. Let's examine how those steps occur in your child.

As an infant, one's needs are internally driven by the sensations of hunger, fatigue, and discomfort. Infants function exclusively in the realm of instant gratification—crying until their specific need is gratified. The crying stops when the need is met—or more accurately, the crying does not stop until the need is met. Gradually, the baby's neurological system starts developing and maturing and the child begins to tolerate a slight delay between need and gratification. Eventually, the ability for expressive language and cognitive development enables the toddler to request what he wants along with what he needs. Pragmatically, parents and caregivers are not always able to drop whatever they are doing and immediately meet the desires of a toddler. It is at this time that the child begins to experience the feelings associated with waiting. Invariably, the child also begins to ask for things he cannot have. The toddler and young child must then also begin to cope with the frustration of *not* getting what they want.

In the healthiest scenario, a child progresses from having her needs gratified immediately, to being able to delay her gratification of needs, to coping with not having her needs (and wants) met at all. But just as in muscle toning, this process does not occur magically or overnight. With experience and practice, children learn to deal with waiting for what they want, or not getting what they ask for at all. Consistent and repetitive exercise is the key factor in developing these mental muscles. Coping with gratification delay is facilitated by the repetitive and consistent boundaries and consequences imposed by parents, authority figures, and institutions like schools. Even social settings such as movie theaters and libraries help shape your child's need gratification system.

To illustrate how other social settings require your child to cope with wants and needs, consider the following scenario: A small child accompanies her mother to the local public library. She knows that in the library, you are supposed to use your "quiet voice," not the regular, boisterous voice you use at home or on the playground. She and her mother pick out several books and join the line at the checkout counter. At this point, the little girl is beginning to lose her patience. She wants to leave the library *now* with her books. Her mother reminds her of the quiet voice rule and explains that they have to wait in the line for the other people to check out their books, but the child becomes impatient and fussy. The mother tries to engage her daughter's attention by asking her to help find the library card in her wallet, but the child begins to whine. She gives her daughter one more chance to wait her turn in line quietly, but the girl begins to shout in frustration. The mother leaves the books behind and takes her daughter home, explaining to her that she needs to learn to wait in line and follow the rules of the library. They will try again next week. The regulations of the library prohibit this young girl from taking her books home without properly checking them out. Yet, her need for immediate gratification prevails and she cannot wait or even delay her need for gratification. Her mother imposes a consequence (leaving without the books) for her daughter's inability to cope with delaying her need gratification.

Accepting "no" for an answer does not occur overnight. It develops gradually, and only if it is worked on consistently. After a few more trips to the library, this mother should be able to teach her daughter to stand patiently in line quietly in order to get her books. Once the child is able to tolerate waiting, it is easier to maintain that dynamic, and parents can become more flexible or indulgent. Like a person who's trying to build muscular strength, this mother may experience some initial pains, including embarrassment (a screaming toddler in the library is never fun) and the fallout from the grumpy, disappointed child. But with time, both she and her child will become stronger as a result of their training.

Understanding the process of developing the need gratification "muscle" is the first step in helping your children cope with their wants and needs. It is important to keep the following principles in mind:

- ► It is a gradual process that usually takes several years.
- ► There is usually pain (in the way of objection and anger) until your child "gets" it.
- ► There is often anguish and guilt felt by you until your child "gets" it.
- ► The gratification muscle needs to be maintained throughout adolescence.
- ► Once it is well established, the gratification muscle is easier to keep honed.

Now that you know more about how need and want gratification affects your child, let's turn our attention to why it has become such a problem for Generation Text.

TWO SIDES TO THE WANT GRATIFICATION COIN

When it comes to the developmental issue of want gratification, the very nature of our fast-paced, push-button culture has created a huge problem for kids and parents alike. There are two sides to the want gratification coin. On one side, kids want more and more. Generation Text kids are exposed to more things and more social options than any other generation, which causes them to ask for more. As technology continues to advance, so does their ability to get more of what they want—and get it immediately. On the flip side of the coin are the current lifestyle circumstances causing parents to give into their kids more and more. Both factors—kids wanting more and parents giving more—disrupt the healthy adjustment to want gratification, and both factors can potentially create behavioral problems in your child, as well as cause difficulties in their relationships.

Let's examine how and why this occurs and, more importantly, how you can go about addressing gratification issues in your children so that they can effectively cope with the delay or denial of something they want. I'll use a case study to highlight many of the reasons Generation Text kids have difficulty delaying or denying need gratification. These issues are incredibly common and pervasive, so please don't be alarmed if you strongly identify with the situation. If you are able to identify with Marc and his parents in the following story, then eventually you will learn how to modify your current approaches.

Twelve-year-old Marc is the sort of child I meet with on a daily basis. His mother complains that he has a meltdown over the littlest thing. If she says "no" to him, or if things don't go exactly the way he wants them to, Marc goes ballistic. He's twelve, but sometimes he acts like he is two, asking for the same thing again and again. And if his parents remain firm, he starts to negotiate. When that doesn't work, terrible things come out of his mouth and then he takes it out on his younger brother. In the process, Marc's parents witness whining, crying, feet stomping, and yelling. Sometimes, his parents tell him that he can have what he wants, but he has to wait until the weekend to get it, and yet he still has a fit. Marc's difficulty accepting "no" for an answer has resulted in his parents' indulging his requests to avoid yet another confrontation. They also, admittedly, change their response to diffuse the volatile situation, giving him what he wants.

In counseling Marc, I first tried to understand him by asking him to describe a typical day in his life and putting myself in his mind-set. What I discovered was that Marc performed dozens of actions every day that fed his needs instantaneously. Technology within a finger's reach has literally met his need for immediate gratification. In Marc's twelve years of life, his family has purchased three new computers—each one processing information faster than the previous model. Programs and Internet sites are loaded by those computers in split seconds. If the Internet connection is slow one day, Marc will bang on the computer desk, frustrated that a website is taking extra seconds to load.

Marc is a very social youngster. Wherever he is, at any time, he can access his friends with the touch of a speed-dial button on his cell phone. If Marc is in the car and he wants to talk to his best friend, he doesn't have to *wait* to get home and call. When he does get home, he simultaneously instant-messages his friends and talks to several of them at once. He doesn't have to wait to call his friend back if the line is busy. He sends and receives e-mails so that he doesn't have to wait for snail mail through the post office. On several occasions, he forgot homework papers at school, but he simply had one of his friends scan it and e-mail it to him. Another time a friend sent the homework by fax. Marc downloads music and shops on the Internet. He doesn't have to wait to go to the store. Marc tells me that he often makes frozen pizza after school. Instead of waiting thirty to forty minutes to cook pizza in the oven, it takes him ninety seconds in the microwave to heat up his afternoon snack.

Internet, scanners, faxes, cell phones, and other technologies have redefined the concept of immediate gratification for our kids. The remote control (a very common topic of discussion in my office) has all the buttons a child could ever need. With TiVo digital video recording technology, he doesn't have to *wait* for his favorite TV show to come on—he can watch it (and pause, rewind, and fast-forward) whenever he likes. It is no wonder that he has learned how to push his parents' metaphorical buttons to get what he wants! Marc literally pushes buttons all day long, constantly massaging his immediate gratification "muscle."

As the immediate gratification muscle flexes with one technological device after another, children have become conditioned to expect getting what they want—and expect it now. Waiting has virtually become a concept of the past, and the fast-paced world in which they function is the only lifestyle they have ever known. This generation of children takes it for granted that their needs and wants are met immediately through technological access, and the result is that they interact with people in much the same way that they interact with machines. Some of Marc's impatience with his younger brother and his parents is due to this kind of intermachine conditioning.

Against their better judgment, Marc's parents have altered their parenting approach due to their child's inability to effectively cope with want gratification. In effect, they are doing a poor job of establishing boundaries and imposing consequences to help shape his gratification muscle, which can never become toned if it isn't exercised frequently and consistently. But why do they do this in spite of their knowledge that it is inappropriate?

Perhaps you say "yes" to your kids even when you know you should be saying "no." Or you change your "no" to a "yes" because your child is protesting excessively. Marc's parents, and you too, have probably fallen prey to two Generation Text issues that are having pervasive effects on parenting styles. I have identified these two issues as *child-centered families* and *yes parenting*.

CHILD-CENTERED FAMILIES

Marc's parents are very loving and attentive to the needs of their two children. Both parents work hard to make a modest living, and they jockey and negotiate between themselves to make sure the boys are not left alone, that they have rides to their activities, and that they are provided with "Generation Text equipment" like iPods, Nintendo DS game consoles, trendy clothing, and so on. Money and time are managed well, and a yearly vacation is always planned to a child-oriented destination. Marc's parents socialize with friends on occasion, but they have not been on a childless vacation since the kids were born. In addition to scraping to save money for vacations, his parents have financial allotments for summer camp tuition, tutoring, tae kwon do classes, guitar lessons, and the weekly expenses associated with preteen social life: bowling, movies, fast food, and arcades. Marc's mother made a conscious decision to be available to her kids, which has hindered her career. She has turned down business trips and a promotion that involved more stress and a longer workday.

After they spend the majority of their time and money on their kids, not much remains for either parent. The lack of time these parents have to spend with one another, or to socialize with friends, and the constant doing without so that their kids will have things, has started to create resentment and anger between them. The discrepancy between how much they give to their kids and how little time and effort they spend on themselves and their relationship has caused the parents to become short-tempered and somewhat burned out.

The devotion Marc's parents demonstrate is admirable. The problem is that this devotion may be backfiring for their family. It may be very subtle, but it is clear that Generation Text children have been elevated to a very high status within the family, gaining a ubiquitous sense of importance. Of course, children need to feel important, and to a degree this is healthy. But today's child has taken it to an extreme far beyond healthiness. The pendulum has swung far from the archaic adage that "Children should be seen and not heard" to "Children should be seen, and heard, and given in to." It is quite typical for contemporary parents to go overboard in creating a child-centered family. Generally, in today's society, there is an inordinate amount of attention and unbalanced focus on the children, and it is not only a detriment to the parents' own needs, but a major contributor to the child's inability to cope with delay and denial of need gratification. There has been an excessive expenditure of family resources on the children, causing the parents to sacrifice their own needs. It is a sacrifice of time, money, emotions, and the very notion of self.

The effect of child-centered parenting on gratification issues is obvious. If there is an excessive focus on meeting the child's needs in the family, the gratification "muscle" is indulged more frequently, and the more it will "need" to continue being indulged. Remember, when a child never experiences the frustration and disappointment of waiting for (or maybe even never getting!) something she wants or needs, she will become increasingly unable to cope with the delay or denial.

This pattern becomes extremely empowering for children and

makes them even more demanding. Children learn that if they ask enough, if they push enough, if they challenge the word "no" enough, they can eventually get what they want. Generation Text parents, in their child-centered orientation, have inadvertently enabled their children to expect immediate gratification.

Maintaining a healthy balance between your kids' needs and wants and your own is crucial. If you experience too much self-denial as a parent, you run the risk of feeling regret, resentment, and burnout. Perhaps you are already there. The marital relationship in particular stands to benefit from creating a healthier balance in the family. In the long term, attending to your own relationship while your children are still young will not only set a positive example for the children, but it can help you avoid the empty nest syndrome later in life. Although the compulsion to please and give to your children is natural, the tendency to spend excess money and time on them has disrupted the proper conditioning and development of healthy need gratification in the Generation Text child. The result is a generation of enabled children who are used to getting what they want, and a generation of parents who are used to giving it.

There are ways you can create a healthy shift from an overly child-centered family to a more balanced family life. Naturally, I want you to continue loving and caring for your children. Your goal should always be to find ways to maintain your children's sense of importance and self-worth, while refuting the notion that family life revolves solely around them. The task at hand is to remember to spend some of your financial and time resources on yourself and each other, so that your children learn your time is also valuable and that sometimes they need to sacrifice their own needs for you. It is easy to say, "I don't have the time or the money right now," or, "We'll do those things when the kids get older." Instead, find ways to make the time and shift some of the spending your way. The following are examples of how you can take time for yourself and as a couple on a regular basis:

- ▶ Make working out part of your weekly routine.
- ▶ Go for a walk alone or with your spouse.
- ▶ Set aside time to read books, newspapers, or magazines you enjoy.
- ▶ Enlist the help of babysitters (paid or family members) so that you can go out together on dates.

▶ Have friends come over for dinner without their children.
▶ Periodically, set aside a day for just you and your partner.
▶ Take a vacation without your children. A weekend away doesn't have to be expensive or elaborate.

The second strategy to help create a more balanced family is to include your children in making certain family decisions regarding how you spend your time and money. In this way, the children become privy to the big picture of family life and begin to appreciate a sense of budgetary limits on time and money.

The Johnson family provides an excellent example of how to put these tactics to work. In a discretionary fund, the Johnsons managed to save a sum of $2,000 earmarked for general family use. They told their two children that they were going to purchase a treadmill for the basement because they wanted to begin exercising. That left $1,000 in the account. The parents posed two options for a family decision—a new flat-screen television for the family room or a jungle gym for the backyard—both items the kids had been asking for. They explained that they only had enough money to purchase one item and that it was up to the family as a group to decide which to choose.

What the Johnsons accomplished here was making their own needs as parents clear to the kids, while emphasizing the children's feelings of empowerment and importance. In terms of need and want gratification, the children are forced to deny themselves one thing in order to gain another. After choosing the jungle gym, the Johnson children coped well with not getting the new flat-screen TV.

When your kids participate in a more democratic family decision-making process, you are able to maintain their sense of importance and simultaneously underscore the importance of your needs. Your children will begin to understand and appreciate how families make decisions with their children in mind, and how sometimes compromises must be made in order to meet the group's needs, parents included. Intermittently emphasizing parental needs is important to help establish give-and-take in family relationships.

YES PARENTING

Why do you say "yes" to your child? The reasons may be obvious or hidden. There are the right reasons for meeting or denying their requests (rewarding good behavior or grades, punishing for the opposite), and there are the wrong reasons (giving in just because you don't want to hear them whine). Examining your decision-making process when acquiescing to your children can be helpful in developing their skills for coping with need gratification. As you start that process, keep in mind that there are several factors present in today's culture that create overindulgent "yes parents," most commonly: guilt, unhappy marriages, divorce, stress, competition, and fatigue.

Consciously or subconsciously, perhaps the biggest factor that drives the "yes parent" is the feeling of guilt. Parenting by guilt, or allowing guilt to taint parental decisions and judgments, has had a negative effect on the Generation Text child's ability to develop healthy gratification responses. Marc, for example, seemed to learn at an early age how to play the guilt card when confronted with not getting what he wanted. He perceived the presence of guilt and viewed it as a means of changing a parental "no" into "yes." He would regularly say things like, "You are always too busy to drive me places," or, "John's mom buys him any video game he wants," or, "I can never have a play date after school because you work all the time." Sound familiar?

The first thing Marc's parents needed to learn was that these statements were nonsense. Kids love "all or nothing" thinking. The fact is, parents are not *always* too busy, John doesn't *always* get what he wants, and they don't work *all* the time. Parents need to listen for trigger words such as *never, always, everything,* and *nothing,* which signal the need to challenge false statements and deflect the guilt card. An easy intervention, and one I use quite frequently in therapy, is to simply respond to the all-or-nothing inference with a single-word question. For example, "You *never* let me go to the movies with my friends!" would receive the response, "*Never?*" In other words, "Let's get real."

But why do parents feel guilty in the first place? Consciously or not, the basic core belief behind guilty feelings is that the parent is doing something wrong or is being a "bad parent." This belief is irrational and untrue. What circumstances could possibly have engendered Generation Text parents to formulate a negative belief about their parenting skills? The answer lies in the parents' need to compensate for their driving misbelief that they are falling short or missing the mark in doing all that they can for their children.

As dedicated to their children as they are, parents often feel that

they are not doing *enough*. Every parent juggles professional demands, financial needs, the needs of their partner, their own needs,
their social life, and the different needs of each of their children. As
if that were not enough, many of today's parents have the added
responsibility of caring for their own aging parents. This involves
yet more time and money. The Sandwich Generation experiences
huge time crunches, caring for both their children and their parents, which makes them feel like they are not spending enough time
with their children. Time itself has become the biggest commodity
in the "family economy." Consequently, the lack of it leads to the
"I'm not being a good parent" feeling.

Yes parenting can also result from an unhappy marriage. Parents
in unhappy marriages, as well as separated and divorced parents,
are no strangers to the Generation Text family dynamic. Although
divorce does not automatically mean that your child will have problems, kids are common casualties of marital strife and divorce.
Exposing children to disruptive family situations like unhappy marriages or difficult divorces contributes to the guilt parents may already feel for other reasons, resulting in compensation with
indulgence. The belief that one is doing something terrible to one's
children, coupled with the competition between parents for the
child's love, often leads to excessive giving to the child. The thinking is that in such an unhappy home, the least you can do is give
your child things to make her happy. It is natural to feel this way,
and the intentions are good, but by indulging children in this way,
you are ultimately doing them harm. Your child needs you to say
"no."

As parents navigate through their fast-paced, complex social
structure, they experience a great deal of stress. Dealing with your
job's demands, your boss, your workload, and your kids can be
overwhelming. Even if you are a stay-at-home parent, daily demands can be taxing. Stress has a direct impact on parenting. It
causes you to feel tired, and fatigue often creates a lack of tolerance,
irritability, and an overwhelmed feeling that lowers your energy
level. This sometimes translates into a lack of fortitude and firmness
in dealing with children, particularly in the evening. Generation
Text parents just don't have the fight left in them by the time evening rolls around. It is easier to say yes and give in than to fight
with your children or teach them a lesson. The energy and tolerance

it takes to maintain firm limits and rules at home is diminished because of a lack of stamina.

Finally, there is the issue of competition. Competition is inherent and healthy in a capitalist society, and it pervades all aspects of our culture. For kids, competition is healthy when it fosters motivation to work hard or attain an appropriate goal. Unfortunately, when it is applied inappropriately, it can be detrimental to the child's healthy development. Many Generation Text kids want everything their friends have, and parents want to give them those things, and more. The belief that a child must have as much or more than their peers is ever present among many parents and children. As if that is not enough, the highly visible, glamorous lives of entertainers, athletes, and CEOs provide enticement for parents and children to engage on an extremely competitive level.

Competitiveness is not limited to material items. The need to be the best or a star also applies to academics, athletics, the arts, and so on. In order to help their children attain these high levels of performance, parents often provide their sons and daughters with enrichment activities that can include, but are certainly not limited to, dance classes, private academic and SAT tutoring, tennis lessons, art classes, music lessons, and sports clinics, to name a few. All of these activities are beneficial for the development of a well-rounded child. They also provide an edge in the child's ability to achieve in many areas of life. I applaud and even recommend these competitively based activities in order to facilitate identity formation. The problem is not that competition readily accompanies these worthwhile activities; the problem is the unrealistic attitude and high expectations Generation Text parents place on their kids when they engage in these activities.

Generation Text parents are trying to compensate for their guilt feelings of not being good enough by trying to make their children prodigies and superstars. My brother experiences this every day in his work. Parents hire him to videotape their high school athletes, creating a DVD of their son's or daughter's on-field highlights. The parents send their youngster's streaming video resume to NCAA Division I colleges with dreams of a scholarship. My brother relates countless stories of mediocre athletes, at best, aggrandized by their parents as the best since Tom Brady or David Beckham.

To maintain their social edge, parents provide children with the latest name-brand fashions, expensive automobiles, the best sport equipment, state-of-the-art computers, and expensive musical in-struments. The desire to give their children every possible advantage to attain a high level of performance and achievement is another motivation for yes parenting.

But the prevailing competitive atmosphere creates a climate of excess for children, who become accustomed to getting much of what they want, even when those desires are unreasonable. The plethora of opportunities and possessions that Generation Text children receive makes it difficult for them to develop effective coping mechanisms when denied something they want.

TUNNEL VISION SYNDROME

Putting it all together, the following issues have contributed to the difficulty Generation Text kids have as they try to cope with need and want gratification:

► Technology-enhanced, push-button, "get what you want, when you want it" culture
► Immediate access to the things they want and "need"
► Exposure to an excess of material goods and privileges
► Child-centered families
► Yes parenting

As a result of all of these factors, Generation Text kids often experience what I call "tunnel vision syndrome."

In recent years, increasing numbers of families seek therapy because of a child's inability to deny or delay need gratification. Kids of all ages are tormented by the frustration they experience when their needs are not immediately met. They have tremendous difficulty accepting "no" from their parents. Even waiting a short time for something they want is intolerable. It's not just the *numbers* of kids having trouble with need gratification, but the frequency, intensity, and duration of their protests when they do not get what they want that makes this issue characteristically different today than it was ten or twenty years ago.

Tunnel vision syndrome is characterized by a relentless drive to change the parental "no" to a "yes" and the phenomenon of not being able to see beyond the object of desire. The slogan for the

Lexus automobile is, "The relentless pursuit of perfection." The child with tunnel vision syndrome touts his campaign to get what he wants as "the relentless pursuit of *yes.*" It is as if the child has blinders on. He has his sights set solely on what he wants, disregarding logic or potential consequences.

For example, a seven-year-old patient was obsessed with seeing the movie *Ratatouille*. When his parents finally found the time to take him, they found the theater unexpectedly closed because a pipe had burst and the building was flooded. The child began to have a meltdown, insisting his parents try to convince the manager to let them see the movie anyway. He went on and on and ramped up his anger and the volume of his voice. The reality of the movie theater being closed did not dissuade his need to get what he wanted, nor could he even comprehend his parents' offer to locate another theater to see the movie. He just kept his sights on *that* movie, to be seen at *that* time, in *that* theater. Finally, his parents had to threaten punishment if he didn't stop, but he couldn't respond to that, either. This kind of situation can be quite trying on parental patience. When the tenacity of the child's tunnel vision exceeds the ability of the parents to remain steadfast, the parents tend to give in. The intensity of the desire in the child causes him to pull out all of the stops in an attempt to get his need met. Children freely use negotiation, manipulation, and intimidation in the process.

I have found that children who have tunnel vision usually follow the same mode of operation each time. For example, nine-year-old Glenna always begins with negotiation: "How about if you let me play PS3 now and I won't play for the rest of the weekend?" When that tactic fails, Glenna progresses to manipulation: "Tracy gets to play on school nights and you said her mom is a very good mom." The persistence usually continues even when the parent threatens punishment. Since Glenna's focus is only on the target, she restricts herself from seeing reason.

Anger, frustration, and disappointment are the prevailing feelings experienced by the child with tunnel vision syndrome. These feelings become extremely magnified when the parent stands firm. When they don't get what they want, kids move on to intimidation as a final tactic. I have witnessed many kids in my office shout hurtful things like, "I don't love you anymore," "You are the meanest mommy in the world," and "You are the worst daddy in the world." Frightening statements such as "I'll kill myself" and "I'll run away from home" are frequently used as intimidation tactics. The anger sometimes turns into rage and the child starts throwing objects. Eventually, tunnel vision can take on a life of its own, with the child's need to feel gratified superseding her need to obtain the actual object or privilege she originally asked for. In other words, she becomes driven by the need to feel that she is getting what she wants—no matter what it is—rather than being driven to get the cookie she is demanding to have.

To avoid falling into the tunnel vision trap, you first need to identify your child's predictable sequence of tactics. The initial reaction can be to negotiate and try to make deals. When that fails, your youngster may move into manipulation mode. Next, he tries intimidation, which can get scary at times. These tactics can come in any order, but each individual child usually uses the same sequence with each episode.

Once you realize the steps your child predictably takes in the tunnel vision sequence, identify them to your child by name. Sit him down at a calm, conflict-free time so that he will be most receptive and attentive to understanding the problem he is having and how you are going to help him. It is permissible to use sophisticated words like "manipulation" and then explain what they mean. Once your child understands his own actions, you will be able to identify them as he uses them. For example, when your child says, "If you buy me that action figure I will clean my room today," you respond by saying, "You're negotiating to get what you want." Another strategy to break the cycle is to reflect the child's feeling of disappointment by saying something like, "Kayla, I realize how disappointed you feel when you can't get what you want."

When neither of those interventions work and your child begins to turn disappointment into anger, the next appropriate course of action is what I call *disengagement.* Disengaging is a two-step process. Step one is to calmly say, "You are having trouble accepting the word 'no' right now, so I am going to walk away. When you feel calmer you can come see me, but I am not going to discuss it with you anymore." When you start to use this step, your child may be so far gone that he doesn't hear you. But as you enact step two— walking away—your actions will undeniably be understood. Withdrawing your attention without much delay can be quite effective. If you are not present you eliminate the child's ability to negotiate or manipulate. In cases of tunnel vision syndrome, I explain to parents that "less is better."

The young patients I have helped with tunnel vision syndrome are the lucky ones because their parents were able to reach out for professional help. But these patients are just the tip of the iceberg. I believe tunnel vision syndrome is a pervasive problem for Gen Text, and it is only getting worse with time. The good news is that with an understanding of how need gratification develops, and what factors contribute to it, parents can begin to avoid and correct it.

EXERCISING THE MUSCLE

To understand how you can further combat the forces of child-centered families, "yes parenting," and your child's tunnel vision syndrome, let us look at another example, in this case a conversation between five-year-old Steve and his mother:

STEVE: Mom, can I have a cookie?
MOM: No, honey, not now.
STEVE: But why can't I have a cookie?
MOM: I said, No! (*Her voice begins to elevate.*)
STEVE: But I want one now! (*He begins to whine and cry.*)
MOM: Why don't you go watch television until dinner is ready?
STEVE: Give me one! (*He continues to challenge, whine, cry, demand, and yell that she give him the cookie immediately.*)
MOM: Okay, if you stop crying you can have just one cookie. And don't ask me again.

This mother is not training her child to delay his need gratification—the muscle is simply not being worked. She indulges Steve, reinforcing the need for immediate gratification. In a way, she is giving into her own intolerance for the stressful situation.

Now consider how she might have handled the situation differently:

STEVE: Mom, can I have a cookie?
MOM: No, honey, not now.
STEVE: But why can't I have a cookie?

MOM: Because we are about to have dinner. You can have one after dinner.

STEVE: But I want it now!

MOM: I understand that you want it now, but you can't have it until after dinner.

STEVE: Give me one! (*He continues to challenge, whine, cry, demand, and yell that she give him the cookie immediately.*)

MOM: (*ignoring him for a minute or so, then speaking*): I know it's hard to wait, but you will just have to be patient and have your cookie after dinner. If you continue to cry about it, you will have to go to your room and there will be no cookie after dinner.

In this scenario, the mother initially responds to Steve in a respectful manner. She explains the reason for denying him the cookie. Kids deserve to understand why they cannot get what they want. You should explain why you are saying "no"—but only do so one time. If your child disagrees with your reasoning, you need not explain any further; you don't want to get into a debate. Next, you should offer a possible solution. When the child refuses to wait, or to delay his need gratification, and continues his inappropriate behavior, you can offer him a choice. I call it the "either-or strategy." Steve can either stop crying and asking and get the cookie after dinner, or he can go to his room and not get the cookie at all.

At this point, the control is in the hands of the child, but within the parameters established by the parent. Steve has a decision to make, which forces him to contemplate the consequences of his next action. Teaching your child the invaluable skill of how to think through his actions is one of the most important lessons you can instill as a parent. Whatever choice Steve makes will be a step in the right direction, because he will be learning how to wait for something he wants. Yet another strategy used in this second scenario is identifying Steve's feelings. Identifying and reflecting the child's unpleasant feelings helps him cope with them. Eventually, his mother will start to hear what he's really saying, "It's so hard for me to wait for it," instead of inappropriate whining and crying.

The fact is that more of us gravitate toward the first kind of interaction with our children, rather than the more productive second scenario. As a result, Generation Text children are not put through the test often enough to condition their need gratification responses. In everyday life, children have quick and easy access to whatever they want, and such a lifestyle is the only one they have ever known.

If you are just starting your adventure in parenting, you have the advantage of shaping the gratification muscle before it starts to get flabby. If you have made some mistakes along the way, don't worry, it's never too late to start. You will be met with much resistance, but if you avoid wishy-washy and overindulgent responses (such as, "We'll see," or "Maybe," or "You deserve that toy, but . . ."), you can begin to help your child. If you address these issues as soon as possible, you will help your child develop a more flexible, easygoing nature and increase the frequency of pleasant interactions. Be aware that if your child is already used to getting what she wants most of the time, shifting gears will be met with more tantrums and protests than ever before.

Take Herbie as an example. Herbie was an adorable albino laboratory rat assigned to me during my professional training. I had to teach Herbie various behaviors, one of which was to press a bar strategically placed in his cage. When Herbie accidentally pressed the bar, a food pellet came down a chute. Every time he bumped into the bar he received a food pellet. Soon Herbie learned to purposefully depress the lever to get his food pellet. He pressed the lever an average of five times an hour. Then, I stopped the food pellet from coming down the chute. Herbie pressed the lever, but the food pellet was denied. I was now extinguishing, or unlearning, his behavior. Strangely enough, Herbie's bar pressing behavior fervently increased to thirty or forty times an hour, even though there was no reward, much as a child will repeatedly whine and beg for privileges that have been taken away from him. Eventually, Herbie gave up and stopped pressing the bar altogether. This can happen with your children as well.

Although your child's behavior, like Herbie's, may become more intense once you start saying "no," the most important thing you can do is to remain firm and consistent with your new reactions. As the demanding behavior begins to wane, the gratification muscle starts to take shape. Remember, a muscle cannot become firm and toned by working out once in a while. The more the muscle is exercised and maintained, the better it is conditioned.

With this in mind, let's return to Marc. When Marc's parents became aware of the forces behind their son's inappropriate behavior, they were astonished. Together, we devised strategies and family policies to help tone down Marc's push-button tendencies. Because he had always been a strong student, his parents had never set firm limits on his television viewing, Internet time, and video game playing. They decided that as long as he was handling his academic responsibilities, they could allow him to monitor himself. This is solid parenting, generally speaking, but considering Marc's difficulty with accepting "no" for an answer and wanting everything immediately, his parents needed to reconsider their strategy. To strengthen the immediate gratification muscle, they began to establish time limits and designated days for electronics usage. It is not realistic, in contemporary life, to eliminate or even significantly reduce your kids' intermachine interaction. Pushing buttons to get what you want is often unavoidable. But parents need to understand that our fast-paced, push-button culture is a phenomenon that has to be reckoned with, and setting definite limits is often the first step.

Most parenting approaches come from a positive place. Even indulgence due to guilty feelings emanates from deep love and a heightened desire to be a good parent. So, in addition to helping Marc's parents understand when they parented out of guilt, I also had them perform an exercise called the "reality check."

USING REALITY CHECKS

Immersed as they are in their complex daily lives, people often develop a skewed view of their own life. Perceptions of situations become impaired and our points of reference distorted. Consequently, we make decisions and judgments based on blurred perceptions and off-center points of reference. I use reality check exercises to help people regain an objective view of themselves.

The reality check exercise I used for Marc's parents was designed to create an eye-opening effect. Remember, guilty parenting is driven by the misbelief that parents are not doing enough or being good enough for their kids. A reality check will help you objectively identify what you are doing well and what you need to improve. In the process, you will be challenging the irrational beliefs about your parenting that you have undoubtedly accumulated.

The first part of the exercise is to compile a bulleted list of the parenting traits you and your spouse consider to be ideal. Of course, these items will vary from parent to parent, but here's a representative sampling of this list:

▶ Be attentive to your children when they talk.
▶ Be aware of what is happening in their lives.
▶ Provide them with the appropriate tools and programs to enhance their education.
▶ Expose them to cultural activities such as museums, plays, and movies.
▶ Provide positive and negative consequences for appropriate and inappropriate behavior.

Next, compile a list of the parenting traits you currently are using on a regular basis. Comparing the two lists is usually a reality check in and of itself, because there is often very little variation between the two lists. This indicates that you really are parenting in the way you want and helps relieve the guilt that may be causing you to be a "yes parent." Any discrepancies you find between the two lists means you have discovered an area of parenting that needs more of your attention. A variation of this exercise might be to simply perform a point-by-point evaluation of your ideal parenting list to get your reality check.

Reality checks should be done periodically to avoid a loss of objectivity in your parenting skills. Conducting ongoing reality checks with your partner is a great idea. Check to see what your partner thinks about your specific parenting decisions and general parenting approaches. General questions to ask each other regularly are:

"Do you think I am being too strict?"
"Do you think I am being too easy on them?"
"Am I overly involved?"
"Am I overly controlling?"
"What am I not doing enough of with the kids?"

The dialogue that follows these questions will help you stay centered, monitor your parenting, and keep you firmly based in reality.

USING NORMALIZATION

Another way to combat "yes parenting" is to take advantage of the normalization concept discussed in Chapter 2. Routines must be established and rigidly adhered to at first, in order for your kids to gradually accept them as a new reality. Evening routines begin with how you and your children greet each other. Eye contact and a display of physical affection, such as a hug or kiss, set an initial tone. Greeting your spouse in the same manner is also helpful.

With Marc's family, we instituted a five-minute buffer time after greeting one another, in which Marc and his brother were able to play independently. This buffer time was needed to allow both parents to debrief from the stress of their day before they began trying to meet the needs and requests of their kids. It also provided a few minutes of "me" time for the parents, even if it was only to change their clothes or lie down for a moment. The point is that each family should decide on what routines work best for them. Establish and stick to these routines because they become normative procedures in the household. Consequently, the number of demands and requests from the children is reduced because the rule structure is clear.

Here is an example of a possible dinner routine and rule structure:

▶ Dinner is served within a specific time frame according to the day of the week.
▶ All family members who are home must sit with the rest of the family.
▶ Dinner is eaten at the kitchen table—not in the family room or bedroom.
▶ No television, toys, or electronic gadgets are allowed during dinnertime.
▶ Only one dinner will be prepared, which will always include at least one item that each person likes to eat. No other meals will be prepared.
▶ Desserts will alternate between healthy and less nutritious choices. Everyone always gets a healthy dessert, but less nutritious desserts are only deserved when a reasonable amount of dinner is eaten.
▶ Everyone participates in cleaning up the dinner.

This particular dinner routine may not work for your family. The point, though, is that when any routine is established and maintained, you will see a decrease in comments like, "Can I watch TV?" or "I don't like pasta, can you make me something else?" or "I want cookies for dessert tonight!"

Beyond dinner, establishing routines for the order of the evening, including homework and bedtime, provides the predictable structure that kids need. Well-established parameters help reduce the frequency of demands from your children. Fewer demands in turn mean fewer reasons to deny them. Once you have established a routine, you will have more stamina with which to respond with good judgment when the kids want to deviate from the routine. Deferring to the rules of the routine is much easier than having to decide whether or not to acquiesce to the request. Once the kids get with the program, there is plenty of room for flexibility. The best part is that the normalization phenomenon works in your favor when family routines are well established. And a bonus is a smoother running family.

EVALUATING YOUR FAMILY

Take a step back and perform a self-evaluation of how your parenting approaches are helping or hindering your child's development of denial and delay of need gratification. Consider the factors within your family that may be perpetuating your children's inability to accept "no" for an answer or contributing to their tunnel vision syndrome.

Are you a "yes parent"? Are you so tired at the end of the day that you don't have the energy to be steadfast with your children? To what degree do guilty feelings govern your parenting decisions? Using reality checks and established routines can help alleviate guilty feelings and reduce the frequency of your child's demands. Examine how competitive you are and how much you emphasize competitiveness within your children. Make sure there is a healthy ratio of power in your family. If you decide that your family is too child-centered, begin to make the shift so that your kids do not feel too much empowerment. Exercise some introspection to assess how factors in your life may be contributing to your child's poor ability to cope with gratification issues.

Make sure you are exercising the gratification muscle by standing firm with your children. Say "no" even when it is easier to give in. The more consistent you are in fighting the fight, the easier it gets as time goes on. Develop effective coping skills for gratification issues and understand how to avoid the pitfalls of raising an "I want it now!" child. In doing so, you will set the stage for teaching your children the value of working for what they want.

CHAPTER 4

Work Ethic

···

Play Now, Work Later

LINDSEY IS A SIXTEEN-YEAR-OLD HIGH SCHOOL SOPHOMORE. SHE IS bright, engaging, attractive, sociable, and, up until now, academically successful. Lindsey had always earned As and Bs in elementary and middle school, but when she entered high school her grades began to slip. She started to get more Bs than As, and Cs appeared for the first time on her report card. At first, her parents chalked up the decline to the adjustment of starting high school. By the time she met with me in the middle of her tenth-grade year, however, the As had disappeared altogether and some Ds were creeping into her grades.

After an assessment that ruled out learning disabilities, drug use, depression, and other psychiatric illnesses that might account for the academic decline, I determined that Lindsey was suffering from a condition you won't find classified in the *Diagnostic and Statistical Manual of Mental Disorders* (the bible for psychiatric illnesses). Lindsey, a mentally healthy teenage girl, is afflicted by a poor work ethic. Even though the "symptoms" did not appear until relatively late in her academic career, her work ethic had never really developed.

Lindsey's profile is characteristic of Generation Text. A lack of an effective work ethic is sometimes seen in early childhood, but often it rears its problematic head in adolescence for the first time. Although the work ethic may have been missing all along, parents might not notice in the case of a naturally gifted child who finds easy success in school, sports, and other activities. Eventually, exertion of effort becomes an essential ingredient for success, and then we notice the absence of a work ethic. I had one patient who was so bright that he didn't face the first academic challenge to his work ethic until he began a PhD program in physics at Princeton! His ability to breeze through school caused him to expect everything to come easily, so he put little to no effort into other activities such as sports and clubs. This young man simply expected success without feeling like he had to work for it. Likewise, Generation Text kids expect to receive things simply because they want them.

If you ask teachers and employers about the work ethic of most of their students and employees, they will tell you that it is substandard. There is a sense that mediocrity is good enough, and expending extra effort is rare. Why should you care about this?

I often tell my patients that the keys to success in any profession are an average or better innate ability, the propensity to treat people respectfully, and a strong work ethic. You don't have to be intellectually gifted or attend an Ivy League college to be successful. In fact, even if you are gifted and talented and attend a tier-one university, it is unlikely that you will be successful if you *lack* a positive work ethic. Such a work ethic, and all of the personality traits that are packaged with it, distinguish individuals as standout performers.

Why is it that Generation Text lacks the drive toward excellence? The answer to this question is complicated, but it starts with the fact that working hard is a learned behavior, not an innate human trait.

THE PATH OF LEAST RESISTANCE

When water trickles down the side of a hill, it finds the path of least resistance. Why climb over boulders when it takes much less energy to go around them? This kind of basic physics makes sense. What you might not realize is that most kids, and in fact most adults, are just like water—if they can, they will find the path of least resistance. The problem with taking the easy way is that it often results in an inferior outcome. It has always been a parental challenge to get the most effort out of our children, but this challenge has become more of a battle with Generation Text kids because of their strong sense of entitlement, as discussed in the previous chapter.

Having a strong work ethic does not come naturally to kids. Instead, it is a learned concept. Working hard to achieve something is a value and an attitude that is constructed over a long period of time. The tendency to find the path of least resistance, on the other hand, comes naturally, especially to those who are used to getting what they want. Access and excess issues enable our kids to obtain material objects and privileges without much effort. Today's kids have their eye on the prize without regard to the expenditure of effort that enables them to receive the reward. And why should they? It doesn't make sense to exert effort when it isn't necessary. And for children who are raised by "yes parents" in child-centered families, children who are used to getting everything they want as soon as they want it, this certainly holds true.

In contrast, the generations previous to this one subscribed to two basic tenets: Hard work will greatly increase the likelihood of reaching your goal, and hard work is virtuous and builds moral character. Many of this country's immigrants and laborers had to work hard just to survive. Their children heeded the example of their hardworking parents and coupled that with their desire to take advantage of the incredible economic growth opportunities of their era. Their children in turn saw hard work as a way to further improve their standard of living and attain luxuries not available to them as children.

Generation Text kids, it seems, don't feel the same need to work hard at all. Lindsey, for example, had informed her parents that they needed to start discussing the kind of car she would drive when she got her driver's license. She assumed that she would automatically get a car without having to earn it in any way. Regarding her school work, Lindsey asked, "Why should I work hard when I am doing okay?" Her attitude toward achievement was that as long as she was doing well enough to get by, she shouldn't waste her time working hard. The emphasis on "good enough" prevents Lindsey from reaching her full potential. Unfortunately, Lindsey is not alone. Working toward potential, or doing your best, is an aspiration that has a dwindling presence among Generation Text kids.

SENSE OF ENTITLEMENT

What happened in the years between her great-grandparents' generation and Lindsey's? Why should today's children feel so little motivation to work hard and earn their privileges and belongings?

Much of this phenomenon can be linked to the strong sense of entitlement Generation Text kids feel. A sense of entitlement is an expectation that you should receive something you want without earning it. For Generation Text kids, it is an intense feeling based on the belief that they deserve things simply because of who they are. A recent survey indicates that about 83 percent of Americans believe that today's youth have a stronger sense of entitlement than kids did ten years ago.* What caused this change? Part of the answer is the empowerment kids experience as a result of child-centered families and yes parenting, in which getting what they want comes easily. Combine those factors with a high-tech age filled with machines and gadgets that make it easier to get work done generally, and we have a generation that is used to getting what it wants with minimal effort. Technology simultaneously brings kids to new heights of knowledge and information, while negatively impacting the development of the basic work ethic. It is one of the major afflictions of growing up in a high-tech age.

Consider, for example, the software you can use to help you compose music. I love all types of music, and so I downloaded a free program on the Internet that allows me to compose my own music using dozens of "instruments." Without actually learning how to play any of those instruments, I am able to produce perfectly performed musical compositions. In this way, I can pursue my hobby without putting in the countless hours it would take to learn how to play, practice, and master those skills in reality.

There is a difference between me and kids in this generation, however. Generation Text children believe they should be able to become concert pianists without ever touching a keyboard. Of course, those are the ambitious ones—the kids who actually have goals of becoming something or other. They also believe they should get what they want based on the fact that they want it, without any larger goal in mind. They don't understand the difference between "wanting" and "needing" something.

These children are surrounded by more devices, toys, games, food, and clothes than anyone needs. Having so much becomes an expectation and soon they feel entitled to vast amounts of "stuff." They also believe they should have the ability to replace or improve

---

*Sacred Heart University, "Majority of Americans Cite Sense of Entitlement Among Youth, Says National Poll," news release, May 16, 2006, http://www.sacredheart.edu/pages/13433_majority_of_americans_cite_sense_of_entitlement_among_youth_says_national_poll.cfm.

on those things when they so desire. They are a generation with a disposable mentality, taught to believe that if they don't like something, they can throw it away and get a better one. The disposable mentality is created by both obvious and subtle factors. In the age of technological evolution, perfectly functioning gadgets such as cell phones, iPods, and computers are regularly replaced (usually every eighteen months) with new and improved models. Fads generated by the fashion industry render last season's clothing disposable, even when it is still in perfect shape, since wearing something that is not "in" jeopardizes one's social acceptance. The overall ethos of the land of plenty is that old can quickly be replaced by new. Kids are equipped with new hockey sticks, tennis rackets, and baseball cleats every season regardless of the condition of their "old" equipment. Parents lease new automobiles every three years as opposed to owning the same car for ten years, which may add to this mentality. The result is a lack of appreciation for what we have, and the general neglect of our belongings.

Without developing a strong work ethic, Generation Text will invariably fail to meet parental and societal demands as children and they will be less than happy adults. We can't have it both ways. We can't have high expectations for achievement and hand over the world to a generation with an overwhelming sense of entitlement. It is vital to take a step back and examine how we might be contributing to our children's poor work ethic. Furthermore, we need to provide our kids with the tools they need to work for what they want.

"GOTTAS" AND "WANNAS"

Many years ago, I sat in on a planning meeting for an eighth-grade patient's high school course selections. The guidance counselor, John Scott, described the eight-period day in terms of subjects you "gotta" take and things you "wanna" take. I have broadened his approach to a general philosophy for developing a work ethic.

The goal for all kids is to develop a sense of industry—an orientation toward work, achievement, and accomplishment. As children are exposed to parental, societal, and institutional demands to perform and achieve, they must negotiate their struggle between engaging in preferred play activities and completing chores and tasks that are required of them. For most kids, cleaning their room, doing homework, going to school, and taking out the garbage are "gottas"—they are things they have to do. Playing baseball, taking horseback-riding lessons, playing video games, watching television, and hanging out at the mall with their friends are "wannas."

The problem is that Generation Text kids have it reversed. They want the wannas without doing the gottas. Lindsey, for example, expects to get a car without having to do anything for it. I explained to her that you have to take care of your gottas in order to get your wannas. In fact, the more gottas you take care of, and do a good job at, the more wannas you end up getting. This was a somewhat novel notion to Lindsey because, up until now, whenever she "needed" new clothes, a new iPod, or money to go out with her friends, her parents found it easy to give her those things—after all, she is a delightful and well-behaved child. Lindsey was also smart enough to master certain concepts and get decent grades without having to work very hard. In her case, the poor work ethic went undetected because her parents were focused on her grades alone, which were good. Only when her grades began to slip did the issue surface for them.

Lindsey needed to learn that high school was just the beginning. In the future, she will be expected to perform and work hard, but if she is unable or unwilling to put forth the effort or go the extra mile, she will fail. Beyond schoolwork and vocational activities, long-term, committed relationships also involve hard work and the tools incorporated in a strong work ethic. If she wants to be successful in these major areas of life, she will need to start developing a work ethic now.

I asked Lindsey to maintain a list of all the things she asks her parents to buy her and of her social activities, both formal and informal. I had her parents compile a list of all of the tasks and responsibilities they expected from their daughter. In other words, Lindsey made a list of her "wannas" and her parents made a list of her "gottas." It became obvious in subsequent family sessions that Lindsey received most of what she wanted, but either refused to meet her responsibilities, or procrastinated and then eventually did a shoddy job. This was an increasing source of consternation and stress in her relationship with her parents. Chances are, if you create the same lists for your kids, the imbalance between their wannas and gottas will be eye-opening. Of course, there will always be an imbalance because kids need their parents to provide them with far more than parents need from their kids. Still, a careful examination of these lists will help you determine how lopsided the giving and taking is between you and your children. Pay particularly close attention to how deficient they may be in meeting minimal expectations for completion of chores, homework, and family obligations. Do your kids have to work for things they want, or are they provided with automatic privileges? How can you help them realize that they have to take care of their gottas first to be able to earn the wannas?

PERSPECTIVE AND HUMILITY

One part of having a good work ethic is not taking anything you have for granted. Having perspective and humility facilitates an appreciation for family and material possessions. No matter how much money you do or do not have, an appreciation for it must be discussed and recognized regularly to impart these values to your children.

I was reminded of this weekly when I met Susan, a thirteen-year-old patient. Susan's family was of modest means and she did not have a closet full of clothes or many other luxuries common to Generation Text kids. Every week, Susan appeared for her session wearing sparkling white Adidas sneakers. When I noticed them, I asked if they were new. Slightly offended, Susan informed me that they were about a year old and that she wore them every day. They looked shiny and new because she cleaned them two to three times a week. She loved them and wanted them to last. Susan's parents obviously instilled in her an appreciation for material objects that allowed her to treat them with respect.

Another way to maintain perspective and humility in your children is to encourage them to do community service and charity work. Giving time to others builds character; it creates moral commitment and a sense of appreciation for the gift of your fortunate lifestyle.

Donating old toys around Christmas and Hanukkah and having your child buy a new toy with his own money to give to the less fortunate is a great approach. Some children have difficulty letting go of their toys, even if they haven't played with them for a while.

When Andie's rather wealthy father asked her to choose three toys to donate to charity, she asked him to go to Toys "R" Us and buy them new toys instead. This is not the attitude we want our children to have. In order to teach Andie a valuable lesson, her father insisted she choose some of her own toys, and brought her with him when he delivered them.

To clearly emphasize the importance of giving to others, he explained to Andie: *"I am proud of you for choosing those toys to give away. You haven't played with them for a long time, which means you probably don't like them anymore. Isn't it great that you can help a child who never had these toys feel so happy?"*

To help Andie share the good feeling of receiving gifts, he told her: *"You know how good it feels—how excited you are—to get new toys. Isn't it great to be able to give that great feeling to a child who wouldn't be getting a new toy if it wasn't for you?"*

To help her part with her old toys and emphasize the importance of people over things, he told Andie: *"I realize that it is hard for you to give up your toys. You have to remember that making someone happy is much more important than keeping an old toy. People's feelings are more important than things."*

To teach the meaning of giving and not being self-centered, he told Andie: *"If you kept those toys, you would be thinking only of yourself. When you are selfish, it usually hurts another person's feelings. When you give something of yours to someone who needs it, it makes it even more special for them."*

That experience is sure to stay with Andie as she matures. You, too, can do similar things to help your own child build an effective work ethic.

STRUCTURE AND TIME MANAGEMENT

Mike, a nine-year-old boy, had been playing his video game system for two hours when his mom asked him to clean his room. Entranced by the barrage of multisensory colors, graphics, visual movements, and sounds, Mike completely ignored his mother, who then asked again. Still no response. Then, the mother started to yell. The yelling finally got Mike's attention, but at this point, his mom was angry when she yet again asked her son to clean his room. This time, Mike graced his mom with a response.

"After I finish this level," he said.

Now, even more annoyed and even firmer in her tone, his mom commanded Mike to go and clean his room.

"But I just have to beat this one boss! I've never gotten this far! If I stop now I'll have to start at the beginning of the level!"

"Can't you save it?" his mother pleaded, proud of the fact that she knew about "save" points in the game, allowing Mike to continue where he left off.

"I'm not at a save point, Mom."

Mike continued to play, never taking his eyes off the screen. Abruptly, his mother shut the game system off. Mike threw the controller down, frustrated by the game and angry at his mother's action. He yelled some disrespectful comment and stomped upstairs to his room. Fifteen minutes later, his mother yelled to Mike to ask him how much progress he had made. No response. She called again. Still no answer. Starting to fume again, she went into Mike's room to check his progress. As she entered the bedroom, she stumbled, trying to avoid stepping on the cordless phone on the floor, then sidestepped the pile of clothing at her feet, barely managing to maintain her balance. Looking up, her rage immediately returned as she caught sight of her son lying on the bed with iPod earbuds on, listening to music while playing Game Boy Advance SP.

Sound familiar? What Mike's mother needed to learn was that her first task should have been helping her son distinguish between work time and play time. Generation Text kids have particular difficulty with this distinction due to the vast number of distractions available to them. They have so many different types of machines with which they can interact that it becomes nearly impossible to attend to their responsibilities in a timely fashion, and the potential for the number and frequency of conflicts multiplies exponentially. During the course of a day, a child can flitter from machine to machine, leaving an angry parent trailing behind. The simple task of cleaning his room becomes a constant test of self-discipline for Mike, who has easy access to his friends, games, and other distractions. In the rather brief interaction between Mike and his mother, Mike was unable to make the appropriate distinction between work time and play time, the result of which was an ugly confrontation leading to anger on both sides. Errors were made by both Mike and his mother.

The following tactics can be used to avoid situations like this one:

1. *Provide schedules and rewards.* Teaching your kids how to organize their time will help them develop a better work ethic. By adhering to an established schedule, the transition from work time to play time, and vice versa, becomes a mechanical process. Having definite blocks of time on school nights and weekends for homework, chores, social commitments, and free time will help your child to become work-oriented while still maintaining play time. Teaching your kids how to budget their time so that they finish their gottas before getting their wannas helps them develop the art of time management. They will learn how to estimate how long a task takes, how to break down a task into multistep projects, and how to meet deadlines.

Building reward systems into such a schedule will help motivate your child and keep him on task. For example, after devoting a block of time to cleaning his room, two hours of free time can be scheduled before the science project time block begins. However, there is no free time until the room is clean. Ideally, your child will begin to build in his own short rewards after completion of a chore, like rewarding himself with computer time after he takes out the trash, gathers the recycling, and walks the dog. It is also permissible for you to offer tangible rewards for task completion, like taking your child out for ice cream once she finishes her homework.

2. *Limit access to electronics.* Teach your child how to make these distinctions by providing her with a structure that makes it less tempting to play. Providing structure entails modifying the physical environment and expressing clear expectations of your child's behavior and clear consequences for straying from the task at hand.

If your child is like Mike, you need to limit her access to electronics. If she is having a problem getting her homework or house chores done, it is unfair to allow her free access to the distractions that compromise her ability to work rather than play. Just imagine trying to stick to your diet if you were asked to spend all day in your favorite bakery shop, or trying to stop drinking while you worked as a bartender. If your child has work to do—homework, cleaning the playroom, or raking the leaves—you must make sure all of her

distractions are out of sight or in your possession. For the less portable distractions such as televisions and PCs, learn how to set parental locks, remove a part of the device that renders it inoperable, and
of course limit those devices to the family room rather than putting
them directly in the child's bedroom or playroom.

Parents need to take back control of the environment. If your
children are well disciplined and can say no to social and electronic
distractions, continue to give them the trust and confidence in their
decision making, which will enable them to keep up the good work.
This strategy borders on micro-parenting, but until your youngster
can learn self-discipline, he actually needs you to implement it. Just
like you used to cut your child's food into small pieces when she
was a toddler because she was incapable of doing it herself, you
need to remove potential distractions from kids when they have
difficulty discerning work and play time. They will not do this on
their own.

3. *Get their attention.* When asking your child to transition
from a play activity to a work activity, you may need to tap his
shoulder to get his full attention. Next, use the Stop, Look, and
Listen approach: "Mike, stop what you are doing. Please look at
me. I am going to tell you two things to do right now. First, I want
you to shut the video game system off, and then I want you to clean
your room. Mike, what are the two things I asked you to do?"

4. *Give them a warning (5–3–1–Off).* To help develop time
management skills and deadline awareness, it is also wise to give
your kids what I call the 5–3–1 warning. Let Mike know that in five
minutes he will have to shut the game off. Give him a three-minute
and then a one-minute warning as well. If this is done consistently
with most transitions, he will eventually learn to plan the termina-
tion of his play activity as his deadline approaches.

Once you have successfully terminated the play activity, you
must set up your child to begin the work task. Escort him to the
area where the task is to be accomplished and give him assistance to
get him started. In Mike's case, this would mean going to Mike's
room with him and letting him know exactly what has to be done.
You may choose to set an example by picking things up off the floor
before actually leaving the child alone to complete the job. Most

kids will finish a job once they've started—the key is getting them to start it in the first place.

As you work on these issues, it is always helpful to remind your children that, although it may be hard to believe, if they do their work first, and do it well, they will actually end up with more time to play. Also, fighting with you and being generally uncooperative about work tasks prolongs the agony and draws out the unpleasant feeling they have about the work: It's like peeling a bandage off very slowly as opposed to ripping it off quickly. Explain that no matter how you slice it, your son or daughter won't enjoy the work, so it's best to make it as painless as possible. You might also add that another benefit of cooperating with you is that there will be less yelling, anger, and nagging from you as a result!

PROMOTING SELF-RELIANCE

Generation Text kids have learned to rely on both adults and technology to help them complete tasks. While some dependence is natural and expected, an *over*reliance hinders the development of a good work ethic. Remember, kids tend to take the path of least resistance. If they can get their parents to do as much for them as possible, or if a machine can do it instead, they will avoid taking on the responsibility for themselves. The result of these tendencies is that kids lack the independence they need to develop an effective work ethic. Let's start by explaining the benefits of self-reliance, then consider the major factors eroding self-reliance and work ethic.

Benefits of Self-Reliance

Whether you are a parent, an employer, or president of the PTA, you rely on others to perform tasks independently and to the best of their ability. Self-reliance in attaining goals is an important component of a strong work ethic. All goes well if the task is an easy one to accomplish. But what happens when your child is working on something and encounters a snag?

For the most part, eight-year-old Alice does her homework without the assistance of her parents, since most subjects are relatively easy for her. Her math homework is another story. As soon as Alice runs into a difficult math problem, she asks for help from her mother. Mrs. Gold easily accommodates her daughter by helping her. This may be a common scenario in your family. On the surface, it seems appropriate and harmless, but Mrs. Gold is unwittingly handicapping her daughter. Alice has quickly learned never ask her father for help, even when he is in the same room. This is because Alice's instinctive responses to frustration are to either avoid the task completely or ask someone to help her. While Mrs. Gold practically hands Alice the answers on a platter, Mr. Gold encourages her to think through the problem on her own, which perpetuates her frustration.

Although well intended, Mrs. Gold is actually hindering the development of an important aspect of Alice's good work ethic—self-reliance. Solving even minor problems requires effort. Overcoming problems, be it a math assignment, an argument with a friend, or a malfunctioning cell phone, requires practice. A certain amount of frustration is involved in independent problem solving, and children need to learn to tolerate frustration so that it does not interfere with their ability to complete tasks effectively. Tolerating rather than escaping the feeling of frustration enables your child to learn how to persevere, be resourceful, and think creatively in solving problems. The willingness to see tasks through to the end and solve problems independently is a big part of developing an effective work ethic.

I encouraged Mrs. Gold to use her husband's approach, which facilitates independent problem solving. Asking questions about how to go about solving the problem instead of directly getting her to the answer (or giving her the solution) provides an appropriate balance of assistance and self-reliance in working it through. This way, Alice is forced to tolerate frustration, persist at the problem, and think resourcefully and creatively to solve it.

Dangers of Micro-Parenting

Micro-parenting happens when parents overstructure their children's schedules, mapping out the details of every step of every task, giving them endlessly detailed instructions. When a parent does too much for the child, it sends the message that the child may not be capable of completing certain tasks himself. This increases the child's dependency on adult assistance; it also communicates a lack of confidence in the child. Consequently, the child will not develop independent problem-solving skills. Ideally, there should be a balance between how much direction and structure you provide and how much autonomy your child has. Allowing him to navigate through tasks within the parameters you establish will promote independent thinking, problem-solving skills, and self-confidence.

Doing too much for your child, particularly when he is capable of doing it on his own, will ultimately hamper his sense of industry and discourage his need to develop ambition. Allowing your children to tackle more on their own means you have to tolerate watching them experience distress, and possible failure, or you may have to accept a substandard completion of the task. For example, having your seven-year-old make her bed as part of the morning routine means she has to make time to complete the task; it also means she may be unhappy about having to do it, while you may have to live with the bed looking like it was just slept in even after she makes it.

Overreliance on Technology

In many ways, life has become easier because machines and gadgets have streamlined everything from daily living tasks, to travel, to the way we do business, and so on. One might think that access to the numerous fascinations in the world through portable communication devices and the Internet would provide more of an incentive to work hard. After all, our kids have extensive exposure to the wonderful things they can acquire in the world, expanding their desire for those things.

But instead of having to work to get those things, for Generation Text they are readily available upon request. When you provide your child with unlimited Internet access, their own computers and cell phones, and your credit card information, why would you assume they would act any other way? As a result, Generation Text kids rely on technology as a natural and almost effortless means to get what they want. Reliance on technology limits the child's experience of putting time, effort, and even inconvenience into actually earning something he wants. The feeling of working earnestly for something you want—another component of a strong work ethic—is somewhat lost.

WHY SELF-RELIANCE MEANS WORKING HARD

Many of us have become overly reliant on technology. Think about how inconvenient or difficult your day would be without a computer, wireless Internet, a cell phone, a microwave, or even an air conditioner. The first step in combating this overreliance is to develop a keen awareness of it. To promote self-reliance and a strong work ethic, kids need to experience the feeling associated with hard work—a feeling that technology has a tendency to eliminate. Once in a while, take the technology away from your children and have them complete a task the old-fashioned way. For example, don't allow them to always use the calculator for computations on their math homework. Once in a while, take them to the library to research a topic instead of doing a search online. Not only will these experiences reinforce concepts and work habits, they will send a message that putting extra time and effort into something can be virtuous and rewarding. It will also promote independent thinking and problem-solving skills. By approaching a task step-by-step, kids obtain a fuller understanding of the topic or concept they are learning about. They not only develop a greater appreciation for the focus of their work, they can utilize this knowledge to build on it or apply it to new concepts.

My fear is that Generation Text kids are subtly learning to feign helplessness because they become unmotivated when the help is unavailable. Promoting self-reliance will help fight the learned helplessness that micro-parenting and technology have created. The proper balance of parent involvement and appropriate use of technology to facilitate task completion will help your kids develop into problem solvers with a positive work ethic.

For example, if your child has a homework assignment to translate a paragraph from English to Spanish, he no longer needs to use dictionaries, context, or critical thinking. Instead, he can go to any number of websites, such as www.babylon.com, type in the passage, click a button, and have it automatically translated for him. True, the passage has been translated correctly. But isn't the idea to learn to fluently read and write in Spanish? And isn't it important to correct your kids when they cheat their way out of doing something?

To combat situations like this one, encourage a child to take on extra credit or other optional assignments when they are offered. This will emphasize the value of doing work with a sense of pride and maximum effort. It is also important to recognize how hard your children work for something. Tell them how proud you are of them when their grades or skills improve as a result of their efforts. Of course, you don't always want to evaluate outcome in terms of grades and performance. What is important is that if they try their hardest, putting significant time and effort into the job, they will undoubtedly do the best that they can.

Ellen, a ten-year-old girl with a math learning disability, represents a dramatic example of emphasizing effort over outcome. Since Ellen feels inadequate in this subject, she is very uncooperative with her math homework. In therapy, Ellen and I worked on the idea that even though she was a poor math student, she should still try her best. At the beginning of one session her father made a point of telling me, in front of Ellen, how well she studied for a big math test. She not only worked uncharacteristically hard, but was extremely cooperative and willing to practice until she knew the material as well as possible. She studied with her father and on her own. She even pulled her math book out on the car ride to school that morning. The next week, her father came into the session alone and informed me that Ellen scored a 67 on the math test. He asked about the appropriate punishment for such a low grade. I reminded him that this grade reflected Ellen's absolute best effort, and that he should be rewarding her based on that effort, rather than punishing her. By positively reinforcing Ellen's conscientious efforts, including her taking the initiative to study, the important message about work ethic was clearly communicated.

Setting Goals

Setting long-term goals and outlining the steps needed to accomplish objectives is a big part of developing a strong work ethic. By doing so, you map out a structure or formula to work toward an objective, do it thoroughly, and complete it on time. Whether the goals are "gottas" or "wannas," the process is identical. Your child must set his sights on the end result, whether it is writing an essay for English class or getting a new skateboard deck. Listing each step needed to meet the goal will ensure that the proper amount of work will be put forth. Inherent in goal planning is the feeling that the outcome is actually earned by the child, not unconditionally received.

Setting goals and devising plans to earn specific luxuries is a way to instill a work ethic and combat the sense of entitlement. Despite the drastic departure from what they are used to, Generation Text kids will eventually adjust to being expected to earn things rather than being handed them effortlessly. Expensive gifts should be reserved for birthdays, religious occasions, and recognition of important accomplishments such as graduations and life-cycle events. If they want the newest technology, toys, and clothing, you should find ways for them to earn the money with which to pay for those things. You might give your kids an allowance based on chores, or implement a rewards system for working up to their potential in school. Not only will a work ethic be reinforced this way, but your children are more likely to maintain, care for, and appreciate the items they worked for. Regular daily and/or weekly chores emphasize the work aspect of life, allow kids to contribute to the running of the family, and incorporate an "earning your keep" attitude that replaces their sense of entitlement. Of course, kids shouldn't have to work for *everything* they want, but nor should they be given carte blanche without setting a goal and a plan to earn *some* of what they want.

Earning It and Enjoying It

After several months of therapy, Lindsey and her parents, whom we met earlier in this chapter, established the goal of buying her a car when she got her driver's license. She agreed to help pay for it by working a part-time job and earning allowance money for completing regular chores around the house. Her parents created a chart in which they matched their financial contribution to the purchase with Lindsey's work contribution. Lindsey was also required to contribute to the cost of gas and maintenance, while her parents would pay for the insurance. The car is now considered a privilege, not an automatic right. If she follows the rules of the road, keeps the car clean and well-maintained, and is a careful driver, Lindsey will be able to keep her new car. This is quite different from her original attitude, and it was made possible by her parents' willingness to alter their parenting style.

The idea of earning the things they want can be expanded to money management skills as well. As your kids accumulate funds with a goal in mind, they must learn how to budget for other purchases that will deplete their savings, prolonging the process of saving for their bigger goal. In Lindsey's case, for example, she had to weigh the pros and cons of a new pair of jeans with the delay in getting her car. There were actually several choices she had to make regarding expenditures that might delay the arrival of her car. She scrutinized each item and bought some of them but denied herself others. As we all know, these are lifelong skills that will be relevant in almost every aspect of experience as our children grow up.

To encourage saving as a family value, I offered my three children a "dollar for dollar" deal when they were young. To motivate them to save money, whenever they earned funds from babysitting, snow shoveling, or as gifts, I matched every dollar they put in a savings account. If they put $50 in their account, they were really saving $100. One day, the most entrepreneurial of my children came to me and asked how much money he had in his savings account. At that time, he had accumulated a good sum of money. I told him he had a great deal of money in there because he had saved so well, and I congratulated him on a job well done. Then I asked him why he wanted to know. He told me that he wanted to take all the money out of the bank. Alarmed, I asked him what he could possibly want to buy with that amount of money. He replied, "Oh, I don't want to buy anything. I just want to take the money out and put it back in so that you will match it." I praised him for his ingenuity, proud of the fact that he had internalized the importance of saving. Still, I couldn't agree to his plan.

WHY WELL-ADJUSTED KIDS HAVE GOOD WORK ETHICS

We have examined the importance of having a good work ethic in children. A good work ethic manifests many of the traits that represent a well-adjusted child, including a sense of industry, ambition, the ability to work independently, and the ability to work up to one's potential. Having a good work ethic also increases your child's potential to be successful at whatever he attempts. Success, as we know, contributes to positive self-esteem.

By employing the many suggestions given in this chapter, you can combat the negative forces, promote a strong work ethic, and develop a sense of pride and motivation in seeing your children succeed. You will need to:

- ▶ Integrate a work ethic into your daily family lifestyle.
- ▶ Actively teach your children the skills needed for a good work ethic.
- ▶ Recognize, discuss, and appreciate what you have—never taking it for granted.
- ▶ Teach by example and by modeling a positive work ethic.

Remember, work ethic is learned. It is something you must teach your children. To do so, try the following:

- ▶ Promote perspective and humility by doing community service and charity work.
- ▶ Provide the structure and time management skills conducive for a good work ethic.
- ▶ Help your child discriminate between work time and play time.
- ▶ Use schedules and rewards.
- ▶ Limit access to electronics so that your child avoids becoming distracted from work and finding the easy way to complete a task at the expense of learning it thoroughly.
- ▶ Promote self-reliance so that your child can tolerate frustration, learn persistence, and think resourcefully and creatively.
- ▶ Set goals so that your child experiences the steps and effort it takes to reap rewards.

You can employ your own work ethic by making an effort to address this issue with your children on a daily basis. It is something that is learned gradually over time, but will be a key factor in raising a well-adjusted child.

CHAPTER 5

Interpersonal Relationships

··

Friends, Family, and Strangers

WHEN KIDS ARE NOT SOCIALLY SKILLED, THEY TEND TO BE AT RISK for emotional problems, social problems, underachievement in school, social isolation, and either becoming a bully themselves or being picked on by bullies. One of the best predictors of healthy functioning as an adult is the degree of social adequacy a person acquired as a child.

One of my eleven-year-old patients exemplifies the extensive problems that emanate from having poor social skills. Gregg desperately wanted to be accepted and liked by his peers. Unfortunately, he repeatedly went about it in ways that drove kids away from him. At the beginning of therapy, Gregg told me that he was becoming friends with a boy named Floyd. At the first sign of this potential friendship, Gregg became overzealous in his interactions with Floyd. He would monopolize his newfound "friend" by interrupting conversations Floyd was having with other kids, call him frequently for play dates, instant-message him voraciously, and text him constantly. He came on so strong it made Floyd feel uncomfortable.

Not only was Gregg suffocating in his social relationships, his behavior and communication was often inappropriate. He would poke other kids, try to wrestle them, make inappropriate jokes, and make off-color comments about the girls in class. Each time Gregg attempted to secure a friendship, he followed this similar behavior pattern. Inevitably, kids became angry with him, often causing them to react with verbal or physical aggression when Gregg went too far. Eventually, the rejection would come, even to the point where Gregg was sometimes bullied. Gregg felt somewhat depressed and dejected. As he sat in class, his mind tended to focus more on what the other kids were thinking about him than on what the teacher was teaching. Subsequently, his grades suffered.

It is easy to see how Gregg's poor social skills led to his depression, low self-esteem, unfulfilling friendships, and even poor academic performance. He needed help in learning more appropriate social skills. Therapy, coupled with the assistance of his parents and school staff, helped Gregg become aware of his repetitive mistakes and inappropriate interactions and enabled him to begin developing a more appropriate social skill set.

As Gregg (and all kids) need to learn, there are do's and don'ts when interacting with others. Social skills in children are also culturally determined behaviors—the manners and etiquette that are specific to situations they encounter will become their default behaviors. The relative appropriateness of a certain behavior varies from one context to another, and children must learn to navigate those variations in order to meet cultural demands. Take the acts of yelling and clapping, for example. If a child yells and claps at a professional football game as a way of cheering for his team, it is both appropriate and normative behavior for the situation. Almost everyone in the stadium is doing the same thing at the same time. But if that same child stands up to yell and cheer for his friend who finishes reading a book while in a library, he will be chastised, punished, and probably asked to leave. The same behavior is either appropriate or inappropriate depending on the culturally defined situation, and children must learn the appropriate behavioral code associated with each cultural demand.

One of the most common problems my young clients face relates to their relationships with peers and adults. Somewhere along the line, they haven't learned or applied appropriate social skills for these relationships.

There are three primary ways children develop social skills: They observe social behavior, they learn directly from adults, and they practice by interacting with their social environment. The child's social environment serves as his classroom for learning these skills, and in fact it can be an overwhelming task for kids to decipher all of the "rules" and nuances of relationships they experience in social interactions.

SOCIAL SKILLS IN THE DIGITAL AGE

For Generation Text kids, the development of effective social skills is even more complicated than ever before. Your children use the same three means to learn social skills as previous generations of children did, but due to modern-day cultural and technological factors (as discussed throughout this chapter), learning social skills through observation, direct teaching, and practice is a very different process. Let's examine the primary reasons for the change in the course of social skill development in Generation Text kids:

▶ *General.* Generation Text kids are excessively aware of and sensitive to their social world. This translates into a magnified impact on Gen Text kids' social skill development. Since Generation Text kids focus excessively on peer relationships, they spend a great deal of their time seeking acceptance and trying to relate to one another. For some, a heightened social awareness hones social skill development. But for many others, social skills become inappropriate or harmful to relationships, without proper adult guidance.

▶ *Observation.* Technology affords the ease and mobility with which to experience the social arena far beyond the immediate, face-to-face world. In other words, today's kids have an enormously broader view of the social world to observe.

▶ *Direct Teaching.* Generation Text kids have layers of privacy when socializing via text messages, instant messages, cell phone calls, and e-mails. If parents are not privy to these conversations and interactions, they are unable to facilitate appropriate communication and social skills in their children.

▶ *Practice.* Because Generation Text kids and their parents have placed such a high priority on socialization, they have an opportunity to practice social skills (both good and bad) more frequently. Furthermore, technology has made it so easy for kids to communicate and socialize that their ability to practice social skills has increased dramatically as compared to kids who grow up without access to as much technology.

If you consider how these issues influence the social skill development in Generation Text kids, you can see how much can go awry. Technology has made it possible for kids to socialize in a private world that excludes parental guidance and instruction. Kids have access to other kids (and adults) from anywhere and at any time, without the benefit of adult supervision. They can say whatever they want to whomever they want, whether they have met in real life or not. While parents recognize the critical importance of social skill development in their children, they usually do not understand how to correct the problems that may arise. In this chapter, we will begin to learn how to raise children who will become adults who maintain healthy, satisfying relationships. To help your children, you first need to understand just how important it is to have good social skills. You must also learn about the nature of communication, how to respect personal space, facilitate healthy relationships, and how technology affects social skill development in your children. Most important, you will learn how to develop ways to take advantage of the rich social arena your kids are exposed to, while mitigating its negative effects.

THE IMPORTANCE OF SOCIAL SKILLS

Social skills, as the foundation for all relationships, are the entrée for a successful life. Children who learn appropriate social skills are known to:

- ► Have high self-esteem and confidence
- ► Feel supported and loved by peers, parents, and adults
- ► Feel included and wanted, not isolated
- ► Have many people to spend time with
- ► Feel included in large, organized social groups such as athletic teams, religious groups, and classrooms
- ► Have people in their lives to share experiences, thoughts, and feelings
- ► Have a positive outlook on life in general
- ► Be outgoing, so other people want to be around them

Learning behavioral codes can be quite perplexing to children, but to eventually function as adults, they will need to navigate and absorb numerous sets of social rules and learn how to distinguish between the various expectations of numerous experiences. If children learn these behaviors in a variety of social situations, by direct observation and instruction and by actual practice, it is easy to see how overwhelming it can be for them due to their easy access to the world and the excess of social interactions they experience. Instead of learning social skills with a limited exposure to peers and adults as in past generations, Generation Text kids have almost boundless availability to the social world.

COMMUNICATION SKILLS

The most important social skill that a child develops is the ability to communicate, both verbally and nonverbally. This is the skill that most sets human beings apart from other life forms and the one that is the cornerstone of any human relationship. Children must learn how to express and receive all forms of communication in order to solidify close, successful relationships. They also need to learn how to work collaboratively in groups. Cell phones and the Internet provide Generation Text kids with a completely new dimension with which they communicate with one another. Getting along with others and problem solving in groups is contingent upon the child's ability to communicate effectively, and technology has changed the very nature of how they are communicating. A brief explanation of the facets of communication will help you understand how this is happening.

The process of complete communication between two or more individuals involves someone sending a message—overtly or covertly, depending on the situation—and someone else interpreting and responding to the message. Communication is the glue that binds the love, honesty, and respect in social relationships; it is also the means of defining necessary boundaries. Communication occurs as speech, written language, nonverbal body language, and behavior, the rules of which vary according to the cultural context. To become effective communicators, your kids have to understand the cultural determinants, learn how to send and interpret messages expressed in words and actions, and attend to the explicit meanings and the underlying social nuances, all in a matter of a split second. For some children, it can be a very complicated and overwhelming process. To illustrate one specific aspect of underlying messages in communication, listen to Laura, a sixteen-year-old patient, as she discusses a problem she is having:

"I try to be friendly and nice to everyone, but they treat me as if I am invisible. Some of the popular girls won't even say hi to me at my bus stop. Now, I just stand there by myself. I overhear kids talking about all this cool stuff they do on weekends and all I do is stay home and watch TV. Sometimes I think bad things about them. I don't understand. Why don't they like me?"

The content of this message is clear and simple. Laura wants friends, but she doesn't have them, and she does not understand why. The affective message in Laura's statement is the unspoken feeling she communicates. Her emotions—which include frustration, inadequacy, loneliness, isolation, jealousy, boredom, anger, and confusion—are expressed as covert messages hidden in the content message. Although Laura does not express any of those specific feelings overtly, they are the basis for her communication. If communication is the "glue" of interpersonal relationships, feelings are the chemicals that make up that glue, facilitating the connection between two people.

For children today, the need to understand messages transmitted in different formats and linguistic styles has created an entire subculture of communication that is unfamiliar to most adults. They must be super proficient communicators using the Internet, e-mail, chat rooms, instant messages, and text messages. If parents are the primary educators promoting appropriate social skills, they must appreciate the difficulties technology presents, and then use that knowledge to promote healthy communication skills in their children. Verbal messages, expressed with the spoken and written word, are primarily overt in their intention. When your child says, "I want to go to the movies," her desire is explicitly expressed. But verbal communication is hardly that simple and certainly not one-dimensional. When a person speaks, she sends several other covert messages in addition to the words, which sometimes transmit different or additional significance. The meaning of that simple verbal communication, "I want to go to the movies," changes depending on the tone, modulation, inflection, tempo, and volume of the person's voice and the emphasis placed on each word. Consider the following sentences, all of which use the same words but communicate different implied messages:

Statement	Method of Communication	Cover Message
I want to go to the movies.	Sarcastic tone	I really do not want to go.
I want to go to the movies?	Upward voice inflection	I'm not sure whether I want to go.
I WANT TO GO TO THE MOVIES.	Shouting	I feel intensely about going.
I want to go to the movies.	Emphasis on "I"	This is what I am choosing.
I want to go to the *movies*.	Emphasis on "movies"	I want to go to the movies and not somewhere else.
I w-a-n-t t-o g-o t-o t-h-e m-o-v-i-e-s.	Slow, deliberate delivery	I want to be heard and understood.
I want to go to the movies.	Whispering	I am trying to be patient.
I want to go to the movies.	Whiney tone of voice	I am exasperated and discouraged because I am not getting what I want.
I want to go to the movies!	Slightly elevated volume	I am annoyed that I can't go.

These nine sentences are all ostensibly the same, but with subtle changes in tone, the meaning of the message is changed or added to. Similarly, body language and facial expression can also be used to alter the real message someone is sending. What happens to the covert messages embedded in communications when a child is texting, instant messaging, talking on the cell phone, or chatting on the Internet? This is a large part of the problem when Generation Text kids communicate with one another.

Whereas verbal messages can be both overt and covert, nonverbal messages are exclusively covert. Commonly referred to as "body language," nonverbal messages have the ability to reinforce the intensity of a verbal message, or directly contradict it. When a person encroaches on the space between him and his listener, he is often doing so to emphasize the meaning of his verbal message. When someone folds her arms while stating how open she is to another's ideas, she is communicating a closed, unreceptive posture that directly contradicts her posture of openness. Most psychologists believe that nonverbal messages constitute a large percentage of every verbal message, communicating the person's true feelings.

Obviously, communication is complex enough even without

our conscious awareness of all of the covert messages we are sending at the same time. With both verbal and nonverbal messages, overt and covert messages, it is a wonder that we understand each other at all! And all this is compounded by the frequency of techno-communications. Interestingly, the most potent messages are received via covert messages such as tone of voice, volume, word emphasis, affective transmittal, and body language. To underscore the importance of *how* people talk to one another, one of my favorite interventions to use in session when one family member is yelling at another is to say, "She can't hear you, you are talking too loud." My intention is to help patients understand that certain aspects of their communication actually *prevent* people from understanding what it is they are trying to communicate.

TECHNOLOGY: HELP OR HINDRANCE?

Social skills are learned through direct observation of others' behavior and direct feedback from peers and adults, a process called "practice effect." If practice makes perfect, then the different situations children find themselves in end up being quite important in teaching appropriate social skills. Considering the new kinds of social interactions kids experience today, it's no wonder that their parents are sometimes at a loss when it comes to giving them feedback. Although social skills have historically been synonymous with inter*personal* interactions, Generation Text kids employ inter*machine* interactions more frequently. The major part of their social skill experiential learning involves communication through e-mail, instant messages (IM), text messages, and so forth, creating a unique challenge for those of us from the previous generation.

Unless you live in a cave, you and your children cannot execute daily tasks without interfacing with many machines. Of course, that's not necessarily a bad thing, and can actually offer many advantages. However, the abundance of machine interactions can have a negative effect on the development of communication skills and social skill development in general.

In years past, without machines, communication with other human beings involved adeptness in a whole set of social graces, like making eye contact, shaking hands, being conscious of allowing appropriate physical space between people when they talk, reading nonverbal behavior, detecting hidden or additional messages in someone's tone of voice, volume, or emphasis on specific words to convey specific meanings. The diminished need for the use of these skills today in turn diminishes the quality of human communication. To get money, you must simply follow the instructions on the ATM screen and remember your PIN code. To make purchases or order dinner, you need never speak to another person or even leave your living room.

Young children are surrounded by technology. Elementary schools have computers in almost every classroom and youngsters spend a lot of their time learning how to use them. By the time they get to high school, the Internet and cell phones serve as a primary means of communicating with friends. An online survey conducted in 2005 by *Media Week* found that seven out of ten sixteen- to seventeen-year-olds own cell phones. Fourteen- and fifteen-year-old cell phone owners represent about half that amount, and thirteen-year-olds one fourth. They also found that cell phone ownership increased 43 percent among teens between 2004 and 2005. Additionally, teenage cell phone users were more likely to have computers in their rooms.* This all adds up to less face-to-face interaction, even as Generation Text children expand their social experiences in other ways, sometimes leading to an actual excess of social contact. For these kids, versatile mobility affords them the opportunity to practice and hone social skills more frequently than ever before. Julio told me that he had forty-seven friends on his AIM buddy list, most of whom he "spoke" with over the course of a week. Ron was excited about his friends list increasing in his MySpace profile. Nancy had over 350 text messages last month. These kids clearly have a sense of social life and interaction.

Although we commonly believe that relationships are about quality and not quantity, our children are beginning to lean in the opposite direction. A child who has 400 other kids on his buddy list and seventy-five names in his phonebook is considered to be more popular than the kid with twenty buddies and fifteen phone numbers. However, your child will only truly benefit from friendships if she learns how to have meaningful, caring relationships based on reciprocity, feelings, time together, play activities, and good deeds. Virtual relationships over the Internet and through

---

*John Consoli, "Teen Cell Subs Heavy TV Users," *Mediaweek.com*, May 3, 2005.

online gaming (e.g., Xbox Live) do not allow for the real closeness required for intimate, more connected relationships, no matter how often they actually communicate.

Intermachine interactions are characteristically different from traditional social skill experiences. The world of text messaging, IMing, blogging, and e-mailing has created an entirely new social skill subculture among our youth, bringing with it a new code of culturally determined rules and written language. Part of the problem is the absence of the ability to read the nonverbal cues in these written communications. Another problem is how techno-talk can affect what kids say to one another.

The mother of twelve-year-old Cara showed me a printout of an IM conversation her daughter had with a boy in one of her classes. Cara's mother was mortified by the content of the conversation, which included graphic sexual references. It was difficult enough for this mother to realize that her little girl was growing up—but even more difficult to recognize that it was Cara who was initiating most of the discussion about "hooking up" with the boy. When Cara came in for her session with me, I asked her what she was thinking and feeling during the IM conversation. Her initial response was, "I don't know—like, it was normal." Generation Text kids are unfazed by this type of techno-talk because it occurs with such frequency. Cara thought that her mother was making a big deal out of nothing. As our discussion progressed, she admitted that the content was somewhat racy.

I asked Cara, "Would you have said the same things to your friend if you were speaking in person?"

She shifted in her chair and immediately responded, "No way!"

Although the anonymity and invisibility of techno-talk helps some kids overcome their timidity, for others it can be perilous. The bravado that accompanies these interactions is an invitation for trouble. When kids enter chat rooms and "socialize" with nameless, faceless people, they are able to be bolder than they would be with actual peers, in person, because of this very anonymity, which dismantles one's sense of appropriate guardedness. The physical and emotional distance inherent in this kind of communication puts kids in extremely vulnerable positions. By sharing explicit thoughts and feelings divorced from a certain reality, kids compromise their personal integrity. Beyond the obvious dangers of sex offenders parading as fellow children and so forth, kids put themselves in the dangerous position of learning how to lie, deceive, and manipulate others. Think about the long-term effects of thousands, maybe even millions, of these types of social interactions, and it is not difficult to imagine that they will have a negative effect on your kids' social skills, relationships, and self-esteem.

But it doesn't have to be all bad. Brittany's story is an example of how social relationships can be enhanced by using technology to overcome powerful, negative cultural messages. Brittany is an eighteen-year-old college freshman who has never had a boyfriend because she has always been shy around boys and has never felt confident that she was attractive. That all changed when she attended her cousin's high school graduation and had a chance meeting with Kyle. As Kyle shuffled through the aisle and sat down next to her, he stepped on Brittany's toe. After apologizing, he introduced himself. Small talk and some banter about high school ensued. The ceremony ended and they parted ways. In the past, that probably would have been the end of a potential relationship.

Fortunately, it was only the beginning for Brittany and Kyle. With the popularity of social networking websites, Kyle knew there was a good chance that Brittany would have an account on either Facebook.com or MySpace.com, along with millions of other people. Without much effort, Kyle was able to locate her account based on the little information he picked up during their brief conversation at the graduation ceremony. He requested to be her friend on Facebook.com. Brittany quickly figured out who he was and clicked on his profile. She responded by accepting his request and wrote on his "wall." Within hours they exchanged screen names and began IMing. After communicating through instant messages for a few days, Kyle asked if he could get to know her better. In our session that week, Brittany admitted that her lack of confidence begged her to ignore him, but I encouraged her to engage. For the next two weeks they talked via cell phone, exchanged many text messages, and continued IMing. Brittany finally became comfortable enough with her new friend to ask him if he wanted to hang out, and they soon developed a relationship.

At the beginning of her next session she was grinning from ear to ear. "I have a boyfriend," she announced. We discussed the process and discovered that her newfound comfort level and ability to be socially bold was due to the feeling that she could "hide" behind the computer. Her inhibitions were reduced to a minimum with intermachine communications. Without face-to-face interaction, she was able to focus solely on written communication, not worrying about her physical appearance, body language, or other nonverbal covert messages she may have sent or received in person. The Facebook profile provided information about Kyle's interests and personality. His profile described a young man who was compatible with and attractive to Brittany. If she wasn't privy to this information or hadn't liked what she'd seen, she would never have pursued a friendship with him.

Brittany, like other shy kids, was able to overcome her shyness through cyberspace socialization. The opportunity to socialize behind the emotional safety net of a computer helps these kids overcome the anxiety they experience in person, while also providing them with a vehicle to practice and develop their social skills, which ultimately helps them build confidence in their ability to handle face-to-face social interactions.

Socially awkward Generation Text kids have the advantage of being able to test and practice new social skills and comfortably engage with peers, family members, and strangers using techno-talk. For them, potentially risky social situations can be replaced with appropriate and judicious use of online social skills. Beyond that, even socially successful kids can benefit from online communities like Facebook and MySpace. For one, it stands to reason that socializing on the Internet has reduced the amount of time kids spend aimlessly hanging out in malls, diners, and parking lots. Although there are certainly dangers lurking in computer connections, parents have a better chance of keeping their kids safe at home than in the peer-pressured climates of the local hangouts. The sheer volume of users on websites like MySpace, furthermore, ensures that our kids stay in close contact with one another, forging relationships and building friendships at all hours of the day and night. In this respect, there are certainly benefits to online and mobile phone relationships, as evidenced by Brittany's situation.

But the question remains: With the ease and frequency of techno-socializing, are our kids only learning how to have superficial, impersonal relationships? What are the pitfalls of technological access and techno-talk?

SOCIAL RISKS OF INTERMACHINE INTERACTIONS

Ironically, kids today are using technology to seek out increased social interaction, yet the rise of intermachine communication has caused many kids to spend less social time with actual people. The break point comes when their time spent on the computer goes from being social and positive to isolating and stressful. If your children rely almost exclusively on technology as a social medium, they are likely to have more difficulties in school. Due to easy and excessive social access outside of school, kids tend to experience a higher frequency of social conflicts, bullying, peer rejection, emotional difficulties, and concentration difficulties in school. As the heavy reliance on technology for socialization increases, some children even begin to avoid face-to-face contact altogether. These kids eventually experience a strong sense of depersonalization, or loss of one's own sense of self and identity, and feelings of social alienation.

Although there are definite advantages to the prominence of intermachine interactions for children who are emotionally stable or those who need to overcome social anxieties, they are certainly in the minority. The majority of today's kids may not have significant social problems, but they do face obvious disadvantages in the face of the same technology. Cell phone conversations may help your children learn how to interpret covert messages hidden in voice intonations, but the cell phone does not afford the opportunity to experience and perceive a host of other nonverbal messages. Written communications in text messaging, IMing, social networking sites, and e-mailing are also extremely susceptible to misinterpretation. In general, these new means of communicating cheat our children out of the experiences we took for granted in our own childhoods. You might even worry that the subtleties of conversation will soon be lost to them. The absence of these nonverbal cues in written social interactions can negatively affect the quality of their social relationships. The following story is an example of how this can occur.

Lena, a seventeen-year-old patient, once described to me her "on again, off again" relationship with her boyfriend, which included many arguments through IM and text messaging. Lena would recount the conversations verbatim to me, using an angry tone of voice when explaining her complaint about something her boyfriend did or did not do. She would then read his written words using a warm, loving, caring, soft tone of voice to express his sorrow or love for her. Lena would then be taken aback when I would ask her if she truly thought he was being so sincere in his messages. Perhaps, I suggested, he was being sarcastic, rolling his eyes and writing with an irritated or defensive tone of "voice."

Lena needed to realize that written communications do not determine sincerity. She soon began to realize that she was interjecting her own interpretation of her boyfriend's written communications based on what she was hoping he would be saying to her. Lena couldn't understand how he could be so mean when they argued in person, yet so sweet during text fights. Written communications altered her perception due to the lack of nonverbal social cues, which kept her in an unhealthy relationship far longer than she needed to be.

I once asked Lena why she and her boyfriend used IM and text messaging as the medium for the discussions that more or less defined the status of their relationship. A blank look came over her and she simply shrugged her shoulders. Kids are simply unable to decipher the unspoken or additional messages *because* they are so heavily reliant upon these imperfect forms of communication. Their text and instant messenger conversations are written in a code. For example:

"Ht what u doin?"
"My hw. But wca"
"did u hear ab Tracy and barry? She said she would never bfwp"
"I no. she's a glg 2"
"nmp g2g"
"b4n"

In case you didn't follow what these two boys are saying to one another, the translation is:

"Hi there, what are you doing?"
"My homework. But who cares anyway?"
"Did you hear about Tracy and Barry? She said she would never
    be best friends with privileges."
"I know. She's a good-looking girl, too."

"It's not my problem. I have got to go."
"Bye for now."

Virtual written communications require kids to possess a heightened sense of social nuance, without the benefit of facial expressions, body movements, or vocal intonations to interpret. They not only have to learn face-to-face communications as all other generations have, they now have the challenge of interpreting the written word on an increasingly large scale. This fact, in and of itself, creates more difficulty for today's kids to develop the most important social skill of all—communication.

PERSONAL SPACE

Ricardo, an eleven-year-old client prone to fighting with other children, came to me to work on his social problem of aggression. In getting to know Ricardo, I quickly discovered his strong attraction to the violence found in the movies, video games, and television shows he preferred. Unlike some aggressive children, Ricardo was not an angry or mean child. Rather, he was a kid who just wanted to be friends with others, but never learned how to respect other people's personal space. He frequently crossed boundaries, which became quite threatening to his peers. Instead of reaching out to them, he reached in.

I used Ricardo's interest in and knowledge of *Star Wars* movies and the *Star Trek* television series to help him understand physical boundaries. Each person, I explained, has an invisible force field around him, much like the Starship Enterprise does in *Star Trek*. He was not allowed to break the force field unless he had permission to do so. We role-played this scenario many times until he was able to improve his behavior.

Culturally defined boundaries—both physical and psychological—are essential to healthy relationships regardless of the nature of that relationship. Your children need to learn about physical space and comfort zones so that they become aware of appropriate physical boundaries in relationships and can practice them face-to-face. Intermachine interactions are simply no substitute here.

In the United States, when people talk to one another they maintain a distance of about eighteen inches between them. A greater distance than that conveys a lack of attention to the speaker, and a lesser distance creates much discomfort for the listener. We look for social cues giving us permission to cross the personal space boundary and to touch other people. If someone puts their hand out in greeting, they are giving you permission to invade their personal space and shake their hand. Touching is also culturally determined. When you greet someone in a business environment, a handshake is expected and appropriate. When you greet your spouse after not seeing her all day, a kiss is expected and appropriate. You would not consider kissing a potential client when greeting them for the first time or shaking your wife's hand when you see her at the end of the day. These are all lessons we have internalized over many years of practice and experience. Children who spend their days on the computer are not learning these important lessons.

As with physical boundaries, psychological boundaries vary according to the nature of the relationship. It is generally considered inappropriate to share your innermost secrets with someone you barely know (unless that person is your therapist!). Even the most intimate relationships require a certain degree of psychological distance so that each person can maintain a separate sense of self and identity. When psychological boundaries are appropriate, mutual and self-respect are also present. When there is invasiveness or a poor sense of boundaries, the relationship will usually be problematic for one or both people, leading to feelings of being taken for granted, abused, controlled, and worthless.

Learning how to navigate appropriate physical and psychological boundaries determined by the nature of the relationship as well as by the culture has always been a difficult task for kids. Today, establishing and regulating boundaries is even more difficult due to the easy and immediate access our kids have to one another as well as to complete strangers. Access is a two-way street, and Generation Text kids don't always have control over the people with whom they come into contact. The second problem with easy social access relating to personal space and boundaries is the loosening of social inhibitions due to the "safety" of intermachine interactions. Remember how twelve-year old Cara was willing to be far more explicit with her boyfriend when instant messaging him than she would ever have been with him in person? Now, consider what happened to Camille, a fourteen-year-old who found herself in an uncomfortable situation due to boundary problems.

Camille was chatting online with several of her friends. Unbeknownst to them, other kids entered and exited the chat group regularly. Keith, a fifteen-year-old, asked to be invited into the group. Camille and Keith seemed to hit it off and soon moved their conversation to a private IM format. Their online relationship began with innocent and typical teen talk about their dislike for school, their music preferences, and their friends. Conversations quickly moved to their thoughts and feelings about parents, siblings, and what they each look for in the people they date. A few IM conversations later, explicit sex talk began, including their experiences with the opposite sex. A steady dismantling of personal barriers had begun, despite the fact that Camille was fabricating 90 percent of her stories.

Camille and Keith met at a local mall, each bringing several friends with them. That day they spent the afternoon together, having only limited physical contact holding hands, walking arm in arm, and hugging. Over the next two weeks they had multiple IM, text, and cell phone conversations. A familiarity and closeness with one another accelerated and they decided to meet at a party of one of Keith's friends. It was at this party that Camille found herself in the bedroom with Keith, where things started moving too fast for her comfort. She was able to pull the brakes, but only after she engaged in sexual activities that went far beyond her comfort level.

Sure, this type of accelerated sexual contact could have happened in 1980. It could even have happened in 1960. But it would not have happened to as many kids as it does today, when the possibility of meeting perfect strangers is just a click away. Generation Text culture, filled with sexual images and messages, rapidly permeates the boundaries of inhibition and moral standards among youngsters.

WHAT PARENTS CAN DO

Parents have the unique opportunity to teach their kids essential social skills during the most vital developmental stages of childhood and adolescence. Nurturing and parental responsiveness are key elements of any child's development, and parents have the unique ability to teach their children appropriate social skills via modeling, vicarious learning, and direct teaching.

> ▶ *Modeling* is the way children learn through observing your behavior in social situations within and outside the family.
> ▶ *Vicarious learning* is taking advantage of opportune situations and teachable moments, such as when your child is watching television and you take the time to point out the positive or negative implications of SpongeBob's boss, Mr. Krabs, doling out orders that test SpongeBob's better judgment.
> ▶ *Direct teaching* is explicit instruction and guidance regarding specific social skills or social situations.

You will use one or more of these methods to teach your children the right social skills. These three approaches are discussed in greater detail below, with examples, followed by additional recommendations on specific social skills you need to work on with your kids—from assertiveness training, to handling inappropriate conversations, to showing good manners.

Parents have always had the responsibility of helping their children develop healthy relationships, but parents have more to contend with today. Allowing your kids to use cell phones, IM, the Internet, chat rooms, and e-mail without specific guidance is an invitation for trouble. You would never allow your teenager to drive a car without learning the rules of the road or first practicing with a supervising driver. You would never give your ten-year-old a buzz saw and tell him to go make firewood, or allow your five-year-old to use the oven without supervision. In much the same way, computers and cell phones must be regarded as useful machines that require adult instruction, guidance, and supervision before they are mastered.

The impact of technology on your child's social competence is largely contingent upon your role as an instructor and coach. Your involvement has enormous positive consequences for your child's ability to establish and maintain healthy relationships.

Modeling

One of the primary ways kids learn how to relate to others is through observational learning. They watch what other kids do on the playground, at lunch, during play dates, at dances, in the halls between classes, and in many other social situations. But while other children play a major part in your child's development, you as parents are the most frequently observed individuals, making you the most influential. This even applies in adolescence, when the peer group is increasingly significant. At all stages of childhood, parents need to stick to the adage, "Do as I say and do as I do." Teenagers have the cognitive ability to discern hypocrisy in your actions. They take delight in pointing out discrepancies between parental wisdom and behavior.

The way you conduct yourself in front of your kids is a primary teaching method in all facets of raising healthy kids. Your behavior and the way you treat others becomes ingrained in your child's psyche. Treat your kids, your partner, your friends, your colleagues, and even the cashier at the local A&P with honesty and respect. Let your kids witness these interactions, even when they are unpleasant. Spats between parents or disagreements with friends or professionals should be handled in such a way that your kids learn social conflict resolution in a positive way. Show your kids that you feel empathy for others, happiness for their good fortune and achievements, consideration, and altruism.

When you make a mistake, let them know that nobody is perfect. Hold yourself accountable for your actions in social situations by verbalizing your culpability and apologizing to whomever you hurt. Show your kids that it is okay to laugh at yourself without being self-denigrating or ridiculing. Above all, show them integrity. One parent told me that a recent trip to the bank resulted in a good modeling opportunity. When this mother got to her car, she realized that the bank teller had accidentally given her $100 more than she asked for, and she immediately went back inside to return the money, teaching her children the vital lesson of honesty. Try to remember that your child scrutinizes your social interactions even when you do not realize it, so it is all the more important to model good behavior when they are watching.

There is no such thing as the perfect parent, but good parents reflect on their actions and parenting strategies. By reflecting on your actions you can verbalize the mistakes you make in front of your child. Just as important as recognizing the mistake is letting your child know what you *should* have done instead. Better yet, tell or show the child how you will correct it if possible. For example,

Mary Beth was late in picking up the kids for car pool one morning. One of the mothers was upset because her daughter was very anxious about being late for school. Mary Beth apologized but made excuses for her lateness, blaming it on traffic and the fact that her husband left for work early, leaving all the morning preparations for her. Later, she explained to her son, who witnessed this exchange, that although she did the right thing by apologizing, she was wrong to have made excuses or to blame Dad for her mistake. She should have apologized and let Mrs. Post know that she would leave earlier next time and try not to let it happen again.

Vicarious Learning

Vicarious learning as a means to understand and develop social skills is tantamount to learning from a distance—seizing the moment or using what I call teachable moments as they occur. Teachable moments occur when your child is not directly involved yet is able to observe a social situation and learn from it. Learning vicariously using teachable moments can happen anywhere, such as when you and your kids are shopping in a supermarket, playing in the local park, watching television, or walking down the street. So if you and your child are walking through a mall and you see two kids teasing a third, make sure you take the time to identify the inappropriate social behavior and explore how the teased child must be feeling. The advantage of vicarious learning is the absence of direct emotional involvement in the social situation, so your child will tend to be more receptive and less defensive when discussing the situation.

The three most common times your kids will talk to you about what is going on in their lives are during dinner, on car rides, and at bedtime. These are the best times to stimulate conversations with your kids regardless of their age. They are also times to sit back and listen to what they have to tell you, and to observe their discussions with their siblings and friends. Take advantage of these distraction-free moments to hear about behaviors and social dilemmas their friends and classmates experience. Participate in their discussion as a way to teach them your family values and appropriate social problem-solving strategies, asking for their opinions rather than lecturing.

The following exchange between thirteen-year-old Chris and his mother at dinnertime is a good example of a teachable moment:

CHRIS: Nigel got suspended today for yelling at Mr. Randolph. He really went off on him.
MOTHER: Why did he get so mad at the teacher?
CHRIS: Mr. Randolph gave him a zero on his lab because he said Nigel didn't hand it in. Nigel argued with him because he did hand it in. He claims the teacher lost it.
MOTHER: Do you think Nigel handled it well?
CHRIS: Duh! He got suspended, didn't he?
MOTHER: How could he have handled it so that he would not have been disrespectful to Mr. Randolph, but so he could still try to get credit for the lab?
CHRIS: Well, I wouldn't have yelled at the teacher. Nigel told me that his mother helped him with the lab and when he handed it in he remembered asking Mr. Randolph if he was putting it in the right pile.
MOTHER: So, what would you do if you were Nigel?
CHRIS: I don't know. I guess I would have explained it to Mr. Randolph in a calm voice. I would have had him call you, to let him know I was telling the truth. If that didn't work, I would have gone to my guidance counselor and asked her for help.

In this case, the mother urges Chris to put himself in Nigel's place and imagine how he could have better handled the same social situation. This discussion may serve Chris well if he faces a similar scenario or other conflicts with authority figures in the future.

Another way to use vicarious learning is to use yourself as an example. Periodically, point out the social skills you use in different situations. It doesn't matter if you handled the situation appropriately or not. Provide a short analysis of the situation as an instructional tool for your child. For example, if a waiter apologizes after spilling soda on the table, point out to your child how you helped him feel better about it by letting him know that you realized it was just an accident and by telling him not to worry about it. Or, let's say you are in a hardware store and you cannot find the paintbrushes. An employee is speaking to another customer and you interrupt their conversation to ask where the paintbrushes are located.

Let your child know that it was rude of you to interrupt and that you should have either waited for the employee to finish with the other customer first or said, "Excuse me, can I ask you a quick question?"

Aside from your own example, you can teach your kids valuable social skills by commenting on the television shows and movies they love to watch. Kid-oriented media provide a plethora of social situations, conflicts, values, and behavior that can be instructional for your kids. Take advantage of these teachable moments by discussing them with your kids. Have them evaluate and make their own judgments about each situation. Avoid judgmental questions such as, "Was it a *good* thing or a *bad* thing to do?" Instead, ask questions such as, "Was it *helpful* or *harmful*? Was it *appropriate* or *inappropriate*?"

Vicarious social skills teaching can also be conducted by discussing the behavior of friends, colleagues, and relatives. As long as you are careful to avoid a gossipy discussion, the people in your lives can prove to be quite topical in terms of social analysis. The real lives of famous entertainers and athletes are also often newsworthy. Their stories are rich in "do's and don'ts" lessons for your kids, especially regarding the way they handle their relationships.

Direct Teaching: TACT

Direct teaching of social skills is certainly a viable way to help your kids learn how to get along with others and cultivate healthy relationships. TACT, which stands for Teach-Apply-Congratulate-Teach, is a general formula to guide your instruction. For every social strategy you want to impart to your kids, first *teach* them the skill, prompt them to *apply* it, *congratulate* them, and then *teach* them again using encouragement, coaching, and reinforcement.

Reinforcement includes both positive and negative feedback. The feedback is usually verbal, where you say something like, "That was very considerate of you to let James have that last piece of pizza," or, "You are being too selfish by not sharing the computer with your sister." Although used judiciously, feedback can come in the form of tangible rewards or punishments. For example, if you have been trying to encourage your teenager to spend more time with the family and he starts doing so over time, you can reward him with a privilege or the new CD he wanted. For a negative consequence of showing no improvement, you can deny him a privilege. Identify the social behavior you are trying to teach, and be clear about the contingency between the behavior and the consequence. Generally, I prefer a positively framed, educational approach to learning social skills. However, there is a place for criticism and punishment. Try to praise and emphasize your child's efforts as opposed to the outcome. As we already know, it takes time and repetition for your child to learn a new behavior. If you withhold praise until he achieves a successful outcome, he may give up before such an outcome occurs. Using TACT involves three methods of direct teaching: verbal discussion, role-playing, and behavioral rehearsal.

Verbal discussion identifies and clarifies the desired social skill or behavior you are trying to teach your child. Again, try to avoid the lecture format as much as possible. Kids tend to lose their focus and subsequently ignore parental diatribes about their behavior. Even with teenagers, making it short and directly to the point will hold their attention and optimize the potential for the desirable behavior. Encourage your child to talk about her feelings, while being careful not to taint her expression. If a child senses disapproval when she tells her parent that she is angry, she may suppress the feeling instead of expressing it. Consider the following exchange between ten-year-old Rosie and her father after Rosie's play date.

FATHER: Rosie, when you have your friends over it is nice to let them decide what to play sometimes. How would you feel if Charlotte got to decide what to play with all the time?

ROSIE: I would feel like she was bossing me around.

FATHER: How do you think Charlotte felt today?

ROSIE: She didn't get mad or anything, she just kept playing with me.

FATHER: Still, she may have just tried to be nice even though she felt annoyed inside. Why is it so important that you always do what you want?

ROSIE: Because then I have more fun.

FATHER: I want you to have fun, but when you have a friend, it is nice to sometimes do what you want and sometimes do what she wants.

In this dialogue, Rosie's father gently but clearly identified her bossy behavior and how it affects people. He helped Rosie understand her own feelings as well as her friend's feelings through discovery instead of lecturing.

Encourage your children to express both positive and negative opinions about the social situations in which they are involved. By asking them for their opinions regarding a social dilemma, their self-esteem is boosted and their confidence and sense of security is strengthened so that they will be more likely to assert themselves in other social situations. Coaching and helping your children decide on the best course of action in various social situations is one of the best weapons parents have against their children's submission to negative peer pressure. The more confident and secure your child is, the stronger her own convictions will be, so she'll be less likely to succumb to the pressure of being accepted at any cost.

Role-playing is a therapeutic tool that enables the child to experience and practice the behavior set, verbalizations, and emotions associated with a social situation. In the case of the conversation between Chris and his mother, a role-play exercise would have involved the mother playing the part of Mr. Randolph and Chris playing the part of Nigel. A dialogue ensues focusing on appropriate behavior and a positive solution to the conflict. Role-playing involves direct involvement and a practice effect for the child.

Behavioral rehearsal is similar to role-playing because it involves a practice effect. Instead of playing specific roles, however, the parent asks the child to practice her part in preparation for dealing with a specific social situation. In other words, whereas role-playing is a means for the child to understand different options in any given social situation, behavioral rehearsal is direct teaching with a specific script to prepare for an imminent social situation. For example, if your son is being teased by a classmate at the lunch table, you can provide him with a set of retorts along with specific action he can take, then you have him practice them so that he knows exactly what to do the next time he's being teased. This is particularly helpful in problematic social situations your child may be encountering. For example, when dealing with a bullying situation, whether it be in person or via techno-communications, provide the verbal and behavioral responses to deal with the situation and have your child actually rehearse those lines. When the situation arises, your child will barely have to think because she will already have the script and actions right at her fingertips.

Modeling, vicarious learning, and direct teaching are the tools you can use to help your kids develop appropriate social skills and have healthy relationships. Keep these techniques in mind as we address some specific social skills needed by Generation Text kids to ward off exposure to the negative influences experienced through the technological access and the cultural excess.

Assertiveness Training

The list of specific social skills a child needs to learn is enormous. There are certain methods and basic tenets your child needs to learn that will assist him in developing happy, healthy relationships. One of the major techniques is called assertiveness training. Understanding the difference between being aggressive, passive, and assertive is instrumental in your child's social development. Being assertive is a way to stick up for your rights in a respectful manner, maintaining your self-respect and averting situations in which an adult or a peer tries to take advantage of you. Encouraging your child to express his needs, demand respect, and uphold appropriate boundaries in his relationships is invaluable. This is especially true for Generation Text children, who fall prey to unwanted real-time and virtual negative influences.

Jeff, a fifteen-year-old high school student with a social learning disability called Asperger's syndrome, kept "lending" lunch money to another student who never paid him back. Jeff innocently told his dad about his new friend. When his dad suggested that Jeff refrain from lending his "friend" any more money until he paid what he owed, Jeff revealed that the boy refused to be his friend if he didn't give him money. Jeff's father and I decided that rather than report the student to stop the shakedown, we would help Jeff learn how to assert himself. We wanted Jeff to internalize the Chinese proverb, "Give a man a fish and he eats for a day. Teach a man how to fish and he eats for a lifetime." His dad explained to Jeff that a true friend would not base his friendship on whether or not someone is giving him money. He coached Jeff and rehearsed assertive statements such as, "I won't lend you any more money because you really aren't my friend," and, "If you were my friend, you would pay me back the money you owe me."

Previously, Jeff was being passive and letting the boy take advantage of his good nature and hunger for friendship. Your kids need to know that being passive in their relationships at school, and even in their relationships online, allows others to manipulate and control them. Aggression is a force that dominates relationships; it is the unwanted behavior that crosses relationship boundaries. In Ricardo's *Star Trek* terms, aggression breaks one's invisible force field. Your kids need to know that if they feel uncomfortable, it is possible that they are being too passive, or that someone else is being too aggressive, and they need to learn how to correct the situation. Aggression can take the form of physical actions or verbal communications.

Recognizing Inappropriate Conversations

One of the first things you can do is to help your child recognize inappropriate conversational content, both in techno-talk and real-time talk. Your kids need to understand when someone is being invasive or disrespectful, making them feel bad or uncomfortable. Role-play with them, or actually give them a script to help them respond to unacceptable intrusiveness in a variety of social situations.

Eleven-year-old Tracy and several of her classmates created a private chat room. Their chat sessions were going well until a few of her friends invited cousins and out-of-town camp friends into the chat room. As it turned out, three of the outsider girls began dominating and influencing Tracy's friends and they started ganging up on her. Tracy came to her mother feeling upset and confused. She told her mother how the girls were making fun of her because she wouldn't use inappropriate language and go out with a boy. Tracy felt betrayed by her friends because they joined the "faster" girls in ridiculing her.

Her mother praised her for staying true to herself and not letting the girls pressure her into saying things that made her feel uncomfortable. Tracy did not want to stop chatting with her friends, but she didn't want to continue to be taunted. They decided that honesty was the best retort, where Tracy would simply tell her friends, "I'm not ready to go out with boys. I'm sure I will be one day, but right now I like doing other things." She went on to list some of the things she likes to do, and recalled funny stories that involved some of her friends in the chat room. Tracy was able to engage her friends in a positive way as they recounted the fun times they had had together and she quickly diffused the social attack. Eventually, her friends aligned with her and the stronger girls gave up and faded out of the chat room discussions.

In another situation, Jesimin, an astute fourteen-year-old, came to her mother after a woman in South Africa instant-messaged her with a problem. Apparently, this woman's boyfriend left her stranded without any money or credit cards. Could Jesimin send her $480 for an airplane ticket home? Thankfully, as this was obviously a scam, Jesimin heeded her parents' instruction to come to them if she could not handle any online situation or if an annoyance persisted. Her parents praised Jesimin for immediately informing them. They advised her to ignore the IM query and not respond to any IM whose sender she was unable to identify.

The reality is that Generation Text kids are skilled at socializing via writing. And because there is a permanent record of every online conversation your kids have, it is imperative to be careful about what they say. A cyber-social life is a real necessity for Generation Text kids, but nonetheless they need to understand the different degrees of their relationships so that they understand how much to reveal and to whom.

One exercise I use in therapy is particularly useful for parents to employ at home. First, list various people in your child's life, such as a best friend, a close cousin, a casual friend, a teammate, the guy sitting next to her in Spanish class, and even a stranger she may encounter online or in person. Next, make a list of many statements ranging from basic factual information about your child, to superficial information and thoughts, to very personal or intimate feelings and thoughts. Examples might be:

"My address is 7 Laurel Dr., Groton, Ct."
"I like to wear bright colors, even in the winter."
"I think Elaine's boyfriend is so hot. I would go out with him in a minute."
"I would have sex if it was the right person."
"I hope we have a snow day tomorrow."

Have your child match the statement with the appropriate people with whom she could share that information. Discuss the reasons why she should or should not make certain statements to certain people, so she begins to get a feel for what is appropriate and inappropriate. This exercise serves as a guideline for your child when she goes online to communicate.

Another way to facilitate your kids' online social life while guarding them from hurtful conversations is to teach them how to engage in appropriate chitchat or small talk. Providing them with an arsenal of conversational topics—recent movies, sports, television shows, celebrity gossip, school happenings, the latest pictures posted on Facebook, and weekend events—gives them a safe way to initiate and maintain a new social connection. Chitchat, small talk, and simply asking other people questions about themselves are ways to establish new connections and allow kids to express interest and give attention to another youngster, while not disclosing sensitive information too early in the friendship.

Emphasizing Good Manners

Once they understand how to speak and respond appropriately in conversation, teach your children that peers and adults always appreciate good manners. As annoying as some kids may think it is, you must explain what they need to say and do in situations as they occur. When you coach your kids ahead of time by saying things like, "Don't forget to thank Mrs. Pratt for driving you," you are encouraging good manners. Certain situations occur infrequently, so you will need to remind your kids what to do (i.e., "Please send Brett a thank-you card for the Communion gift he gave you"). Of course, modeling appropriate manners is a surefire way to teach social graces. Learning the basic niceties, such as saying "please," "thank you," "excuse me," and "I'm sorry," will go a long way in aiding your children's social interactions. Attend to their behavior and manners in public places as well as at home. Correct them when they speak too loudly or run around inappropriately in a store or do any number of culturally unacceptable things, so that they gradually adapt to society's expectations.

Some of the suggestions I am making may seem basic and simplistic, but I am spelling them out because they are quickly becoming lost social skills in our culture. As you go through your week, take notice of how many times you, your children, and others fail to display appropriate manners. If you are happy with what you see, maintain it. If you are surprised at the absence of good manners, it is time to start actively working on it.

Looking Good

While adults tend to judge kids based on their manners, adults and children alike judge one another on the basis of appearance, for better or worse. Generation Text kids are acutely aware of fashion and the latest "look." Their identity is so strongly connected with physical appearance that it is prudent to help your child make choices that present an image of pride, confidence, and moral character.

Make sure you teach your kids appropriate grooming and hygiene so that they are better able to make a positive first impression. They will then stand a chance of other people wanting to get to know them better. Although some kids will invariably use their appearance as a means of protest or a way to establish a unique identity, you will be less likely to battle them over such things as body piercings, tattoos, and purple hair if you establish positive grooming and proper hygienic habits when they are very young.

Providing a Supportive Family Environment

The family unit is at heart a training ground for social skill development. The unconditional love inherent in family relationships creates a risk-free environment to try out and experience a variety of relationship issues and emotions. Learning how to express love, deal with competition, share possessions and attention, express anger, hurt, and disappointment, and take turns are all skills that can be strengthened within family relationships. Once a child has a strong sense of belonging to his family group, he will be more willing and able to function in groups outside of the family.

When it comes down to it, if the family environment is supportive and strong, the social behaviors and skills demonstrated within it will be ingrained in your child. It will be more difficult for the massive amounts of messages from the media, the Internet, and peer groups to penetrate and permanently alter the positive lessons your child has learned through family social interactions.

Facilitating Social Opportunities

Children have the opportunity to practice social skills in both informal groups (play dates, family gatherings, and recess play) and formal groups (organized athletic teams, extracurricular classes, and religious institutions). You need to initiate and orchestrate your child's involvement in both types of social groups at every stage of development. Generally, the younger the child, the more the need for play date suggestions, where you will be involved in coordinating their social activities. Teenagers need your involvement and guidance in terms of group safety and accountability issues. Balance a fair amount of informal play with organized formal social groups, since both provide a relatively structured environment for your children to learn appropriate social skills. Even informal gatherings such as play dates, hanging out at the mall, and attending a get-together at someone's house can be instructional when the right limits and supervision are imposed.

Playing with Your Kids

While making sure that they have the opportunity to play with other children, you should also make sure that you play with your children for the pure sake of having fun with them. For younger kids, that means getting down on the floor with them and using their toys. Periodically, act like a child their age and use the play situations as opportunities to help them learn to deal with typical problems they face. Playing with older kids means listening to their music and then discussing it, surfing the Net, and playing video games with them.

Teaching Empathy

Relating to your children is most effective when it comes to teaching them about respect and empathy. Not only must you show your own respect and empathy for what they are experiencing, but you should ask your children to put themselves in another person's shoes, so they can understand how they would feel if someone was treating them inappropriately. Considering the amount of time kids spend on intermachine interactions devoid of emotional cues, their ability to develop empathy—which is primarily expressed through verbalization—may be stifled.

While some kids seem to acquire empathy naturally, this is the exception rather than the rule. Empathy is an abstract social skill that takes a long time to develop. In order for your child to learn how to consider and care for another's feelings, you must focus on modeling, vicarious learning, using teachable moments, and direct teaching. Providing your kids the language of empathy will help them immensely. The following are examples of empathetic statements that can be modeled, vicariously learned, or directly taught:

"I feel so bad for you."
"That must have been a very difficult experience for you."
"I hope you feel better soon."
"Can I help you with that? You look like you're pretty frustrated."

Empathy requires a degree of selflessness because your child must look beyond himself and think of the other person. Teaching your children to be considerate and to give of themselves in a balanced manner in their friendships will go a long way in their personal development. It is just as important to help them recognize when they are not being respected and to give them permission to feel sorry for themselves without resorting to a pity party. Teach your kids to look for friends and romantic partners who have similar values and interests, since being friends with or dating someone simply because they like you isn't enough of a reason to have a healthy relationship with them.

MEANINGFUL RELATIONSHIPS

There is no doubt that the digital age and today's cultural pressures create a greater challenge for parents who are trying to help their kids learn appropriate social skills, maintain family values, and develop healthy relationships. Techno-communications gadgets are the new forum for social skills practice. Talking on cell phones, text messaging, and social networking on blogs have emerged as a primary means for kids to socialize. They are as embedded in their subculture as air-conditioning in cars has become in ours. As a result, Generation Text runs the risk of being unable to handle the essential face-to-face aspects of communication.

The bright side is that techno-communications have enabled communities to expand and grow closer as it becomes increasingly easier to maintain contact with one another. While this may be true, we must be in tune to the quality and healthiness of these relationships. Although our kids have numerous ways to frequently contact one another, it doesn't necessarily mean they have good social lives. Abbreviated, invisible social interactions on blogs and instant message boards are not as personal as they seem.

It is very important that our children learn to value their relationships and treat people with care, honesty, and respect. The high-tech age makes it too easy and too tempting not to do so because people are not seen face-to-face. By developing sound moral character, appropriate social skills, and strategies to develop longevity in committed and satisfying relationships, our kids will be able to take full advantage of the opportunities that abound.

CHAPTER 6

Starting Early

••

The Generation Text Child

IT'S NEVER TOO EARLY TO START ADDRESSING THE EFFECTS OUR CUL-
tural climate has on the psychological development of our children.
Starting this process in early childhood not only increases the likelihood of success, it is a proactive, preventative strategy. Of course,
parents of older children will still be able address these problems
very effectively, although they will be combating current forces
rather than working preventively.

The good news is that the basis of effective parenting is really
the same as it has ever been. Once you establish a strong foundation
of tried-and-true traditional methods, you will be well on your way
to effectively parenting your nontraditional Generation Text child.

THE TRIED-AND-TRUE FOUNDATION: BASIC PARENTING STYLES

Raising well-adjusted kids is challenging under any circumstance,
let alone in today's high-tech, socially accelerated culture. Nevertheless, it is imperative to apply the well-established fundamentals
of parenting to a generation of kids that has the ability to explore
the world and push the limits well beyond their parents' comfort
zone. Tried-and-true parenting techniques will help promote appropriate behavior, positive self-esteem, and solid values in your
child.

By utilizing the following strategies, you will be equipped with
a solid parenting approach that will help mitigate the negative in-

fluences of our culture and capitalize on the positive opportunities it has to offer. There are three basic parenting styles: autocratic, democratic, and permissive. The first step in determining your parenting strategy is to identify which of the three styles best describes you.

Autocratic parents are extremely authoritarian, providing a strict and controlling environment with many rules that are rigidly enforced. Autocratic parenting creates a punitive climate in which parents use strong, forceful tactics and leave the children no room to challenge authority or the rules.

The autocratic style provides a clear, consistent structure for the child. Children with authoritarian parents live in a very predictable environment, which helps them develop self-control. Some kids need this kind of rigid rule enforcement to help them with impulse control, including those children who have a tendency to test parental limits, are most cooperative when they know what to expect, function better with established routines, and tend to be anxious or fearful.

Democratic parents are reasonable with rules and demands, more willing to be flexible, and able to provide a rationale for those rules and demands. In a democratic family, the child's input is considered, but the parents remain in control, accepting or rejecting varying points of view. Children who have a more easygoing temperament, are bright, and usually compliant with rules will function best with the democratic parenting style.

Permissive parents represent a very lax parenting style with loose boundaries. They impose very few demands and rules on their kids. Free will and free expression of feelings are encouraged by permissive parents, with little monitoring and accountability for the children.

The permissive style encourages the creative child to think outside the box, giving him the opportunity to explore the world and discover his creative passion. Children who most benefit from a permissive parenting style thrive on creativity, have a natural ability to impose limits on themselves, do not have oppositional or control issues, are intellectually curious and exploratory, and utilize good judgment most of the time.

ALIGNING YOUR PARENTING STYLES

Deciding on a parenting style is not always easy, especially when two parents have decidedly different tendencies and styles. As with everything in life, parenting requires that you stick to your general game plan but be willing to shift and adjust, from circumstance to circumstance and from child to child. For example, if your child tends to wander off into the inappropriate parts of the cyber-world, you need to be more autocratic to impose strict controls. If that same child's identity is entrenched in creativity, a permissive style is in order when it comes to decorating her room. When it comes to this child's cell phone use, a democratic approach might be best. Sometimes, each child in the same family requires a different approach. Such is the case of the Martusso family.

The Martusso parents use all three parenting styles with their three children, each of whom requires slightly different approaches. Jay, the oldest child, needs guidance and suggestion. He is quite bright and sometimes makes decisions with his parents when they directly involve him; although his parents are the ultimate decision makers, they consider his input. For Jay, the democratic style works best. Risa, on the other hand, tends to be irresponsible and impulsive. Her internal controls are weak and she often breaks rules, sometimes knowingly and sometimes accidentally. She is the type of child who requires structure and firmness. Mr. and Mrs. Martusso have found the more rigid, autocratic style best meets her needs. Isaac, the youngest, is self-directed and quite creative. Isaac is the type of youngster who can be given a pile of junk and make something beautiful or useful out of it. At the same time, he is a compliant and responsible child who rarely reneges on his commitments. The Martussos have discovered that the permissive parenting style fosters a climate of free expression for Isaac.

Certain routines and scenarios such as bedtime rituals, the way a child maintains his bedroom, and mealtime interactions help to reveal family dynamics. Because they are basic daily interchanges among family members, these tasks usually represent how the overall family is functioning. By paying close attention to these routines, psychologists are able to assess a family's parenting style, organizational skills, communication skills, family values, and the degree of compliance in the children. You too can learn to assess your own parenting style by examining how daily routines are handled by both you and your children. For instance, you might start by assessing how smoothly routines are accomplished, how decision making is conducted, and how compliant your children are.

In addition to understanding and aligning your parenting styles, keeping your kids safe, compliant, and under control requires you to establish a clear rule structure. With this in mind, picture your child inside a box. The walls of the "box" represent the limits or parameters you impose on the child's behavior in any given situation. Your child has the freedom to roam around the box, make decisions, and display behavior within your guidelines. If he roams outside the box (in other words, if he breaks the rules), there must be a consequence or punishment. I refer to this rather basic, but essential, fundamental of parenting as *box parenting*. Box parenting is not a revolutionary strategy, but many Generation Text parents have strayed from the consistent application of it. All children and adolescents need to have boundaries and limits imposed on them. Since their own internal controls are not well developed, they need parents to tell them just how far they can go. Establishing clear and firm boundaries with Generation Text children is even more imperative due to their ability to access a world that is not adult supervised.

Box parenting should be instituted whenever your child has mobility. From babies who are learning to crawl to teenagers who are learning to drive, all children need boundaries. To illustrate the issues involved in box parenting, as well as aligning different parenting styles, let's take a look at a specific family that came to me for help. Keep in mind that the parenting issues revealed in this example are rather common, demonstrating the basics of parenting, and can therefore be applied to any access or excess issue Generation Text kids experience.

Sean and His Family

Upon my first meeting with Sean, a blond-haired, blue-eyed eight-year-old, I was struck by his slight stature. Because of the way his parents described Sean in their first meeting with me, I expected to meet an aggressive, surly-looking child. Sean had difficulty following the rules of the house. He rarely cooperated with parental requests, did not seem to care about anyone else in the family, and was outright defiant at times. Still prone to temper tantrums, Sean had difficulty when things didn't go his way. Interestingly, Sean did not display behavioral problems at school. On the contrary, when I consulted with his third-grade teacher, she described him as a compliant, conscientious student. There was some minor misbehavior at the beginning of the school year, but no inappropriate behavior had surfaced in months.

Within the first few minutes of our initial session, Sean began to challenge me and test the limits of our interaction. From his chair, he spotted toys and started to walk over to the toy corner. I gently asked him to go back to his seat and told him that we would get to play with the toys in just a few minutes. About two minutes later he got up again. I asked him to be patient for just a few more minutes until we finished talking. Sean complied and eventually we started playing. He built a creative space-age vehicle out of K'NEX bricks, and then he wanted to play a different game. I told him that I would love to play the game with him, but my rule is that after you finish playing with one toy, you have to clean it up before taking out another toy. He continued pulling the next game out. I repeated my request. Sean opened the game box and started removing the pieces.

Using the "if . . . then" technique, I told Sean, "I realize that you are excited to try out that new game, but if you don't clean up the rest of the K'NEX, you won't be able to play with any of the toys today. If you clean them up, I'd be very happy to teach you the other game." Sean immediately cleaned up the K'NEX bricks and we played the next game.

At our second session, I only had to remind Sean about the cleanup rule once, but each week I found myself needing to create another rule in order to maintain control over the session. This meant that Sean needed more structure in order to have a productive session. Sean tended to test the limits of the "box" established in my office, but he became compliant when the rules where clear and consistent. In other words, his behavior improved when he knew exactly what he was allowed to do and what was forbidden, which is probably why his behavior at school was so different from his behavior at home. Teachers and schools enforce strict and consistent rule structures that are often missing at home.

Most parents, at one time or another, have had similar issues of oppositional, uncooperative, and testing behavior in their kids.

While some kids learn to comply, others continue to challenge and rebel against authority and rules. One explanation for this discrepancy is the presence of a childhood psychiatric, neurological, or learning disorder. Fortunately, most kids, like Sean, do not have pathological disorders. They simply have not "gotten with the program." The program, or structure, is the one that needs to be established by the parents. If there are flaws in the structure, as was the case in Sean's family, there will undoubtedly be an undesirable behavior pattern. As I became more knowledgeable about how Sean's parents dealt with rules, his difficulty complying with them became clear.

Take dinnertime, for example. Sean's father, Lawrence, wants his three children to behave during dinner. According to his rules:

► Everyone remains at the table until all of them are finished eating.
► Each child must sit properly in his seat.
► Whatever you serve yourself must be eaten.
► The meal that is prepared is the only option for dinner.
► No one is allowed to leave the table without permission.
► Television, other electronics, and toys are prohibited at dinnertime.
► Getting dessert is contingent upon the table manners you display and how much of your food is eaten.
► Words like "please" and "thank you" must be used.

Sean's mother, Thelma, only agrees with the dessert rule, and saying please and thank you. When both parents are present for dinner, Thelma supports Lawrence's rules, but when Lawrence is working late or on a business trip, she only enforces the two rules with which she agrees.

Lawrence is an autocratic parent and Thelma is a permissive parent. Their conflicting parenting styles are having direct effects on their children, especially Sean. Furthermore, each parent enforces a different set of parameters on their children. Lawrence prefers to keep his children in a very small, restrictive box. In his autocratic style, he creates a regimented, rule-oriented climate with little room for the kids to think for themselves. Thelma's box, on the other hand, is too large. She imposes very few rules and boundaries on her kids. She does have limits, but there is still far too much latitude given to the kids, who do not have enough internal control to roam freely around such a large box.

Most of the time, a small box is too oppressive for children, who need the chance to make their own decisions, try out new behaviors, and develop independence. When the box is too small, the child often becomes angry because of the lack of autonomy he feels. This constriction can sometimes make children quite devious. The only way they can experience what other kids experience is to find ways to sneak out of the box and break the rules. At the same time, when the box is too big and the limits imposed on them are too liberal, kids generally find themselves in trouble. The healthiest box is medium-size, one in which they can experience a certain amount of self-discovery and experimentation within their environment. If they are overly controlled, they will become handicapped in their ability to cope with the world when they are older. Overly controlled Generation Text kids find ways to break out of their box by accessing their friends and the world without their parents' knowledge, running the risk of premature exposure to values and behaviors that are unhealthy for them, precisely because they lack significant parental structure.

Thelma and Lawrence found that when their parenting styles became polarized over time, they began compensating for one another. Lawrence tries to make up for Thelma's permissiveness by being overly strict, and vice versa. As a result, Lawrence's box became too small and Thelma's became too large. With two different sets of rules and expectations, is it any wonder that Sean is confused and anxious? At home, he protests in an oppositional and sometimes manipulative way. In school, where the structure is appropriate and there are clear and consistent rules, Sean understands the predictable classroom and does not feel the need to misbehave.

Lawrence and Thelma soon began to try meeting in the middle, creating an appropriate and reasonable rule structure that is above all else consistent. Young children like Sean need consistent, safe environments in order to function to the best of their ability. Establishing a unified, consistent parenting style and rule structure with your children sets the stage for easier compliance when they are older and the stakes are higher. For example, when you expect everyone to follow a dress code for family birthday parties when they are children, it will be easier to attain compliance at family gatherings when they are teenagers.

The Importance of Consistency

In addition to the need for both parents to align parenting styles and rules, each parent, individually, must enforce the rules consistently. Being consistent is especially important when you are teaching your child a new behavior. If you provide your child with her first cell phone, for example, you need to express all the rules for its use and stick to that game plan without wavering. There is room for flexibility only once the child is "inside the box" and demonstrating respect for those parameters.

Remember that inconsistency causes low self-esteem and a lack of confidence in your kids. When they are allowed to do something one day, but are punished for doing the same thing a week later, kids become confused and frustrated. For them, when the rules keep changing, they feel inadequate because they are unsure of how to "be good." They "find themselves" in trouble without intending to break rules simply because the rules seem to change unbeknownst to them. Ultimately, they feel bad about themselves. Consistent expectations and rules, on the other hand, create a predictable environment, enabling kids to start thinking ahead instead of acting impulsively. Over time, as they become used to staying within the box, their behavior remains appropriate with hardly any effort on their part.

Sometimes inconsistency is not obvious. Bill, for example, was denied a PlayStation 3 video game system for his birthday because his parents were afraid he would become addicted to it. Instead, they bought him a handheld Game Boy Advance. Their thinking was that they would be able to have more control over a handheld video game system. But for Bill, video games are video games, whether they are a console or portable, and so his parents' caution to him about his proclivity for video game addiction was negated and discarded.

Other times, inconsistency comes in the form of tacit approval. For example, Randi was punished for turning on the television before school on Tuesday, sending the message that such behavior was now allowed, but her parents ignored it when she turned it on Friday morning. Naturally, she will feel frustrated and confused if she is punished for doing the same thing on Monday. Generation Text kids are particularly affected by mixed messages brought on by tacit approval. Because they are so highly driven by want gratification, when inappropriate behavior is ignored they astutely pick up on your mixed signals and interpret the permissive message as the rule.

Expectations and rules are not the only things that need to be consistent. Consequences for breaking the rules need to be administered in a consistent manner as well. If you sometimes send a child to her room for yelling, and sometimes yell back, she will not take your punishments seriously. If, however, yelling is always punished with a time-out, the behavior will eventually stop. You must also be consistent in your tolerance of certain behaviors. If one parent has no problem with a child doing his homework on his bed, with papers and books strewn everywhere, and the other parent cannot bear to let the child do his homework anywhere but at a neat and orderly desk, you must decide as a parental unit how to handle the situation. Consider the needs and ability of the particular child, and know that one of you will have to tolerate something you don't prefer in the best interest of the child, who needs consistent messages about what is and is not expected of him.

Naturally, your own emotional and physical state on any given day affects your ability to be consistent. For example, if you have had a stressful or emotional day, you might snap at your kids for a behavior that you would normally overlook. Be aware of your own physical and emotional state so that you can control your reactions. If you find yourself yelling or punishing the kids for things you normally would not, it is time to pull back, take a few deep breaths, and regain perspective. Your kids need consistency in order to negotiate the world of temptation that surrounds them and to distinguish between what is appropriate and inappropriate on every level—from mealtime behavior to social graces, to work ethic to television programming to Internet and cell phone use. The more consistent you are in communicating and enforcing these parameters, the easier it will be for your child to remain inside the box.

Adjusting Your Rules When You Need To

As important as consistency is, the reality of raising children is that parents need to make adjustments according to their children's age, maturity level, and specific personality needs. For example, allowing your sixteen-year-old to take her phone with her when she goes to a friend's house, but forbidding her from taking it to her SAT tutoring class is a realistic and reasonable inconsistency. Not allowing your nine-year-old to have a cell phone at all is equally realistic, but it would be just as realistic to give her a phone and let her take it to a sleepover party in order to allay her anxiety about being away from home overnight. Though such flexibility is natural and necessary, it can be difficult to discern what criteria to use to decide whether a house rule should be changed or modified, and how to change the rules without creating the confusion and frustration of being inconsistent.

The first thing to consider is whether the rule has been firmly established in the family dynamic. Until a child accepts a certain rule—such as no video games on weeknights—and no longer challenges, breaks, or complains about it, it is not wise to deviate from that rule. Once he complies with the rule, demonstrating respect, maturity, and self-discipline regarding your expectation, you can begin to be flexible once in a while. In other words, when your child understands that he is not allowed to play video games on school nights, and accepts that rule, it is possible to reward him for specific academic accomplishments by allowing him to play.

Rules can be adjusted when it is practical and reasonable to do so. For example, you may have a general rule that your daughter is not allowed to have sleepovers on consecutive nights, but you make an exception when a close friend comes to visit from out of state. You may also choose to adjust age-related rules, such as no going to the mall without adult supervision until the age of twelve. A child's maturity level should also be taken into consideration. While most children should not be allowed to play with video games that contain violence, a child who is able to consistently control anger and aggression may be an exception to that rule, since he will be less likely to emulate that behavior. Similarly, a child who is consistently prompt and responsible may be granted an extra half-hour beyond her normal curfew time once in a while. The bottom line is that there are always exceptions to every rule, and you should exercise your best judgment in finding those exceptions and putting them into practice.

The most important thing to consider when you change the rules is to avoid sending mixed messages and creating confusion about what they are and are not allowed to do. Make sure your child understands why you are deviating from the usual rule, be it a special circumstance, a one-time deal, a special reward for specific behaviors or accomplishments, or a test of that child's maturity and readiness for certain experiences. Adjusting your rules should be contemplated carefully and done judiciously. To maintain control and avoid tacit approval, let your kids know that *you* are the one who decides when rules are changed, then make sure to return to the firm enforcement for that rule to solidify compliance. Remind your child that these adjustments in the usual rules are trials, which, if handled successfully, can be tried again.

SOCIAL LEARNING THEORY

The last fundamental tried-and-true parenting concept has to do with social learning theory. Social learning theory is the principle that shapes everyone's behavior, and it is based on two simple tenets. First, when a behavior is positively reinforced, it is more likely that it will be exhibited again. Second, when a behavior is negatively reinforced, it is less likely that it will be exhibited again. Social learning theory is a process that creates or eliminates behavior for children and adults alike, depending on the consequences that follow. The more immediate the consequence is, the more powerful it is in shaping a child's behavior. Consequences take the form of rewards, punishments, and natural consequences.

Positive consequences, or rewards, occur in three categories— primary, secondary, and tertiary:

▶ *Primary rewards* are tangible, concrete, material items such as candy and toys.
▶ *Secondary rewards* are social reinforcers, such as praise and acceptance into a group.
▶ *Tertiary rewards,* a level to which most people aspire, are intrinsic. That is, you do something because it feels good to you, it makes you proud of yourself, or you believe that it is the moral and ethical thing to do. Tertiary rewards are internal and self-imposed, whereas primary and secondary rewards are external.

Negative consequences occur in the form of internal distress or punishments. Common punishments for kids are the loss of a privilege, specific possession, or freedom (also known as grounding). Distress is an unpleasant internal emotional experience resulting from a parental action. For example, withdrawal of attention usually creates a distressed feeling in a child.

Natural consequences are reinforcers that occur within the child's environment, whether positive or negative, rather than imposed by the parent, and they are extremely effective as change agents for kids. Because parent-imposed consequences are complicated by the emotional aspects of the relationship, they can sometimes lose their impact. For example, if your child is perpetually late for school, you can punish him by taking away television for a day. Losing television rights may make him angry, but his focus will be on the loss of the privilege rather than on accepting responsibility for his actions and making changes. On the other hand, a phone call to the principal requesting strict enforcement for tardiness may have a more meaningful effect. The child will now have to focus on his own behavior in order to avoid the distress of detention imposed by an institution, not by "the meanest parent in the world."

Sometimes the relationship between a child's behavior and how it is positively or negatively reinforced is obvious—such as the correlation between finishing homework and being allowed to watch television. Other times you may not realize that a child is acting out in order to get the "reward" of parental attention. Once you understand and internalize the concept of social learning theory, you can apply it to even the most challenging situations your Generation Text child brings to the table and use it to manipulate the consequences, to foster appropriate behavior, and to curtail inappropriate behavior.

BEYOND THE BASICS: PARENTING THE GENERATION TEXT CHILD

Parenting the Generation Text child certainly requires employing all of the tried-and-true fundamental parenting approaches. But as important as those methods are and always have been, the new and unique challenges you face as a parent of a Generation Text child requires you to go beyond the basics, as we will see by taking a look at the Radnor family.

Six-year-old Diana Radnor came to my office to be treated for night terrors. Diana would wake up in the middle of the night in a state of panic. As I talked to her, it became clear that Diana's troubled sleep was precipitated by specific fears. Apparently, Diana had visited a website that presented animated monster adventures. The site, designed for young children, both intrigued and frightened Diana, and she reacted negatively. Diana also told me that she Googled "Barney" (the Purple Dinosaur) and found a disturbing picture of "Evil Barney" holding a chainsaw in one hand and the decapitated head of another popular character in the other.

Diana's parents were conscientious and possessed sound parenting skills. They scrutinized play-date situations, exposed her to appropriate cultural experiences, and set proper limits. They generally agreed on the "box" of limits and consequences for their kids' behavior. Their sound, consistent parenting skills, however, proved no match for Diana's access to scary material on the Internet. The Radnors had not considered that a website for young children might terrify their daughter.

I asked Diana's parents to visit the website and taught them how to check the computer's history, where they would be able to see which other websites their children visited. When they discovered that the computer's history included visits to R-rated movie trailers, a seedy YouTube video of an actor who plays a raunchy movie character, and several pornographic sites that require membership but offer plenty of free nudity as a sales ploy, they were obviously alarmed. As Diana's parents soon learned, nine-year-old Rick was the one visiting these inappropriate sites. Although relieved to know their six-year-old was not yet exposed to pornography, they were none too pleased about their nine-year-old's access to such adult content.

To help them tackle this problem, I gave the Radnors some "homework." Over a three-week period, I asked them to play at least three video games with Rick, watch several television shows with both children, have their kids show them the websites they consistently visit, and listen to as many songs on their iTunes program and MP3 player as possible. The parents kept a running log of their observations, thoughts, and feelings related to the values and moral content conveyed in the various media, and they soon learned that they had become victims of habituation and normalization. Like most parents, the Radnors were providing their kids with the standard Generation Text entertainment gadgets, but they had neglected to scrutinize material that was in fact inconsistent with their values and sense of appropriateness.

Mr. Radnor played three video games with Rick and found two of them laden with violence and aggression. One game included inappropriate language. The explicit goal of all the games was to kill people or destroy creatures. One of the games portrayed female characters wearing low-cut, skintight, cleavage-revealing clothing. Rick seemed unfazed by the violence and sexuality, but Mr. Radnor still found it unnerving.

Both parents watched television shows with Diana and Rick in an active mode. Although people tend to watch television passively, the Radnors were encouraged to pay close attention to the subtle messages the shows conveyed to their children. Most shows turned out to be acceptable and innocent, with a moral message of good over evil. However, some of the shows had explicit and implicit messages regarding violence, jealous competitiveness, and categorizing kids by group labels. Most of these shows are aired on networks geared especially for children.

In addition to the shows, the Radnors discovered that commercials often conveyed the most disturbing messages of all. Paris Hilton is featured in a Carl's Jr. fast-food restaurant ad wearing a skintight swimsuit, lathering up a Bentley, crawling all over the car in a sensual manner, and then putting her finger in her mouth before taking a bite out of a hamburger. A commercial for Hot Wheels entices children to buy the product and enter a contest to win a $10,000 prize. Although alcohol is not advertised during children's programming, any sports event on television certainly includes commercials that depict drinking as a way to be happy, successful, and popular. Studies show that these ads may be linked to increased drinking among youth.* Finally, when the Radnors watched an episode of *American Idol* together as they did every week, they noticed several promos for network shows that involved kidnapping and violence, and frightening scenes from an upcoming movie. Somehow, they had not noticed the content of these commercials before.

When it came to the music their children listened to, the Radnors found that Rick was on the fringe of listening to songs with

---

*L. B. Snyder, et al., "Effects of Alcohol Advertising Exposure on Drinking Among Youth," *Archives of Pediatrics & Adolescent Medicine* 160, no. 1 (January 2006), pp. 18–24.

inappropriate language and content, and that some of the music videos easily accessed on cable television stations were filled with sexual overtones. Watching YouTube videos was even more unnerving, considering the frequently posted violent acts, risqué messages, and high-risk stunts available for viewing there.

Once they started paying closer attention, the Radnors realized how much time the two children were spending in front of screens that projected harmful, or at least objectionable, material. According to one 2007 publication, kids spend more than half of their leisure time in front of screens.* The three weeks the Radnors spent experiencing their children's world was eye-opening. As I helped them process their observations, they discovered several troubling access and excess issues:

▶ Access to inappropriate messages is obtained passively and easily through the normal course of a day.
▶ Children are constantly and innocently exposed to messages that are contrary to the values and attitudes parents want to teach their kids.
▶ Both parents and kids are so used to having access to everything and so much "stuff" in their lives that these things are taken for granted.
▶ What has become normal in terms of social and moral behavior is not consistent with what you want your kids to believe is acceptable.
▶ Parents facilitate the access and excess issues both knowingly and inadvertently.

Enlightened, the Radnors realized that they had to address their kids' access and excess issues, and we focused on developing key intervention strategies. Those strategies, which you can use with your own children, are discussed next.

ACTIVE PARENTING

The most glaring obstacle to raising well-adjusted Generation Text kids is decreased parental involvement. The combination of the fast-

*George Comstock and Erica Scharrer, *Media and the American Child* (Burlington, MA: Academic Press), 2007.

paced, high-speed culture and ease of private access to the world requires parents to be more actively involved in their kids' lives on a regular basis. In order to do so, you will need to consciously monitor your kids' activities and find ways to actively engage with your kids, as the Radnors did, formally recording your observations over a designated period of time. Active parenting means observing and monitoring your child's Internet use, television programming, video games, music, and social activities.

By listening to music, playing video games, and watching television along with your kids, you can limit their exposure to inappropriate material and promote educational media that will enhance moral character and send messages commensurate with your family values. Studies indicate that children spend an average of four hours a day viewing television programs and DVDs and that 68 percent of kids ages eight to eighteen have televisions in their room, which increases their viewing time one and a half hours more per day compared to kids who do not have TVs in their room.*

The Radnors decided to move the computer to the living room, where they would be better able to see the screen. Rick and Diana were also given rules about when they could and could not use the computer. Both kids were required to disclose all of their screen names and passwords they use so that their parents could periodically monitor their Internet activities. In addition, the Radnors directed their kids to websites like Netsmartz.org, LoveYourChildrenUSA.org, SafeKids.com, FBI.gov/kids/k5th/safety2.htm, and Blogging.wikia.com, which help kids use the Internet properly and safely. Next, the Radnors educated themselves about which sites should be off-limits and which provided their kids with useful, positive information. New websites are posted every day, and kids talk about them. You will need to keep your ears open to keep abreast. Treat Internet use like you would treat a sleepover with a friend—know where the child is, what he's doing and for how long, and make sure that there is adult supervision. When it comes to Internet use, such supervision can be found in the form of monitoring and filtering software such as Spector Pro, IamBigBrother, and eBlaster. These programs record keystrokes for chats and instant messages, as well as monitor MySpace, websites visited, web

---

*D. F. Roberts, U. G. Foehr, and V. Rideout, "Generation M: Media in the Lives of 8–18 Year-olds," Kaiser Family Foundation survey, March 2005.

searches, and e-mails sent and received. Parental control settings offered by most web browsers, including AOL and MSN, are another means to monitor and prevent inappropriate Internet activities.

Before buying your child a video game, CD, or DVD, talk to other parents who may be familiar with the item and prescreen it if possible. Just as you would not buy your daughter a book about sex and reproduction without reading it first, you should not buy her a video or computer game without doing similar research into its contents. It is easy to assess the appropriateness of a television show by reading about it on sites such as TV.com or by actually viewing an episode. Checking for ratings and discussing content with other parents are similarly helpful tactics. Never assume that since many of your child's friends are watching or listening to something, or that because it is entertainment made for kids, that it is appropriate for your child.

When it comes to monitoring your children's social activities, keep in mind that beyond those interactions you can directly observe, there are plenty of daily activities that occur when you are out of eye- and earshot. When you are present, keep track of the overt and subtle inappropriate messages that others communicate through actions and words. Use these observations to teach your kids the appropriate messages commensurate with your values. Talk about what people say to them and how they behave at a later time. Reinforce the healthy and positive interactions and explain why the inappropriate actions are unhealthy or unkind.

To monitor your kids' behavior when they are not with you means setting limits and structures to insulate and keep them as safe as possible from noxious material. Always make sure that they have proper adult supervision, and while your children are very young, make it a point to speak to that supervising adult and ask how much they monitor the children. Never assume that someone else will monitor your children as closely as you would, and be sure to coach your children on how to suggest another activity if they encounter material you have identified as inappropriate. This is easier said than done, of course, and it requires that you invest in teaching your children specific skills.

No matter how diligent you are in monitoring your children, once they are no longer under your supervision, it is up to them to cope with and sift through the myriad messages from media, Internet, and peers. For all their benefits, filtering and parental control monitoring devices for the television and computer are often flawed. Some websites inadvertently avert the software, and savvy cyber-kids can disable them. You may have refused to purchase *Grand Theft Auto: Vice City,* but what is stopping your child from playing it at a friend's house? Similarly, you are not privy to the text messages and e-mails your child sends and receives. Lay down the law regarding inappropriate websites, video games, mature-rated DVDs, and TV programs, and teach your kids to suggest another activity when their friends suggest these things. To avoid embarrassment, encourage them to say things like, "I don't feel like playing this game or watching this show," rather than "I am not allowed to play or watch."

While monitoring is important, it is impossible to insulate your children, even under your own roof. You must work very hard to instill in your kids the skills they need to independently navigate through technology and culture. The goal is for them to develop the self-discipline, self-control, good decision-making skills, and judgment so that when they are alone, they can rely on their own devices to filter inappropriate information and influence. Creating open lines of communication is the first step in providing your child with the necessary tools to not only cope with the negative aspects of the culture, but to take advantage of the wealth of positive information and opportunity it offers.

COMMUNICATION

Though you may not always feel like it, you are the single greatest resource of positive influence on your children. The most powerful ability you have as a parent—beyond serving as a model of good behavior—is effective communication with your children. Successful communication between you and your child enhances mutual understanding, trust, honesty, and respect. Conversely, a lack of communication creates emotional distance, deception, sneaky behavior, and a suspicious mistrust of one another.

There are several key factors in developing a good communicative relationship with your child. From early childhood on, have frequent conversations with your kids about the events of your day—recall what you did (together or separately), saw, thought, and felt throughout the day. Such frequent conversations, while they may seem superficial or uninteresting, establish a pattern of interaction that becomes familiar and comfortable for your child. When talking to one another is a normal and comfortable part of their daily routine, your children will be more likely to come to you to discuss sensitive topics like sex, drugs, and problems in school. When these issues arise, your practice with open communication will improve your chances of having a productive discussion in which you do not immediately react or punish, but listen carefully and address the issue head-on, in a direct, mature, matter-of-fact manner, using clearly understood language.

Most parents dread these conversations. They underestimate their child's knowledge about sex, vulgar language, body parts, and violent acts, and when these topics arise it can be difficult for parents to hide their anxiety. It is important to at least appear comfortable with the topics and to give your child proper words to use instead of vulgar language or slang. Ask your child how he feels and what he thinks about what he did or saw. If your child volunteers information about her misbehavior, praise her honesty, try not to overreact, and instead discuss the consequences. For example, say something like, "I am very disappointed in you because you know you are not allowed to watch R-rated movies. What do you think you should do next time John puts on an inappropriate movie at his house? What should be your punishment if you do it again?" Avoid preaching and lecturing, because both are surefire ways to shut down your child's communication.

As we know by now, your kids will inadvertently encounter upsetting or forbidden material on a daily basis. Encouraging them to approach you with their questions or concerns about these things means clarifying that they should not be afraid of punishment for being honest with you. With that fear allayed, they will be more likely to come to you when they encounter inappropriate material, allowing you to deal with it in a productive way before it becomes truly problematic.

Whether they come to you with information about an Internet site, a movie, or peer pressure, the idea is to praise your children for talking to you about the issue, educate them with accurate information about whatever they experienced, and have your children then make their own judgments about it. Fostering their ability to make their own judgments—with your guidance—will only enhance your communicative relationship with your children. Be receptive to what they have to say by listening with an open mind. If you are critical, judgmental, and close-minded, it is unlikely that your child will continue to approach you with problems or questions. An excellent way to convey a receptive, nonjudgmental attitude is to ask a lot of questions. Open-ended questions like, " *Why* do you think it is dangerous to ride your bicycle on a busy road like Route 47?" will generate a more expansive conversation than a question like, "Do you think it is safe to ride your bicycle on a busy road like Route 47?" to which your child would only respond with a curt, "No."

TEACHING DECISION-MAKING SKILLS

Faced with an unprecedented number of options in every part of their lives, Generation Text kids need to possess sound decision-making skills. Whether they are deciding between forty different styles of sneakers or contemplating attending a party where drugs and alcohol will be available, your kids' well-being depends on their ability to make good decisions.

Many of today's children experience profound distress when faced with making a decision. Used to getting everything they want, kids can feel helpless and even victimized when forced to deny themselves something. Some kids become immobilized when faced with a conflict, and others make the quickest possible decision simply to alleviate their distress. Other children dwell on their choice to the point of frustration. Still others simply ignore the decision, hoping it will go away. Obviously, none of these coping mechanisms facilitates sound decision making; rather, they render the child feeling helpless. The first step in teaching your child effective decision-making skills is to dispel the notion that they are helpless in the first place. Once they realize that they have some control over their own destiny, children become empowered to make smarter decisions.

There are three basic paradigms of decision-making conflicts that Generation Text kids experience:

> ▶ *The Happy Problem.* Here, the child mulls over a choice between two or more positive options, such as being picked for

both the travel hockey and indoor soccer teams, but only being able to play on one.

▶ *Choosing Between Helpful and Harmful.* This scenario would include hanging out with a group of friends at the school playground when they decide to smoke cigarettes. Your child will be forced to decide between a healthy option (refraining from smoking) and a harmful one (joining in).

▶ *The Unhappy Problem.* Your child must choose between two negative options, such as going to an inappropriate, violent movie with friends or feeling left out of the group otherwise.

Generation Text kids need to be equipped with sound decision-making skills so that they can function in all three scenarios. If they don't, more often than not, they will succumb to the negative pressures of media, Internet, and peer pressures.

The following are steps you can take to develop good decision-making skills in your children:

1. *Help your child develop perspective.* Making a good decision requires level-headedness. Strong emotions will negatively affect the quality of your child's decision-making skills. The key to teaching your kids to use perspective is to show them the difference between emotion and cognition. For example, kids may find the act of deciding which pair of sneakers to buy a stressful experience, because they are focusing on the potential of *not* getting one of the many good options available to them. Your job is to help the child gain perspective and to provide a set of rational and realistic statements that challenge the thoughts that may be bogging her down. You need to say something that helps to reframe and counter the Generation Text child's drive for want gratification and her sense of entitlement and feelings of loss instead of gain. A comment, such as the following, will bring the stress level down to a point at which the child is able to make a decision:

> "I understand how difficult it is to choose between these two pairs of sneakers. You probably want them both, but you know you can only get one. You are so lucky to be able to have either one—so many kids don't have these options. Think of how happy you will be to have either one of them. This is not the last sneaker you will ever buy. If it is such a difficult decision, it means that either one will make you happy."

Having perspective in this case helps your child realize that she is gaining something, not losing. Choosing between two sneakers is not exactly a life-altering event, although many kids do experience anguish with this type of decision. It is used here to be instructive. With the excess of material objects and privileges Generation Text kids have, learning a positive decision-making method is essential.

2. *List and prioritize options.* Once you have established the right perspective, have your child evaluate the importance of each option. Using a scale of 1–5, with 1 being the least important and 5 being the most important, concretizes the assessment. List the options on a piece of paper and then assign a number based on the importance of each to the child. Ranking the choices from least important to most important usually stimulates a conversation about just how much the child wants each item. The exercise forces the child to start thinking pragmatically, as he undoubtedly begins to scrutinize the choices.

For example, Roger has five different ways he can spend his Saturday night. To help him decide what to do, his parents asked him to write down the options:

- His father has tickets to a professional basketball game.
- A bunch of kids he is trying to become friendly with (including Jennifer, a girl he is interested in dating) are getting together.
- He has a big physics test to study for.
- His usual friends are going to the movies.
- His mother is going to spend the evening at her sister's house, and his cousin, who is also one of his best friends, will be there.

With his mother's help, Roger then ranked the five options according to importance to him. Assigning number five was the easiest—studying for his test. He realized that going to the movies was also toward the bottom of his priority list. Number three required more thought, but he decided that the basketball game was more important than going to the movies and studying, but not as important as seeing his cousin and spending time with his new group of friends. By the time the list was reduced to the final two choices,

Roger found it difficult to decide which was more important to him. Finally, he ranked seeing his new friends, including Jennifer, to be number one, and going to his cousin's house number two.

3. *Evaluate the options.* Next, you need to teach your child how to consider the consequences of his possible decisions. This is a critical step in helping your Generation Text child develop decision-making skills because of all the potential risks and perils his access to the world brings. Your child is more than likely to encounter situations involving sex, drugs, alcohol, peer pressure, and academic dishonesty. Encouraging your child to think through the potential consequences and implications of his decisions on these matters acts as a deterrent for some very bad outcomes.

Although his dilemma about how to spend a Saturday night was not life-changing, Roger still needed to consider the consequences of choosing one option over the others. The implication of not using the night to study was minimal once he realized that he had all day Saturday and Sunday to study. Going to the movies with his friends was something he could do anytime. Roger also knew that not going to the movies would not jeopardize these friendships in the least. Not going to the basketball game had a minimal consequence since his dad bought a season package of twenty games, so he could go another time. Surprisingly, when he examined the implications of his final options, Roger realized that although seeing his cousin was more important to him than seeing his new group of friends, the consequence of not going to the party loomed as a missed opportunity to connect with Jennifer. He further rationalized that he does see his cousin often enough. Roger decided to get together with his new group of friends—including Jennifer.

TEN STEPS TO BETTER DECISION MAKING

Kids frequently try to avoid decisions that present social and moral conflicts. As the parent, it is your job to teach your child that while ignoring big decisions may bring her immediate relief, it will often create bigger and more substantial problems in the long run. Here are ten steps you can follow to help your children fine-tune their decision-making skills.

1. *Be open to discussing tough subjects.* Help your child feel comfortable coming to you to discuss conflicts, even when they involve something of which you don't approve. Ideally, your kids should come to you first when they encounter difficult situations in school, at friend's houses, in the media, and on the Internet. Establish a caring, supportive environment for open discussion. Periodically, initiate discussions about tough subjects like sex and drugs and seize the moment during a television show or commercial that highlights social or moral issues. By doing this, you will give your child permission not only to speak of such clandestine topics, but also desensitize them to having conversations about them with you. Always interject that you want them to come to you if they are ever faced with any of the issues you discuss. Promise them that they will never be punished if they do so, and that you only want them to come to you so that you can help them.

2. *Identify the problem and the goal of the decision.* Ask your child to clearly identify the problem he is experiencing. Sometimes the actual problem is muddied by other factors. For example, a sixth-grader had to choose between working with her rather social friends on a group social studies project and a group of kids who were more likely to take the assignment seriously. Her mother helped her clearly identify the problem, which was avoiding feeling left out and trying not to hurt her friends' feelings if she chose not to work with them. She then helped her daughter clarify her goal, which was to do a good job on this important project. Clarifying and identifying the problem and the goal made the girl's decision to work with the more academic group easier.

3. *Think creatively.* Your child needs to explore all his options, taking each alternative seriously, and then he must utilize creative, resourceful thinking. Begin with a list of pros and cons as a way to allow your child to evaluate each option and consider possible outcomes, including how each choice may affect other people involved. Whenever your children come to you for assistance with a decision, guide them through it by asking, "Could there be another option you haven't thought of yet?" This type of leading question will facilitate your child's independent decision-making strategies

so that he will be capable of going through the process when you are not involved. Avoid telling him what to do because that tactic will not foster creative, resourceful thinking.

4. *Act when it's decision time.* Now that you have identified the problem, the goal, and the pros and cons of each option, it's decision time. Hopefully, the best decision will become clear to your child and she will choose the option you would otherwise choose for her. Of course, this doesn't always happen. When your child comes to a decision you don't agree with, you are faced with one of the many difficult moments as a parent: whether or not to allow her to follow through with her own decision. The answer to that question lies in the degree of risk, as judged by you. Certainly, if implementing the decision has the potential for physical harm to your child or others, you must intervene. If the consequences are not severe, you can have her reevaluate the possible implications of that choice. A third choice is to allow the natural consequences of her decision to occur, being ready to help her pick up the pieces and learn from her mistake by discussing it afterward.

5. *Follow through.* Ensure that the child follows through on the decisions he makes. This is especially important when the decision is a difficult one. If your child is grappling with a difficult decision, he can procrastinate or even avoid implementing the plan of action he chose. Ask him when he plans on putting the plan into action, and encourage him to set a deadline, then follow through by asking how it went.

6. *Evaluate the outcome.* Following up with your child provides more than just the benefit of making sure her decision was implemented, but it will also help her with future decisions. Evaluate the outcome of the decision with your child so that she can use the experience to help guide her through the next decision she faces. For example, if Molly decides to start her homework after dinner only to discover that she didn't have enough time to complete it, she can use the poor outcome of that decision to start her homework earlier the following night.

7. *Prepare your child to make quick decisions.* Sometimes your child won't have time to work through the many steps of responsible decision making. We all face numerous, split-second decisions on a daily basis, and our kids are no exception. We must prepare

them for making those last-minute decisions when we are not around to help them. Situations involving peer pressure and social consequences are often made away from home, when there is nothing we can do to help.

For these situations, and countless others, your children need to rely on the ability to make an immediate decision. Prepare them by going over a mental script on which they can rely. This involves teaching your kids a list of catch phrases they can quickly retrieve to guide them through questionable situations. Consider practicing the following lines with your children at home, teaching them what they mean and when to use them:

> *"If Mom or Dad were watching right now, what would they say?"*
> *"Is this good for me or bad for me?"*
> *"Go with your gut."*
> *"If it feels 'funny'—don't do it."*

Those catch phrases help guide children toward taking the right path, choosing right over wrong, having confidence in their ability to make good decisions, and trusting their gut.

8. *Rehearse specific scenarios.* You can also rehearse specific scripts with your child to help her get out of potentially dangerous or anxiety-provoking experiences. For example, if you want your child to be secure and confident enough in herself to simply say "No, thank you" when her friends offer her a cigarette, you might discuss the possibility of this happening and have her rehearse the practice line, "I have to go to the bathroom, I'll be back in a few minutes," which creates an opportunity for her to disengage from the situation by stepping away. These kinds of actions will make a child feel proud of herself, and they should be encouraged.

9. *Ask pop-quiz questions.* You can help your child practice split-second decision making by asking point-blank questions like: "Do you think you should do your homework now, or play outside and get your homework done after dinner?" Frequently confronting your child with decisions to make within his normal daily routine will provide the practice he needs to make quick decisions on his own, without getting flustered.

10. *Focus on values and goals.* Finally, help your child focus on her values and goals by constantly reinforcing them verbally. When

a child is clear on her values and goals, she will feel more confident and secure when making hard decisions. If the Generation Text child has a strong conviction to values, decision making becomes less conflicted and less stressful.

By using these ten strategies to arm your kids with good decision-making skills, they stand a good chance of resisting the negative forces that the access and excess culture brings. As they internalize this decision-making process, your confidence in their ability to cope with the inevitable temptations of the world will undoubtedly increase.

We have established that Generation Text kids live in a hectic, high-pressured culture. They constantly balance social pressures, academic demands, and extracurricular activities. Having good communication and decision-making skills in their arsenal is a great step in the right direction, but it is not enough. They need to also have good time management skills, without which they will be unable to juggle the multitude of privileges, responsibilities, and activities we as parents offer them.

TIME MANAGEMENT

Poor time management skills translate into missed opportunities and failure to take full advantage of the rich culture in which our kids live. Effective time management can be the basis for your child's success in social relationships. If your child is on time for appointments and meetings and completes tasks in a timely fashion, he will prevent chaotic crises in his life. In short, effective time managers are dependable, reliable people who project a sense of strength and stability. People who are frequently late and don't complete tasks because of their poor time management skills often must live with disappointment, a contentious feeling, anxiety, unnecessary pressure, and low self-esteem due to the negative feedback they consistently receive.

If you are old enough to remember *The Ed Sullivan Show* from the 1960s (and if you can admit it), you might remember the plate-spinning act. A man held a pole with six or seven tines. One by one, he placed dinner plates on each tine, spinning them so that centrifugal force kept them from falling. Eventually, different plates started wobbling and he had to continuously spin them to keep them from falling. With one hand holding the pole and the other frantically attending to each wobbling plate, he managed to prevent the plates from crashing to the floor.

Surely, as a parent you understand that overwhelmed feeling of juggling so many different things at once and trying to divide your attention among them equally so none of your "plates" crash. Today, kids are so busy that they are like that plate spinner, too, and you as a parent need to help them. We know that time management is an art and a skill requiring creative thought and problem-solving prowess. When I work on time management with kids in my office, I use two different systems—one for daily tasks and another for long-range obligations.

Effective time management begins with learning how to tackle and accomplish daily tasks so that chores from the previous day never spill over into the next. Getting to this point creates a sense of competence, reduces stress and feeling overwhelmed, and empowers your child so that he is running his life instead of feeling out of control. To help your child manage daily tasks, you can use this five-step approach:

1. Make a list of all the tasks that must be done today.
2. Prioritize each item on the list.
3. Estimate how long each task takes.
4. Assign each task to a time period throughout the day, building in fifteen-minute breaks when needed.
5. Hang this daily "to do" list somewhere where it can be easily viewed.

Prioritizing is a skill that applies to homework, household chores, play activities, and family obligations. The variables that determine the priority of a job are specific deadlines, the level of difficulty of the task, and the importance of getting that specific task completed. Take Michelle, for example, who has difficulty prioritizing and organizing. She brought me the following list of tasks needing completion over the weekend:

▶ Do math homework.
▶ Clean room.
▶ Do social studies presentation.

- ▶ Write English essay.
- ▶ Buy birthday gift for best friend.
- ▶ Help Dad clean out the garage.

Considering deadlines, difficulty, and importance of each item, we worked on her list, giving the deadlines first consideration. In deciding how to prioritize, I strongly encourage my patients to do their "gottas" before their "wannas," setting a precedent that will help them in the future. The social studies presentation was not due until the following Friday, so it was placed at the bottom of her priority list. The essay, a more immediate "gotta," proved to be the most difficult for her, so she decided to put that task first. Knowing that her parents would not allow her to see her friends until her homework was complete (another "gotta"), Michelle placed higher importance on completing her math homework. Next, she decided that cleaning her room would also increase her chances of going out. Michelle was at the mercy of her parents' availability to buy the gift and clean the garage, so she placed these items next on her list. Now all she had to do was block times throughout the weekend on a calendar to complete all of the tasks. Her priority list ended up as follows:

1. Write English essay.
2. Do math homework.
3. Clean room.
4. Buy birthday gift.
5. Clean garage.
6. Start social studies presentation (if time allows).

In addition to daily tasks and scheduling commitments, your kids need to manage their long-range obligations, including their social commitments, medical appointments, and extracurricular activities. They need to have an awareness of these obligations so that they can plan other things around them. Although not as common as daily tasks, long-range projects are usually multistep efforts requiring a great deal of planning. I have found the following system to prove quite effective even with my youngest patients.

1. *Make a monthly calendar.* Hang a monthly calendar in your child's room or work area for easy daily access, and make sure to

include all of their appointments, due dates, and scheduled events on it. The calendar can have pictures of a high-interest theme, such as sports, lizards, or ballet, or have your child decorate the calendar to make it more attractive and special to them. You can also use a calendar on the computer. Daily reminders can be scheduled in most calendar programs.

2. *Perform a task analysis.* For those assignments requiring a series of steps to accomplish, perform a task analysis. A task analysis is a way to break down a long-range, complex project into smaller, more manageable components. By segmenting each of the steps and calculating how long they take to complete, a schedule can be made to ensure that the project is done on time, and done well, without last-minute cramming.

Let's take James's fourth-grade book report assignment, for example. The report is due in three weeks and must include a written report, a poster of his favorite scene, and an oral presentation to his class. First, we listed the different elements of his assignment:

- ▶ Read the 125-page book.
- ▶ Write the report.
- ▶ Choose and plan a scene for the poster.
- ▶ Make a list of all materials needed and check with parents to determine when they can buy them.
- ▶ Purchase all materials needed.
- ▶ Make poster.
- ▶ Practice presentation twice.

Next, we broke down two of the tasks into even smaller steps. After determining that James could read about fifteen pages in a half-hour, we calculated that reading the book would take eight sittings. The written report would have four sections, so we scheduled four separate sittings in which to write the report and complete that part of the assignment. Then, James began to estimate how much time each step would take.

3. *Work backward.* Begin placing each step in the task analysis on the calendar, starting with the due date for the project and working backward. Space out each step in accordance with the amount of time it takes to complete it. Don't forget to consider other obligations already on the calendar. James's calendar looked like this:

Sunday	Monday	Tuesday	Wednesday	Thursday	Friday	Saturday
7 Read Read	8 Read	9 Read	10	11 Read	12 Read	13 Read Read
14 Write 1st Section	15	16 Write 2nd Section	17 Choose plan and poster scene	18 Write 3rd Section	19	20 Write 4th Section; purchase materials for poster
21 Make poster	22 Practice presentation	23	24	25 Practice presentation	26 Presentation and written report due	27

What had once seemed like an overwhelming task now looked feasible to James when he looked at his schedule. Having this visual aid also helped him see that he could pace himself so that he could focus on smaller, more manageable goals one at a time. He not only completed the assignment, he ended up having it done before the due date. This was quite a change for him, and quite a relief for his parents.

4. *Refer to the calendar daily.* You can go to the doctor with strep throat, get a prescription for an effective antibiotic, have it filled at the pharmacy, and bring it home. You have done everything you need to do to take care of your problem. But if you don't take the medicine, it is all for naught. The same applies to organizing and managing time on your child's monthly calendar. It must be referred to on a daily basis and coordinated with her daily tasks. You will undoubtedly need to remind her to do so until it becomes habitual.

5. *Use technology.* A good way to encourage better time management habits is to ask your children to use the calendar function on their cell phone. These functions have reminders that pop up on the cell phone screen, or voice memo prompts that help them stick to their schedule. Because kids can relate to the cell phone and

enjoy learning new ways to use the gadget, they may be more inclined to learn scheduling this way than they would be if they were merely keeping an old-fashioned date book or calendar.

When teaching your children to prioritize and manage their time, you can motivate them by reminding them that the better their skills become, the more time they will have for leisure. Learning how to allot time for both work and play will help them create a healthy balance in their sure-to-be hectic young adult lives.

IT'S NEVER TOO LATE

Don't worry if you have read this chapter and discovered that you have a lot of changes to make. It is never too late to start. The uniqueness in parenting Generation Text kids necessitates an active awareness of their exposure to the world through technological access. To make sure your eyes are wide open, start your active awareness by periodically conducting the "observing eye" assignment I gave the Radnors.

It is important that you understand and assess your own parenting styles and that you and your spouse are consistent with one another. Understand how kids learn new behavior using rewards and punishments. The excess of material possessions and freedom for Generation Text kids are here to stay. You can only hope to limit them and help them develop an appreciation for what they have. Why not use their need for things and privileges as rewards and punishments to help shape their behavior, values, and attitudes?

Tried-and-true parenting strategies—such as box parenting, establishing and enforcing rules consistently, and active monitoring—have obviously been important for all generations. Generation Text kids need their parents to apply these techniques more than ever because of the higher risks they face on a daily basis.

The three major skills Generation Text kids need to acquire and refine are: (1) communication skills, (2) decision-making skills, and (3) time management skills. If you haven't actively worked on developing these skills with your kids, today is a good day to start. If they are going to grow up well adjusted in a culture that bombards them with information (helpful and harmful), an abundance of social stresses, and numerous moral dilemmas, they will need to be adept in all three areas.

CHAPTER 7

The Access and Excess Teen

••

"I just started at a new high school, and I'm trying to get my home-work done, but I'm having a hard time. I'm drawn to the Internet and cell phone—I can't help myself."—Jeffrey, age 15

"My history teacher gave us an assignment, and I went online to do the research. I went to CNN.com, NYTimes. com, and Washingtonpost .com, and then I got overwhelmed and couldn't finish. There was too much information."—Carol, age 14

"My dad said that I can't go on a teen tour to Europe this summer because it would be spoiling me. So instead he's sending me to Hawaii to do community service."—Wendy, age 16

"After I broke up with my girlfriend, I took her picture off my MySpace page. People kept contacting me to discuss whether I should have broken up with her. I felt weird about that—no privacy."—Matthew, age 17

ON THE SURFACE, IT MAY APPEAR THAT TODAY'S TEEN IS AS PER-plexing to adults as teenagers have always been. But the age of ac-cess and excess has put a new twist on the developmental issues our teens face.

The environment that kids are exposed to has always influenced the critical adolescent emotional tasks of identity and individuation. The huge difference for teenagers today is that their social environ-ment transcends personal contact within their limited locales. With technology at their disposal, plugged-in teens have the opportunity to be even more tuned-out and withdrawn from their parents. They are also more aware of exactly what is available to them. This access to the larger world creates a constant need for more—and the resulting issues of excess affect the process of identity and individuation.

MARCY: A CASE STUDY

The story of Marcy, a fourteen-year-old high school freshman, provides a useful illustration of the influences of access and excess as they affect teenagers in particular. Marcy's adolescent experience is shaped by her exposure to the world and the abundance of possessions available to her.

In sessions with me, Marcy's parents expressed a level of concern for their daughter that was significant but not dramatic. They described her as a caring, conscientious child, a better-than-average student with a loyal set of friends. She had always been close to her mother, but also enjoyed a positive relationship with her father. "So why consult with me?" I asked. "She sounds wonderful."

"Recently things have changed," the father said. "Marcy just doesn't seem herself." Both parents went on to say that Marcy had changed dramatically over the past year, and they feared she might be depressed. She was spending much more time in her room. She spent hours a day on her computer, after school and in the evening. Whenever her parents entered the room, she would abruptly minimize the screen or stop talking. She had her cell phone with her at all times, and when she received a call she would quickly leave the room. Sometimes the phone would make odd beeping sounds, and she'd look at it and start frantically pushing buttons. When her parents questioned her, she retorted with annoyance. Instead of watching TV with the family, she now chose to watch her own shows in her bedroom.

In general, Marcy had become curt and easily annoyed with her parents, often giving one-word answers to their questions. She resisted family activities, from nightly dinners to family outings. She was easily angered, particularly when she didn't get what she wanted, and was irritable with her family. (This irritability magically transformed into the old sweetness whenever she talked to her friends.) Her grades had dipped; teachers began reporting missed homework assignments and Marcy's overly social behavior during class time. She defied parental rules and recently quit the field hockey team and dropped out of a religious youth group.

In addition, Marcy drifted away from a group of girls she'd been close to for years, and was developing a new set of friends. Her new peer group included boys for the first time. She changed her hairstyle and the way she dressed; she wanted to highlight her hair and have her belly button pierced. She asked her mother to buy her thong underwear, skintight pants, and stomach-baring tops. Once-pleasurable shopping excursions with her mother had turned into screaming matches and abrupt mall departures. Marcy's temper flared when her parents denied her requests, and she typically stomped off and mumbled under her breath. Even when her parents gave in to her requests, she soon demanded something else, or something better. Her parents bought her an MP3 player for Christmas, and by March she was asking for an iPod—and eventually got it. By summer, she wanted a new iPod with a pink casing that held more songs.

Recently, Marcy had come home from a sleepover at a friend's house with blonde streaks in her hair. Her mother also discovered that at school Marcy sometimes changed into a friend's shirt—one that her parents would not have accepted. Though they didn't suspect drugs or alcohol, Marcy's parents were concerned about where she was headed.

I started seeing Marcy in weekly sessions. It didn't take much time for her to discover that I wasn't the enemy. Marcy sensed that I was trying to understand without judging or criticizing her. We explored her interests, her goals and dreams, and how she spent her time. Beneath the anger and rebellious behavior, I found a kid begging for help in sorting out her confused thoughts and feelings.

Marcy began confiding in me, which gave me insight into what the issues were and how she was coping with them. Her chief complaints were that her parents were too strict and didn't understand her. Her new friends, she said, knew more about her than her parents. Her old friends, the ones her parents wanted her to have, were "immature." She no longer felt close to her mother or father, for a number of reasons—she didn't like the same things they did anymore; they treated her like a little kid; they were unreasonable and holding her back socially. The only way she could have any semblance of a normal social life, she said, was to do things behind her parents' backs.

When asked what she did for fun, Marcy rattled off a list: chat rooms, instant messaging, going on MySpace.com, visiting websites that featured her favorite TV and movie stars. "What about hanging out with your friends?" I asked. "Oh, I like that, but I don't get to do it much," she said. She denied alcohol or drug use, but admitted to trying cigarettes. Though she denied any physical involvement with boys, and I believed her, Marcy discussed sexual issues openly.

Marcy's extensive sexual knowledge, and her comfort level in discussing it, was not surprising to me. Repeated exposure to sexual connotations everywhere she looked easily led to normalization and habituation of blatant sex talk. Sex was a predominant topic among her friends, in face-to-face conversations, when instant messaging and texting, and in private chat rooms. A study conducted by the Kaiser Family Foundation found that 70 percent of all Americans fifteen to seventeen years old have been exposed to pornography online.* Sex, in all forms, has become a normal part of most teenagers' lives. As a therapist, I have found that many kids have a breadth of knowledge of sexual activities that extends even beyond the awareness of some adults. And it's not just older teens. Even today's preadolescents and young teens have a more expansive knowledge about sex than ever before.

Over time, it became clear to me that Marcy was enamored of her new best friend, Alyssa. Alyssa appeared to be a strong influence on Marcy and the other girls in their group; it was at Alyssa's house that Marcy highlighted her hair. When Marcy was not hanging out with her friends between classes and on weekends, she was in constant communication with them on her cell phone and computer. She described as "friends" not only the kids at school, but the kids she "met" online.

When she got home from school at 3 P.M., Marcy typically turned on her laptop and AOL Instant Messenger (AIM) and talked to friends intermittently until she went to sleep at around 10 P.M. She instant-messaged as she did her homework, talked on her cell phone, constantly sent and received text messages, and watched her

---

*"Generation Rx.com: Teens and Young Adults Surfing the Web for Health Info" (survey findings presented by The Henry J. Kaiser Family Foundation, December 11, 2001, New York, NY), http://www.kaisernetwork.org/health_cast/uploaded_files/kff121101.pdf.

favorite TV shows. In the afternoon she tended to communicate with school friends, but in the evening she IMed with people she knew only peripherally or had never met in person or lived far from her town. Most of this IMing was conducted in her room, without her parents' knowledge. Marcy did not believe she was hiding anything, but liked talking to friends in privacy. It was also typical for her laptop and cell phone to be in close proximity while she watched TV in the family room.

In addition to talking to friends online, Marcy surfed the Web and visited sites associated with her favorite music groups and TV and movie stars. For this impressionable fourteen-year-old girl, in the throes of solidifying her identity, these websites often provided borderline risqué material. The TV shows Marcy watched had themes relating to casual sex, drugs, alcohol consumption, denigration of authority, and manipulative personalities. When asked to talk about the shows she watched, Marcy described a reality show about teens in California. These kids were in sexual relationships, using drugs and alcohol, deceiving and defying parents, driving luxury cars, buying expensive clothing and jewelry, and generally expressing contempt for authority.

WHAT HAPPENS IN ADOLESCENCE?

On the surface, Marcy's conflicts with her parents during this period of her life are fairly typical. The teenage years can be both exciting and tumultuous. During this time there are hormonally based physical and emotional changes that affect family relationships, mood, interests, and a teen's attitude toward authority.

Adolescence, a stage of development that every teenager goes through, is a transitional period that bridges childhood and adulthood. It begins with the onset of puberty (usually age 13) and ends when the teenager reaches the age of majority (age 18 or 19) in which legal responsibilities such as voting, emancipation, and adult privileges are given. The onset can vary, with some kids starting adolescence as early as age 10. Interestingly, the onset is determined by a physical milestone but the ending is more culturally and legally determined. In essence, when they reach age 18 or 19, teenagers are expected to be able to accept the responsibilities of adulthood even though they may not be psychologically ready.

What, then, are the factors that determine that adolescence has been sufficiently resolved to enter adulthood? During adolescence the teenager is engaged in two critical psychological tasks—defining his identity and beginning to separate from his parents. You can think of these as a psychological "agenda." Adolescence, as a stage of development, truly ends when these issues of identity and individuation are resolved. That can occur at age 18 or at age 48.

The Task of Identity

The task of identity has to do with a crystallization of how teenagers define who they are and where they are going in their next stage of life. Included in critical identity issues are sexual orientation, vocational path, and the type of social relationships they choose. Teenagers actively seek out personal characteristics to identify with from their social environment. As they go through their teenage years, kids will "try on different hats" to see which one best fits their personality. Instead of you, the parent, as their primary identification figure, they now look toward the peer group and the rest of the world outside of your family.

As discussed in Chapter 2, identity is a lifelong process. Adolescence is one particular stage in life in which identity formation is heightened. Teenagers are particularly sensitive to how they are projecting their image and how others perceive them.

The Task of Individuation (Separation)

Individuation, or separation from the parent, is the second major psychological task to be resolved before adolescence can truly end. The way teens execute separation from parents is to transfer their emotional needs to their peer group. That's why their friends become so much more important to them than their family. Instead of seeking nurturance, self-worth, validation, and love exclusively from you, they now look toward their peer group and may even discount these needs when they come from you.

Trial and Error

Crystallizing identity and individuation involves almost constant experimentation for teenagers. That is why a teenager's ability to judge appropriate ways to assert his identity and transfer social-emotional needs from his parents to his peer group is often inconsistent and can even appear bizarre. In fact, it is an ongoing trial-and-error experiment. You'll notice that your child's behavior is all over the map. He'll act mature and responsible one minute, and then act like he is seven years old the next. In asserting their uniqueness and separateness from their parents, teenagers sometimes believe they must adopt morals and values that are the opposite of their parents—a clear refutation of parental and familial values. This is often manifest as a battle between teens and parents, causing much anger, frustration, and confusion on both their parts.

The inner tension teenagers feel is also due to the fact that they are at an age when they can simultaneously be a child and reap the benefits of dependence and nurturing, while also exploring the freedom and privileges offered by the adult world. This conflict causes them tremendous angst—and it drives parents crazy. Teens are not children, but neither are they adults. They are quasi-adults. Establishing appropriate parameters and expectations for those quasi-adults who are your teenage children is difficult—especially when they are fighting you much of the way.

WHAT'S REALLY GOING ON WITH GENERATION TEXT TEENS?

Generation Text teenagers must address the same psychological tasks as previous generations. But the process is more intense and difficult for several reasons. Today, the normal adolescent process of crystallizing identity and separating from parents is complicated by constant access to friends and exposure to cultural variables, including role models on TV and the Internet. Think of the tasks of identity and separation as a journey for teenagers. As they embark on this journey, they latch onto any behavior, physical appearance, persona, and whatever they see that looks even mildly attractive. Of course, they reject some of these things, but for the most part, teenagers are vulnerable and susceptible to social influence in their quest for identity and independence. Generation Text kids have a bird's-eye view of the world at their fingertips. It is a world that offers exponentially more exposure to a diverse array of behavior, values, and attitudes that have an impact on their identity. As we discussed in Chapter 1, more choices make the process of choosing more difficult.

The ability for the Generation Text teenager to separate has also become tainted by access and excess issues. Remember, separation involves an inner struggle between the desire to remain a coddled, nurtured child and the healthy desire to grow up and become more independent and responsible. The teen's ability to be with friends, either face-to-face or virtually, has accelerated the process of separating. At first thought, you might see this as a good thing to hasten the process of individuating from the parents. After all, that's what teens have to do when they enter adulthood. The problem is that they are able to be with their friends too much, too soon. Parents provide teenagers with faster and more powerful conduits of social access—computers and cell phones. The access they have to friends is excessive, and they are not ready for it because their judgment is not sound and their self-discipline is underdeveloped. In other words, they are prematurely separating, causing social acceleration. That is one of the reasons we are seeing fifteen-year-olds having coed sleepovers. It is why kids are drinking younger, getting expensive Japanese hair straightening done, and asking for spa treatments with their friends—a luxury even few adults can afford.

Effortless access through technology and an abundance of material possessions have become primary influences. Returning to Marcy, a typical teen, we can see how her parents must compete with an entire culture that is wreaking havoc with her identity and separation issues.

The good news is that Marcy was not depressed, as her parents feared. Beneath the layers of inappropriate behavior and emotional confusion, the caring, motivated child was still present. A normal, healthy need to have more freedom and control over her life was being expressed inappropriately. The unrealistic "real" lives of teen idols seen on Internet sites, in teen magazines, and on TV provided Marcy with a distorted ideal. At one point, Marcy said, "I want to bleach my hair like Jessica Simpson, but my parents won't let me." She not only wanted to look the part—she wanted to act the part as well. In our discussions, she often referenced MTV videos and specific personality and physical characteristics of entertainers. Her desire to emulate them was obvious. The sophisticated, sexualized messages in song lyrics, TV shows, and movies fueled Marcy's rebellion. She and her parents were engaged in a tug-of-war: Her parents, with the values they were trying to teach her, held one end of the rope, while Marcy, inundated with exciting, novel messages by friends, media personalities, and the Internet, held the other.

Marcy's parents needed to accept and understand that her need to separate from them and create a sense of self was a healthy, necessary process. The role of parents is not to insulate their teens from the overwhelming amounts of information, peer influence, and options available to them, but to help guide them through it. All of these things can be helpful to teens, provided they have the proper parental guidance and controls.

Before I counseled Marcy and her parents about how to move forward, I wanted all three to understand what was happening. Marcy needed to know that her goals of becoming her own person and having more freedom were age-appropriate—she was just going about obtaining them in inappropriate ways that included deception, defying rules, and lying. Her methods were backfiring because her parents ended up trusting her less and pulling in the reins on her privileges. Every time Marcy was caught breaking a rule, they grounded her, did not let her attend a party, and took away her cell phone for a day. Marcy's parents needed to understand that all of her behaviors were an expression of either procurement of identity or separation. They also needed to see that, like many parents of teenagers, they were having difficulty with the fact that their little girl was growing up. The combination of all of these factors had led to anger, hostility, and conflict.

We had to find a way for Marcy to pursue her social life and express her identity within her parents' comfort level. In session, that discussion between Marcy and her parents was conducted by me, but it is wise to have the same dialogue with your teenager if you are having similar battles.

In some ways, Marcy and her parents wanted the same thing. Her parents wanted their daughter to become a happy, secure, independently functioning adult. Marcy had the same goal. As she separated psychologically from her parents, it was natural for her to look toward other sources for a new set of values and attitudes. Marcy was receiving messages from the outside world in a quantity and intensity that her parents had to understand and acknowledge. They needed to educate themselves about what Marcy was going through.

WHO'S CLUELESS?

Parents believe that their teens have no idea about the real world. Teens believe their parents are the clueless ones. Both are partially correct. Parents certainly need to give their kids the tools to function successfully in "real" life. But to understand their kids, parents also need to learn as much as they can about their kids' world. Keeping up with fads, decoding teen jargon, and understanding the use of technology at their kids' disposal will help parents construct a bridge between them and their teenage kids.

Staying Current

Do you know who the latest celebrity idols are? Who are the rock stars, rappers, professional athletes, and movie and TV personalities that your teenager is emulating? Which professional athletes are making fashion and behavioral statements? What interests, activities, and behaviors have become cultural norms for your kids?

If you do not know the answers to the following questions, it behooves you to find out as soon as possible:

- ► What does "friends with privileges" mean? (Answer: Having casual sex with a friend without any romantic involvement.)
- ► What are the latest drugs popular with teens, and their slang names?
- ► What are the trendy alcoholic drinks or drinking games?
- ► What happens in the back of the bus on field trips?
- ► What is a "plate party"? (Answer: A random array of prescription drugs placed in a plate or bowl, so everyone can take a handful.)
- ► Which video games are currently popular?
- ► What is "grinding"? (Answer: A style of dancing characterized by the dancers rubbing their bodies against one another in a sexual manner closely resembling intercourse.)

Though they may not interest you, you should watch music videos, listen to song lyrics, read teen magazines, watch teen-oriented TV shows, and visit entertainment-oriented websites. I believe there are two reasons for you to make an earnest attempt at really trying to understand your teenager and the teenage subculture. First, if your teen feels that you "get" him, he will not feel that you are so far outside of his world that he cannot come to you with questions and problems. The second important reason to understand your teenager is to improve your relationship by expressing a sincere interest in his world—a world that has an intimate connection to his changing identity. Your teenager's music is *him*, his clothing is *him*, his interests and even the way he talks are *him*. Talk to your teen to understand the significance and uniqueness of all of the symbols that assert his new identity.

As a parent, you need to be aware of the pressures your teenager faces. Teenagers tend to classify one another using superficial criteria. They judge one another on the quality and quantity of their possessions. They define each other by the labels on their clothes, the designer of their handbag, their hair color and style, the music they listen to, the TV shows they watch, and the model of cell phone they own. If you observe groups of high school students before school or between classes, you'll see striking similarities in the way kids dress in each specific group. Members of each group tend to wear the same style of sneakers and jeans, listen to the same music, and affect the same dialect.

Keeping abreast with what is "in" helps you understand the social pressures your child faces. But understanding the situation is a lot different from giving in to these pressures.

Talking the Talk

Teenagers desperately want their parents to understand them. Their motivation for wanting to be understood is so that their parents will see the wisdom of their need for more freedom, and so they can validate their newfound identities as separate from their parents. To understand them, you should familiarize yourself with the typical lingo your kids use. Since teenage vernacular is such an important part of their identity, start by understanding their jargon. That is one of the first things I had Marcy's parents do.

I encouraged Marcy's parents to ask her the meaning of any terminology that appeared to be "teen talk." Teen talk might occur during carpooling conversations, telephone conversations, electronic communications, or while watching TV, listening to music lyrics, or looking at various forms of advertising media with your teenager. By doing this, Marcy's parents sent a clear message that they wanted to understand more about her.

Speaking the language—or, at the very least, understanding the language—of teen subculture is important. The easiest way for parents to keep up with what's current is to listen to their kids. They can also pay close attention to advertising, which quickly figures out and mimics the latest trends and fads for teenagers. I don't recommend that parents use teen phraseology; it will seem contrived. What I do suggest is that parents understand teen vernacular so that when kids use phrases like "my bad," "knocking boots," "mad good," "that's whack," and "baggin," they can follow the conversation. When Marcy's parents started asking her the meaning of specific teen slang phrases as she used them in conversation, it communicated a sincere attempt to understand her. They avoided using the slang, but it facilitated communication when she would say, "Mom, we were just kickin at Josie's house," and her mom could reply, "Who was hanging out at Josie's with you?"

Teenagers of every decade since the 1950s have used socially oriented slang. The major difference with Generation Text teens is that the jargon is not restricted to verbal conversation. There is a whole new addition to the spoken and written English language associated with the technology they use.

Learning IM, e-mail, video game ("gamer"), and text-message talk is important—and all of them are different. Marcy's parents printed out the following IM conversation accidentally left on Marcy's computer:

BOONSTER [BOY FROM SCHOOL]: TLYK I was leveling up with Jon MMORPG
LAGUNAGRL [MARCY]: lol. Sorry. Ilu. Kol
BOONSTER: Fomcl and ur crbt
LAGUNAGRL: ipn . . . jk
BOONSTER: gtg paw
LAGUNAGRL: musm
BOONSTER: luwamh

LAGUNAGRL: lmirl 2morrow
BOONSTER: ilu
LAGUNAGRL: ilu2

In plain English, this is what the conversation meant:

BOONSTER: Just to let you know, I went up a level with Jason on a massively multiplayer online role-playing game.
LAGUNAGRL: I'm laughing out loud. I'm sorry. Kiss on the lips.
BOONSTER: I fell off my chair laughing and you are crying real big tears.
LAGUNAGRL: I'm posting naked . . . just kidding.
BOONSTER: I've got to go. My parents are watching.
LAGUNAGRL: I miss you so much.
BOONSTER: I love you with all my heart.
LAGUNAGRL: Let's meet in real life tomorrow.
BOONSTER: I love you.
LAGUNAGRL: I love you, too.

It may be shocking as to how foreign to parents the written IM language can be. It may also be surprising to see the intensity of the words written by these young teenagers, but it is important to realize that instant messaging tends to remove inhibitions and promote the use of extreme emotions in a casual manner.

The National Center for Missing and Exploited Children publishes a pamphlet that tests parents' knowledge of IM abbreviations. There are also websites such as IMHut.com and NetLingo.com that provide dictionary-style interpretation. Periodically, parents of teens should update their knowledge of their kids' spoken and written vernacular.

The right to privacy is a delicate issue with teens. I am particularly sensitive to it with the patients with whom I work. But to keep teens safe—and I don't just mean emotionally safe—monitoring Internet activity is extremely important. Initially, Marcy felt that her parents were being invasive. We had many discussions about how the Internet, mass media, and her friends were influencing her. As they came up in our discussions I was able to educate her about the cultural barrage of messages that she had to sift through. Once I empathized with how difficult and overwhelming it was for her and other teenagers, Marcy become more receptive to working on changes with her parents. We began to distinguish the cultural messages that were positive and negative influences on her. After a while she told me that she realized her parents' involvement in general, and even their monitoring of her Internet use, made her feel that they cared enough to try to understand her.

Staying in the Loop

Staying in the loop works both ways. Your teenager's need to break away from you can pull her further away from family life. Although you need to allow this to occur to some degree, you must keep your son or daughter in the family loop and the values associated with it. To do so, you must require their involvement in certain family activities such as special outings, family birthday dinners, extended family member visits, and sibling sporting events or music and drama performances. You must be reasonable in your expectations for their involvement so that you balance their separation from the family with their connection to it. Not only do you need to keep your teenager connected to the family, but for you to stay in their loop you need to keep up with what is going on in their lives.

Generation Text has its own subculture that is significantly different from the teen subculture you probably remember. Adolescents by nature believe that their parents don't know anything about what it is like to grow up *now*. And to a great extent it is true. One of the most important messages in this book is for you to realize that times have changed for your kids—and changed dramatically. They are growing up in a world where the standards for social behavior and influences outside of your purview are completely different from what you are accustomed to. Teens are interacting with a different social and moral code than you are used to, and many parents of teens endorse these changes. You should also be aware—whether you agree with this or not—that many parents allow boys and girls to sleep over in groups, and a surprising number of parents allow their teenager's boyfriend or girlfriend to sleep over in the same room. Some parents even rationalize that since their teenagers are going to drink anyway, why not provide them with alcohol in their own home, take away the kids' car keys, and keep them safe under their supervision.

It is for these reasons—their belief that you don't understand them, the markedly different world and all its influences, and what other parents are permitting—that you need to stay in the loop when it comes to your teenagers. Staying in the loop means asking a lot of questions. The problem is, teens despise questions. Remember, one of the teenager's missions in life is to separate from you. That means going to the extreme and keeping you as far out of their personal business as they can. So when they are in the mood to talk, use it as a window of opportunity to expand the conversation to other topics about their friends, what's happening in school, and what they are up to in their social life. You can also open up a conversation by starting with something innocuous, emotionally safe, and of interest to your teen. Here is an example of a conversation I had with a sixteen-year-old football player who was not very forthcoming about what was happening in his life.

Dr. Osit: How did the game against Lewisville go?
Dennis: We finally won our first game on Saturday.
Dr. Osit: Great. How did you play?
Dennis: Good.
Dr. Osit: Did you catch any passes?
Dennis: I had two balls thrown to me, but only one was catchable.
Dr. Osit: You told me your quarterback doesn't throw many passes. Was your girlfriend at the game?
Dennis: Yeah. She is finally off grounding.
Dr. Osit: What was she grounded for?
Dennis: She got two Ds on her report card.
Dr. Osit: How did you do on yours?

If I started the session by asking how he did on his report card, Dennis would have probably gone into his usual one-word answer mode. Even with open-ended questions, he is a master at using the least amount of words to respond. But instead, I began with his football game. The information about his girlfriend was an unexpected bonus for me. I learned that she is not applying herself academically, and that her parents value education and are involved enough to discipline her for doing poorly. That was an entrée for my asking about Dennis's academic performance, which we ended up discussing in depth.

Even when teenagers are not in the mood to talk, try to ask questions in a very conversational, matter-of-fact manner so that they don't feel you are being invasive. If you sense they are becoming agitated or annoyed, it is okay not to push the conversation any further.

Staying in the loop also means keeping your eyes and ears open. Listen when they are in your car talking to their friends. Teenagers are sometimes so self-involved that they forget you are in the car. I don't support eavesdropping, but if they are in your presence and talking on the cell phone, I suggest you listen in a discreet manner. Believe me, if they don't want you to know something, they have many avenues of privacy at their disposal. Sometimes, you can gain much information by talking with their friends. Many teenagers find their friends' parents to be very approachable because the emotional struggles of identity and individuation are absent. They even tell their friends, "Your mom is so cool," to which the reply is usually, "Yeah, because you don't live with her!"

Finally, staying in the loop means talking with other parents. This is also a sensitive area for teens because they don't want you calling their friends' parents. It makes them feel like you are treating them like a child. Just as I have recommended seizing the moment to talk to your kids, you can do the same when you run into the parents of their friends. Take the time to talk to them. Ask questions without appearing nosy. You may already be friends with the parents of your teenager's friends. Make sure you take the time to talk with them about your kids and what they have been doing. Listen for stories about other kids who may be friends with your youngster. Unfortunately, teenagers are so group oriented that they are often guilty by association. In other words, if you learn that your son's good friend is smoking marijuana almost every day, there is a chance that your son might also be smoking.

As you learn more about what is happening within your teenager's circle of friends, you need to start discussing it with your son or daughter. Staying in the loop decreases the chance that your youngster will slip through the cracks and become too deeply involved in unhealthy activities. Some of these activities are completely off-limits, and some need some discussion and negotiation.

The key is to find common ground between what you are comfortable with and what your teenager wants to do.

Standing Firm

It can be quite difficult for you, as a parent, to remain well grounded in your decision making. Many parents who come into my office, despite their personal values, capitulate to requests that may be inappropriate for their kids' age and emotional development. For example, I am amazed at the number of parents I have worked with who have let their sixteen-year-olds take a train into New York City and go to clubs with fake IDs. A surprising number of parents allow their high school juniors or seniors to have massive parties at their houses, going so far as providing them with liquor and then taking away their car keys to avoid drunk driving. These representations of social acceleration and inappropriate social activities are due to a combination of Generation Text kids pushing the envelope and their parents using poor judgment. It is a function of Generation Text teenagers wanting more and more freedom and having no qualms about asking for it. Why do parents endorse these inappropriate social activities so readily? In addition to the "yes parenting" issues of guilt and competitive-driven parenting, Generation Text parents have a need to ensure popularity in their kids. They have a fear that their teen will be excluded, so they agree to these outlandishly risky social activities. Their need for their teenager to keep pace socially supersedes their good judgment.

It is important for parents to maintain their morals and values and not get caught up in what has become normative teenage behavior. "All my friends are going" or "Everybody's doing it" is simply not good enough. If you acquiesce to this rationale, you are supporting the underlying message that anything is okay as long as your friends are doing it. These pleas also play to the guilt card: "Don't you want me to have friends and be popular?" By giving in, you may be negating all your efforts trying to instill the morals and values you believe will keep your kids safe and help them grow up well adjusted.

FINDING COMMON GROUND

Marcy needed to communicate without yelling, slamming doors, and acting defiantly. Her parents needed to communicate without being close-minded and with the intention of "winning." I coached both Marcy and her parents to approach each other in this manner.

After some coaching, we had a session in my office as a first attempt to find common ground. Marcy's parents told her, in a calm and respectful tone, that they understood her need for more freedom and control over her own life. Instead of her usual reactive anger, Marcy responded calmly, listening and contributing positively to the discussion. As surprised as her parents were, Marcy was equally surprised to hear them say that they agreed that she should be more independent, have more freedom and control over her life, and have more fun.

The issue of trust was critical in this discussion. Marcy had been breaking rules, neglecting her schoolwork, and defying her parents' authority. As I explain to kids in my practice, irresponsible behavior puts their parents in "No" mode—saying no to things they could easily say yes to, because of their lack of trust. To put parents in "Yes" mode, kids need to show that they are responsible and will follow the rules.

Marcy and her parents provide a perfect illustration of this. Marcy's curfew on nonschool nights was 11 P.M. She frequently broke curfew, often with creative excuses. Her parents responded by grounding her or cutting her curfew by as much time as she was late. Once in a while, she'd call them on her cell phone and ask to stay out later. They always said no.

I explained to Marcy that by complying with her curfew, she would gain more than she'd lose. Yes, when she defied the curfew she got to stay out longer. But she usually lost her chance to go out at all the following night. Her parents had consistent follow-through whenever she was noncompliant. I supported their consistency, as it is as important for teenagers as it is with younger children. I also used it to appeal to Marcy's ability to reason logically. We came up with a plan for her to adhere to her curfew for the next few nights. She did so, and her parents acknowledged the change in her behavior. A few weeks later, she called her parents at 10:30 and asked if they would extend the curfew to 11:30, so she could finish a movie at a friend's house. Remarkably (to Marcy), the parental response was "Sure."

Once kids understand that they can obtain freedom and control by being compliant and respectful, it is up to the parents to reward them. I warn teenagers that they probably won't get everything they ask for by becoming more compliant, but their parents will have more trust and confidence in them and will slowly allow them to do more. Interestingly, whenever I ask teenagers if they think they should be allowed to do whatever they want, they always say no. Their response to this question is a testament to what I believe is the reasonable and healthy side of teenagers. Deep down inside, they really want to have limits because the world is far too scary for them to have free rein. I don't think most of them would admit it, and it is probably difficult for a lot of parents to believe it. But look how out of control teenagers become when they have loose supervision and few boundaries. I often believe that their acting out with defiance, drugs, sex, and academic failure is a way to say to adults, "Please control me because I can't."

COMMUNICATION 101

David, a thirteen-year-old patient who had been with me for a year and a half, had developed enough trust in me to speak openly and candidly about what was going on in his life. He visited porn sites and viewed adult shows on the family's satellite TV stations, and when he wasn't watching them, he was thinking about these images. As David's newfound pastime replaced his homework time and distracted him in school, his grades floundered. Report cards were coming out soon, and David was getting nervous about his parents' reaction. Not only was he concerned about his grades, he was starting to worry about his obsession with sex.

I worked with David to muster the courage to discuss what was happening with his parents. He wouldn't do it on his own, so we agreed to discuss the problem in session with them.

When the time came for David to tell his parents, he nervously talked about his preoccupation with sex and his lackluster grades. His parents were not extremely shocked—they'd caught him on porn sites several times—but they became quite angry. They demanded my guidance in setting an appropriate punishment for defying their rules about porn sites and schoolwork.

Though I tried to help David's parents understand what their son was going through, they completely missed what was happening. They lectured him about the perils of pornography and breaking the rules, and the lecture was not restricted to my office; it continued in the car and throughout the week. In our next session, David announced that he would never confide in his parents again.

Parents plead with me to get their teenagers to communicate. They complain that their kids are always plugged into electronics, constantly on their cell phones, in their bedrooms with the doors closed, playing video games for hours instead of being with the family, and watching endless amounts of TV. One father told me that it seemed as if the video game controller was attached to his son's hand. When their teens do talk, parents say, they converse in one-word sentences. But here were David's parents, squelching any potential for future openness from him. And in my experience, these parents are typical. Perhaps you would have reacted the same way David's parents did. But if you want your teenager to be open with you, she has to feel that you are not going to "freak out" when she approaches you. You must remain calm and steady, always prepared for shocking information. Manage your own feelings, keeping them on an even keel. Ask questions if you need to bide time to remain calm. Avoid being critical and judgmental. If you cannot discuss it without reacting negatively or frantically, tell them you need to go to the bathroom and that you will be right back. Collect yourself enough to return as quickly as you can to discuss the subject rationally. This may be very hard to do, but if you work at it, you will be amazed how open your teenager can be with you. I experience this everyday in my office with the kids I work with.

There are some basic concepts that can help parents facilitate rather than inhibit communication.

Reflective Listening

The first basic skill in communicating with your teen is reflective listening. Reflective listening is keying into the feelings behind what your kid is saying. When people speak, they communicate both through content (what they say) and affect (the feeling behind their words). For example, a teenager says:

> "All of my friends are going to the movies tonight, and I have to go to my nerdy cousin's birthday party! This is the second week in a row that they're getting together and I can't go. *It's not fair!*"

A sympathetic—but ineffectual—parental response might be:

> "I'm sorry for the way it worked out. I'm sure you'll be able to do something with your friends next weekend."

This statement might evoke either a sarcastic response or another complaint from the child, which would prompt the parent to react defensively, escalating the conversation into an argument. In contrast, a parent using reflective listening would respond to the feelings behind the words, in addition to the content:

> "I understand how upset, even angry, you feel because you're unable to be with your friends. Are you afraid that since you couldn't go twice in a row, they won't include you anymore?"

This parental response, which highlights the teen's feelings of being *upset, angry, afraid,* and *excluded,* will likely defuse the negative feelings. The teenager might respond, for example, "That's what kids do. If you don't hang out with them, post on their wall, or go to their chat room, they stop being your friend." The parent can then problem-solve to alleviate the child's anxiety.

Incidentally, even if the feeling reflected by the parent is inaccurate, expressing it is helpful. The teenager will correct the parent and share what he is really feeling. Using the example above, the teenager might respond:

> "I'm not worried that they will stop being my friend. I was just looking forward to going because I haven't gone out with them for a long time."

To which the parent might reflect and say:

> "So you were really excited to see them and now you are disappointed."

By focusing on his emotions, the teenager gets in touch with his feelings—and feelings are the glue of healthy relationships.

Creating a Climate

The second basic way to get your teenager to communicate with you is to create what I call a "climate" in the relationship. A positive climate is created when the parent conveys love, respect, and honesty. Trust is a fragile issue between parents and teenagers. A trusting relationship ensues when all three of these factors are communicated through both words and actions. A crucial component of trust is maintaining a nonjudgmental and uncritical posture when your teenager discloses pieces of what is happening in his life.

Marcy's parents made judgments about her behavior. In addition, when Marcy told her parents about her friends' activities, they reacted with disapproval and criticism of the friends as well. To make matters worse, they gave her a hard time whenever she socialized with these friends. A more constructive way to address Marcy's behavior would have been to ask her to make her own judgments about her friends' use of alcohol and cigarettes. Instead of lecturing her about the dangers of drinking and smoking, they could have said, "Marcy, what do you think about how alcohol and cigarettes affect your friend's body?"

Teenagers often tell their parents about their friends as a backdoor way of sorting out what is right and wrong for them. When parents are quick to judge and criticize, kids tend to go on the defensive and adopt an opposite stance. Instead of automatically responding critically, ask your kids what they think. In this case, they are really in the process of working through whatever the issue is, and you just need to listen and ask questions to stimulate more thinking and an eventual conclusion. Kids, I've found, generally want to do the right thing. Let them know that you have confidence in them to do the right thing, without always reminding them what that is.

The mother of a fifteen-year-old boy, Seth, placed a stack of pictures he had downloaded from the Internet on the coffee table in my office. The pictures were of nude men in various positions of sexual bondage. Having found the pictures, the mother handled the situation beautifully with her son by opening up a calm and accepting discussion of homosexuality and Seth's feelings. She asked Seth what he thought about visiting the site, and he admitted that he knew it was probably wrong. His mother, careful not to judge Seth's sexual interest, expressed her belief that it was inappropriate for someone his age to view such material. Throughout the conversation, Seth's mother managed to be nonjudgmental and uncritical while maintaining her authority. At the same time, she maintained a level of honesty and respect for Seth's feelings. She was amazed that he had knowledge of this type of sexual activity. After her conversation with Seth, the mother and I discussed the use of software to restrict Internet access and monitor Seth's computer use. As a result of his mother's rather appropriate response to Seth's Internet encounter, Seth was able to relieve the burden of his secret regarding his sexual orientation. While his mother remained neutral about his sexual preference, her disapproval of visiting sexually oriented sites, regardless of the nature of their content, became quite clear to him.

Some parents are shocked at the knowledge their teenagers have. As stated earlier, it is often wise to hide your astonishment when your teenager presents information or asks questions that surprise you. It is often the case that they are telling you provocative information because it either makes them feel uncomfortable or they are indirectly asking you to put the limit on it. The truth is, teenagers need and respect limits. In your quest to create a climate that is conducive for communication, be sure to maintain the parent–child relationship. You can't be your teenager's friend. They don't want you to be their friend—they need you to be their parent.

When my daughter was sixteen, she came to me for permission to attend a party. I thought this request was odd because the party was at the home of a family we knew extremely well, and normally she would just let us know that she was going over there. She told me that lots of kids would be there, and that some would probably be drinking. She also told me that at one of Jeremy's parties, the police had been called. With all of this information, I told her she was not allowed to go. A few minutes later, I overheard my daughter on the phone, telling her friend how mad she was that her parents wouldn't let her go to the party. It was clear to me that she was feigning anger and was actually nervous about going to a party that might get out of control. She saw her parents' authority as a way to stay safe—she needed me to say no.

Seizing the Moment

The third way to get your teenager to communicate is to seize the moment. Whenever your kid is in the mood to talk about what's happening, stop what you're doing and give her your undivided attention. Kids will talk, but it's usually on their own terms, on their timetable. Parents often try to force their kids to communicate with them, which results in a battle and often yields little more than a few words—those words being "Leave me alone." When your kids approach you or open up a discussion, use reflective listening, don't judge, and ask questions to promote their own critique of the topic.

A good time to seize the moment is after you've watched a television show or movie together. Discussing the relationships and actions of the characters is a nonthreatening way to communicate morals and values about how to treat the opposite sex, authority figures, drug and alcohol use, criminal behavior, and countless life lessons. You can use TV shows, movies, and even advertisements to your advantage, instead of passively allowing them to influence your teen's behavior in a negative way. Don't be afraid to ask questions about sex, drugs, suicide, self-mutilation, and eating disorders. Parents are sometimes afraid that they'll plant an idea in their teen's head by asking questions. But your kids already know far more than you probably realize—maybe even more than you do. By asking questions, you give your teen permission to talk about subjects he might have considered off-limits.

FAMILY MEETINGS

One of my most important recommendations for Marcy and her parents was to conduct regular meetings that would be mandatory for all family members. Family meetings provide an opportunity for each person to maintain a sense of belonging and connectedness. They afford a designated time for sharing and problem solving amid everyone's busy and highly scheduled lives.

I have developed a specific format for family meetings to fit the changing needs of today's teenager. This model mirrors a therapy session format. Meetings should be conducted weekly, biweekly, or monthly, depending on the need and general level of conflict, and they should be limited to about thirty to forty-five minutes. Before the meeting, you should post a blank sheet of paper in a common area labeled "Family Meeting Agenda." Throughout the week, any family member can post an issue they want to discuss, typically a request or a complaint. Some common topics kids include are curfew, bedtime, disciplinary actions, and unfair treatment. Parents often post chores, reminders about respectful behavior and being considerate, and school-related topics. No topic is off-limits. Parents lead the meetings, but not in a controlling or autocratic way. They should keep order in the meeting while being receptive and nonjudgmental about their teenager's ideas and requests. The goal is to decrease the psychological space between them and their kids.

As issues are discussed, only one person speaks at a time. No interruptions are allowed. Parents are encouraged to use reflective listening, remain open and receptive to their kids' ideas, and brainstorm with them to find a reasonable solution. If an agenda item is a complaint about a parent, that parent needs to model receptivity, a lack of defensiveness, and possibly remorse, and suggest a plan for change.

In a successful family meeting, the message to the teen is clear. The teen has a sense of belonging to the family; he believes that what he says has credibility, his status in the family is elevated ("I'm not a child anymore"), and he is respected. Problem solving occurs by brainstorming with the teenager and other family members, not by the parents dictating or barking out denials. Once a decision is made, parents should be clear about how and why they came with their conclusion.

For the parents, family meetings:

- ► Let them know what their teen is involved in
- ► Allow them to gain an ongoing understanding of the progress of adolescent issues
- ► Give them a way to communicate effectively with their teenager
- ► Provide a civil atmosphere in which to solve problems

For teenagers, family meetings:

- ► Give them a means to assert their separation and identity in a respectful manner
- ► Provide an atmosphere in which their parents are receptive to their ideas
- ► Educate them about what their parents are worried about
- ► Help facilitate their parents' understanding of what they're asking for

For Marcy and her parents, the family meetings provided a forum in which to communicate with minimum conflict. For you, family meetings can serve as a force to combat the negative influ-ences of access and excess on your Generation Text teen.

SETTING LIMITS AND MONITORING

While it is important for parents to encourage open communication and hear what their kids are saying, it is also important that they establish limits and boundaries, as well as consequences when those boundaries are crossed. In today's world, this means actively moni-toring their teenager's access to technology.

Teenagers have more autonomy today than ever before. Their ability to maintain a private, even secret, life is easier than ever, as is their ability to get what they want. Parents, who are often busy with their own complex lives and ignorant of cutting-edge technology, tend to parent passively. Parents need a high degree of awareness, communication, limit setting, and monitoring so that they stay in-formed without being overly controlling or invasive.

Cell phones, the Internet, TV, and even video games have merit in contributing to your teen's cognitive and social development. But without proper limits, any and all of these resources can be detrimental. Parents need to be proactive, establishing clear param-eters for cell phone, TV, Internet/IM, and video/computer game use. If you establish limits of use when your kids initially receive these devices, it is more likely that they will follow the rules. Rules for the frequency and duration of use, as well as specific blackout times, should be established. Time limits for cell phones can be easily established using the monthly allotment based on the service contract.

Be sure to address talk time, text messages, and picture-sharing when discussing the monthly limits. Outline what you consider ap-propriate language and topics of cell phone, Internet, and text mes-sage conversations. Caution them against posting any pictures depicting inappropriate poses involving "partying" or sexual innu-endo. Time spent on other devices should be for a specific duration. A good guideline might be one hour a night upon completion of homework, and three hours a day on nonschool days. Blackout times refer to specific times kids are restricted from watching TV, talking on cell phones, going on the Internet, or playing video games. Generally, my guidelines include:

- ▶ A blackout time during the school day (for cell phones)
- ▶ A blackout time during established homework hours
- ▶ An evening curfew for turning off electronics that is appropriate for your teenager and family
- ▶ One screen-free day a week, except perhaps for family TV viewing

To Marcy's parents, I suggested that she be allowed to use the Internet for IM chats in the afternoon hours after school. Talk during these hours tends to be with school friends and is usually relatively harmless, whereas late hours tend to bring out the dangers of the Internet—not unlike going out in the afternoon, as opposed to the evening.

I don't believe in applying the same hard-and-fast rules to every teenager. How often and how long your teenager gets to use these devices depends on the needs of your teenager. The more responsible they are, the better self-discipline and self-judgment they use, the more liberal you can be. The limits can vary, based on your kid's specific academic needs, sleep needs, and family routines.

Once the rules are in place, close and aggressive parental monitoring is necessary. Cell phones are easiest to monitor; the monthly bill clearly indicates compliance. It is easy to view sent and received calls and text messages, which are stamped with the date and time. It's a good idea for parents to pay attention to any unusual calls, noting if and when their teen is talking to someone repeatedly and at length.

I recommend telling your teen that you may periodically check text messages and cell-phone pictures. Doing so will help you understand the interactions and activities in which your teen is engaging. Some kids may consider this an invasion of privacy. But considering the kinds of things kids get themselves into, and how vulnerable they are to the evils of the world, such monitoring is wise. As long as you inform them ahead of time, the assumption is that they are not doing anything inappropriate, so there should be nothing to hide. As suggested in the previous chapter, teenagers will more easily accept monitoring and limit-setting practices when they are established early on.

It's more difficult to monitor Internet use, because the Internet and computer are often used for homework assignments. How do parents know if their teen is using the computer for homework rather than surfing the Web or instant-messaging friends? There are two ways to monitor surfing. First, parents should check up on their kids while they're doing homework. Second, they need to learn to check the history on the Internet browser, which will provide web addresses, dates, and even the times that sites are visited. Sites such as WiredSafety.org provide easily understood information about the Internet. Commercial software like Net Nanny restricts and records activity on the computer.

It is particularly difficult to monitor IM conversations. Recent software releases such as SpectorSoft IM Monitoring Software and Chat Watch 5.0 can record all instant-message conversations from both ends. Monitoring IM conversations has become easier, but these programs do not decipher your teenager's special code. Again, it is wise to inform your children that you have installed the program.

The "community of Internet friends" phenomenon taking place on MySpace.com and Facebook.com reveals a lot about your teenager. Kids naively post personal information about themselves including:

▶ Home and e-mail addresses
▶ Age
▶ Sexual orientation
▶ Favorite movies and songs
▶ Religious and political views
▶ Name of their high school
▶ Relationship status regarding a boyfriend or girlfriend
▶ Recent activities—often inappropriate or even illegal activities

Someone could easily use this information to prey on your youngster either online or in person. Not only that, but most kids don't realize that when someone types messages to you, it can appear on a news feed for all to see. These sites also serve as an important socialization vehicle, facilitating an active, healthy social connection with peers. They have become a primary way for kids to stay connected. Forbidding your child from using social networking sites is not realistic. It will probably socially handicap your child. Being involved and knowledgeable is really the answer.

I recommend that parents, with advance notice, inform their

kids that they'll periodically visit their blogs and MySpace page. A sixteen-year-old patient, Ally, informed me that her mother visited the MySpace entry of one of Ally's best friends, and discovered that he had used LSD on several occasions. Ally's mother told this friend that he had three days to tell his parents, or she would. As difficult as this was for Ally, her friend ended up feeling glad to have gotten help for his drug problem.

I suggest that parents learn as much as they can about the electronic games that their kids have access to, both those played with a console and those played on the computer. Learn the rating system; spend time playing the games with your teenager. This effort will not only help you monitor what they're exposed to, but also determine the appropriateness of the game. If you decide that the game is appropriate, only time limits need to be established. But if you deem certain games to be inappropriate for your child, you will have to remove them. Many games include scantily clad women and violence, promoting illegal acts and antipolice attitudes, dismemberment of characters, blood splatter, and inappropriate language. Repeated exposure to these types of video games can normalize rebellious and aggressive behavior or antiauthority attitudes.

TV shows should also be monitored this way. You need to periodically watch some of your teenager's favorite shows to evaluate the appropriateness.

Parents and kids can hash out together what is reasonable for them to be permitted to do. The most important thing is that when parents educate their kids in a way that communicates an understanding of the teen world, kids will discover how to get more of what they want using appropriate means. They will also be better able to reap the infinite benefits electronics have to offer because they will be used safely and appropriately. The most important thing is to help your teenager negotiate adolescence so that he can transition to adulthood with less emotional scarring.

WHAT HAPPENS WHEN THEY BREAK THE RULES?

A final note: If parents ignore their teenager's breaking of the rules, the teen receives tacit approval to keep crossing the line. The consequences should be related to the infraction. As a general guideline, breaking preestablished rules should result in the loss of any electronic privileges for one to three days. I don't recommend increasing the amount of punishment if the same rule is repeatedly broken; I find that punishments work best when they are frequent and short, not infrequent and severe.

If persistent infractions occur with a specific device, a modification is probably needed until the teenager demonstrates more integrity. For example, I recommend keeping the computer in a public area of the home until your teenager demonstrates responsible use. After you have regained trust you can return it to his room, but continue monitoring how he uses the computer. Most kids are now getting laptops, which makes them mobile and more difficult to monitor. If your teenager owns a laptop, you need to implement the monitoring suggestions posed earlier in the chapter, such as periodically checking the computer history and installing filtering and monitoring software for instant messaging, chat, Web surfing, and e-mail. Also, once in a while, take a peek when they are on the laptop.

Stay Positive

A parent in my practice once told me, "I love my daughter, but I'd like to give her away until she's done with adolescence." As turbulent as life with teenagers can be, this is the time when they need their parents most. The stakes are high—teenagers can make mistakes that have implications for the rest of their lives. Maintaining perspective is crucial. Try not to get caught up in daily (or hourly!) arguments. Step back and try to recall your teenager's positive attributes, even if they are overshadowed in the moment by self-centered moodiness. Try to find humor in your teen and in the situation—it's probably there, if you look hard enough. Keep in mind that eventually they will not be a teenager any longer. Staying positive, keeping your eye on your core values, and maintaining perspective will help both of you get through what can be a rather tumultuous stage.

Don't Regress

I often find the parents of difficult teens acting like their teens. They start overreacting to minor infractions, use inappropriate language, use passive-aggressive behaviors as an expression of control or resentment, and become self-centered, losing sight of their teenager's quest for identity and independence. Modeling mature and appropriate behavior is essential for maintaining your teen's respect. Even though it is a different world, try to remember what it was like when you were a teenager. The better you understand the way your kids feel and think, the more effective you will be in dismantling their irrational notion that you are the oblivious enemy.

Because of his exposure to mature social material, today's teenager is an expert in analyzing parent–child dynamics. He will use this knowledge to shift the focus to his parents' behavior from his own. It's important for parents to maintain focus and avoid getting caught up in these kinds of conflicts where your behavior becomes the focus of the discussion. Be careful not to fall into the trap of defending *your* behavior. Immediately return the focus on your teenager's actions. Consider the following dialogue between a mother and her son:

> MOTHER: You should not be IMing while you are working on that English essay.
> SON: Mom, you can't just walk into my room and spy on me.
> MOTHER: I wasn't spying on you, I was checking on you . . . and your door was open.
> SON: Well, don't. I don't need checking.
> MOTHER: Just get back to work and finish the essay.

This youngster very cleverly put his mother on the defensive by focusing on her behavior. Although she was able to get him back to work, she never really addressed the issue that the instant messaging was distracting him. She should have either ignored her son's accusations or stated, "We're not talking about my behavior, we're talking about having instant messaging open as a distraction from your English essay."

BASIC TIPS—A REVIEW

Some basic tips for parents of Generation Text teens are:

- ▶ Give your teens respect and credibility, even if they might not deserve it at the moment.

▶ Explain how and why you came to your decisions.

▶ Try to recall your own feelings as an adolescent as you work to understand your teen's identity and individuation issues.

▶ Be aware of your own authority and control issues. Avoid power plays. Instead of saying, "I won't let you do it because I said so," say, "This is because I love you and care about what happens to you."

▶ Remember that you are the gatekeeper of privileges, so you don't need to have the last word. You have the *lasting* word.

▶ Do reality checks with your spouse or extended family and friends who have teenagers, to see if your response to and interpretation of your teen's behavior seems accurate.

▶ Keep your kids involved in family life, and stay in the loop of teenage life.

EPILOGUE: MARCY AND HER PARENTS

Marcy's parents used all of the basic tips mentioned above. It took some time to turn things around, but the healthy part of Marcy eventually flourished. Open communication was a key factor in moving parents and daughter toward common ground. Marcy became newly aware of the bombardment of messages telling her what was "in" and "cool." She began to appreciate how desensitized, even brainwashed, she was becoming by this overabundance of information. She began to scrutinize and challenge what message was appropriate for her and what was not, instead of simply adopting it without question. Marcy's parents learned more about teen subcultures, the need to keep up socially, and the sources of influence on their daughter.

Marcy's parents increased their time with her and mitigated the influence of access and excess in her life by establishing:

▶ Family meetings

▶ A relationship climate conducive for communication

▶ Mandatory family involvement, including a minimum number of dinners per week and family days twice a month

▶ Healthy and reasonable limits and boundaries regarding technological access, privileges, and material excess

▶ Consistent follow-through, with consequences for noncompliance with established rules

▶ A high degree of parental awareness, communication, limit setting, and monitoring—executed in a way that is not too invasive and does not impair the teen's individuation process

Eventually, Marcy became less hostile, more reasonable, and more communicative. She still maintained an active social life, but with more balance and proper limits. She started coming to her parents with social dilemmas, instead of seeking answers solely from her school and Internet friends. Her schoolwork improved and her peer group gradually changed again. She did not return to her old friends, but became involved with a healthier group of kids than Alyssa and her friends.

Even if your teenager doesn't appear to have overt problems or symptoms of turmoil, the influence of access to the larger world may be quietly wreaking havoc with his psychological development. Stepping up your involvement in your teenager's life, as Marcy's parents did, without being controlling or invasive, can help you establish limits and reduce the risk of missing something that could get worse.

CHAPTER 8

Walking the Tightrope

....

Balancing Wants and Needs

"Sometimes I feel like my family is a three-ring circus and I am the tightrope walker."—Father of three boys, ages 8, 11, and 14

"I constantly struggle with helping my kids fit in while keeping them grounded."—Mother of a ten-year-old girl and twelve-year-old boy

"My mind hurts from going back and forth trying to decide if I should allow my kids to do the things their friends are allowed to do. I don't want to risk hurting their social life."—Mother of two girls, 14 and 16

"I can't believe I endorse—and even play with—the morally repugnant video games my son asks for."—Father of an 8-year-old boy

THERE IS A TENUOUS FEELING UNDERLYING ALL OF THESE STATE-ments. Parents often describe the delicate dilemma of determining what is healthy or appropriate for their kids while also considering the social norms those same kids experience every day. Generation Text children don't make walking this tightrope any easier. Unlike any previous generation, kids present their parents with countless requests and appeals, many of which seem both outlandish and alien to parents. Many of these requests come from a place of naiveté and innocence. After all, if their friends are showered with everything they want, children naturally assume they too are entitled to those same objects and privileges. In a sense, Generation Text kids have no idea how much they are "pushing the envelope," because they are constantly inundated with options and opportunities. Asking for things is second nature to them. They persistently ask for outlandish things, and as a result, it has become second nature for parents to give them these things just to keep them in the social mainstream. Thirteen-year-old Jodi has a belly button ring, seven-year-old Ella has a television and PC in her bedroom, and sixteen-year-old Bart has his own credit card. Chad, fifteen, has a 1:00 A.M. curfew, Ariel and her friends rented a limo for their eighth-grade dance, and Bob, seventeen, has a fake ID paid for by his parents. What has become the norm for Generation Text kids is disconcerting in terms of developing a healthy self-image, moral character, social skills, and work ethic.

It's time to take a step back and evaluate how much and what you are providing your kids. The trick is, how do you balance the demands of a distorted social norm your kids face every day with what you really believe is good for them without compromising them socially? This is the tightrope today's parents experience, and you need help learning how to walk it.

TUG-OF-WAR

There is a constant struggle between what your kids ask for and what you feel comfortable giving them. Consequently, you are in the position of having to negotiate the conflict between your own parenting preferences and your kids' requests based on the new social norms. The problem is that you must also consider the social ramifications of granting or denying your child's various requests. Parents are naturally concerned about their children's friendships and their ability to fit in socially. Some of the questions posed to me by the parents of my patients are:

> *"A bunch of her closest friends are going to Disney when school lets out. Should I let her go?"*
>
> *"My daughter asked me for the pill. Should I give it to her?"*
>
> *"He keeps asking for the Xbox 360 game called The Club. It's rated M, but he says he has played it at his friend's house. Is it okay for him to have it?"*
>
> *"Is it okay to take my six-year-old to a Hannah Montana concert?"*

The tug-of-war between what kids believe is normal because all their friends are doing it and what you believe is appropriate for

their age and maturity makes walking the tightrope of parental decision making even more precarious.

In this chapter, you will learn when to say yes and when to say
no. The first step in learning how to make these distinctions is to
recognize what is considered "normal" according to contemporary
culture. For example, you may think giving your child his own cell
phone when he is still in elementary school is not age-appropriate.
However, in today's world, it is considered normal and acceptable,
making the decision to provide your child with a phone that much
more difficult. As you have no doubt told your children time and
time again, just because most people are doing something doesn't
necessarily mean it is good for them. So how should you decide
which things to allow and which to deny your children? Not all
parents believe that children should be given everything they want
when they want it. Some requests are so off the chart that it is easy
to deny them, even if the decision excludes them from their group
of friends. Others fall into the gray area created by the drastic
change in social and moral codes that has taken place in the last few
decades.

THE NEW SOCIAL NORM

Let's go retro for a moment and think back to our own childhoods.
Chances are, when you recall your various struggles as a child and a
teenager and your relationship with your parents, you conjure an
image completely different from your own child's reality. Of course,
your generation was fraught with its own problems, but the realm
of influence was considerably smaller. Cell phones, Internet, and
laptop computers were yet to be invented. In some ways, you had
fewer restrictions in terms of roaming the neighborhood unsupervised. However, Generation Text kids can roam the world unsupervised. The other major difference is that you likely never felt entitled
to go wherever you wanted without parental permission. Perhaps
you went places and to parties that your parents did not know
about, but you wouldn't dare ask your parents' permission to do so
because you know they would say no. Your kids, on the other hand,
might regularly seek permission from you to attend a coed sleepover, or to go to parties where alcohol will be served, or ask you to
provide beer for a party at your home. In a way, it is good that they

ask because it keeps us informed about their social activities. They are still hiding plenty, though, and are able to do so thanks to their technology-enabled privacy. But because they live in a new social norm, they simply expect to be able to do these things, as well as receive the latest electronic gadgets and games, and they desperately "need" the latest in designer fashion. The new social norm has magnified and intensified their desire for everything they want, and they expect to get it. So, they let you know what they want, placing you in the position to either perpetuate or challenge the new social norms.

One of your first challenges as a parent is to accept these realities as the new norm and learn a new skill set with which to deal with that norm. Parents of Generation Text kids face the following types of dilemmas every day: A ten-year-old asks permission to go to a PG-13 movie with his four closest friends; a thirteen-year-old girl wants to go to a local salon for a manicure and pedicure; a nine-year-old asks for a Kate Spade handbag; a fourteen-year-old wants permission to attend a rock concert in a stadium; an eleven-year-old and her friends want to go to the mall without parental supervision on a Saturday afternoon; as a post-prom event, a high school junior wants to rent a house at the shore with her friends for the weekend.

When your child comes to you with these requests and others, you have to figure out how to determine what is appropriate for your child, and what is not. How do you put the brakes on without socially alienating your child? What privileges and possessions can kids at various ages handle so that they can be socially accepted and grow up well adjusted? The following case study answers all of these questions.

CASE STUDY: THE DAYTON FAMILY

Leigh and Hy Dayton have been married for sixteen years and have three children—Lance, fifteen, Nina, thirteen, and Janet, nine—and Hy has a twenty-one-year-old son named Douglas from a previous marriage who visits regularly and has good relationships with his stepmother and half siblings. Leigh grew up in a middle-class suburban town in the Midwest and comes from a secular Presbyterian family. Hy was raised in a culturally Jewish family, and when he and

Leigh became engaged his parents disapproved of their religious differences. Eventually, Hy's parents grew to accept and even like Leigh because of her pleasant, easygoing personality, and because of how happy she makes Hy and their grandchildren.

The Daytons describe their marital relationship as "better than most of our friends," but they struggle with one specific aspect of parenting their three children: determining what is appropriate for each of their children to own and to be allowed to do. Although Hy and Leigh agreed on the basic values and morals they wanted to instill in their kids, they argued with each other and with the kids as they confronted each new situation, unsure of how liberal they should be. Many of their friends tended to be more lenient than the Daytons wanted to be, and they felt that they were in a parenting minority. This caused them to give in to their kids more often than they wanted. The Daytons decided to seek my help because of their disagreements and increased second-guessing over parenting decisions. By the time they arrived at my office, the Daytons had articulated the questions they needed to answer:

▶ How do we know what is normal for kids today?
▶ How do we deny our kids things that their friends have without making them social outcasts?
▶ How can we decide what is appropriate for each of our kids without compromising safety issues and the morals and values we want them to have?

To help them answer these crucial questions, I asked each of the Daytons, the parents and the kids, to compile a list of as many specific situations (past and present) as possible that had led to a conflict.

Lance, the fifteen-year-old, came to the next session with an extensive list of conflicts he has had with his parents, including the following:

▶ He wanted to go to New York City (about thirty miles from his home) with two of his friends and walk around Greenwich Village on a Saturday afternoon. One of his friends was seventeen and had a driver's license, so he would drive them in.
▶ Another time, he asked for his parents' credit card so that

he could go shopping for clothes at the local mall with his friends.

▶ An avid music fan, Lance wanted to see one of his favorite bands perform live at a local stadium—on a school night.

▶ He often asked for permission to sleep over at friends' houses two nights in a row.

▶ Finally, because he was once allowed to go with his girl-friend's family to their lake house for the weekend, he wanted permission to sleep over at her usual house as well.

Nina, the Daytons' thirteen-year-old daughter, presented the following conflicts:

▶ She wanted Japanese hair straightening, which costs $600 and lasts for six months.

▶ She wanted to see an R-rated movie with her friends, and their plan was that one of her friends' dads would buy the tickets (including one for himself), take them into the theater, and then leave, solving the issue of no one under the age of seventeen being allowed in the theater alone.

▶ Like most Generation Text kids, Nina is very fashion-conscious, but she finds herself fighting with her parents over her clothing choices, particularly with clothes that fit tightly, reveal part of her body, and cost much more than the average garment.

▶ Nina, like Lance, enjoys an active social life and asks for sleepovers almost every weekend. She sometimes asks to have two overnights in a row on weekends and school vacation weeks.

▶ Finally, she has recently requested permission to go to an Avril Lavigne concert with two friends and one of their mothers.

Janet, the nine-year-old and youngest, wants the following:

▶ To attend a friend's birthday party at a spa catering to young children, where they will experience stress-releasing massages, facials, and other treatments

▶ To wear eye makeup

▶ To watch television shows that are questionable for her age,

but which most of her friends watch and talk about frequently
- ▶ To have her own cell phone
- ▶ To wear clothing like Nina's
- ▶ To have a TV set in her room (because Lance got one when he was twelve and Nina when she was eleven)

Like most kids, Lance, Nina, and Janet certainly do not *need* any of the things they are asking for. Their requests fall into three categories, all related to social life: material possessions, freedoms and privileges, and social activities. The major conflict arises when parents try to reconcile the culture their kids live in with what they believe is appropriate, leading to parental uncertainty and second-guessing. The self-doubt also stems from parents' own insecurities, perhaps related to their experiences growing up unpopular or having less than their peers. Perhaps some parents are even living vicariously through their own kids, missing being a kid themselves or feeling as if they have a second chance, through their child, to accomplish something that they were unable to attain in their own childhood.

Understanding how cultural influences affect child development is the first step in tackling the problems facing families like the Daytons. Gaining insight into how parents are contributing to social acceleration is another step, as is learning about what motivates your child to ask for questionable objects and privileges. Finally, parents need to establish applicable criteria that will help them maintain their integrity while keeping their children safe and engaged in age-appropriate activities. In the following sections, we will follow Hy and Leigh as they tackle their family's issues.

CULTURAL INFLUENCE

The norms and values of the culture dictate how children behave and what parents reinforce in order to produce well-adjusted adults who function independently. To some degree, culture affects entire stages of development. For example, adolescence as we know it is characterized by rebelliousness and turmoil, whereas it is a stage of development in other cultures that is characterized by the ability to develop hunting and survival skills. To understand what has happened in our society, you need to examine the global picture as well as the specific issues.

Two Types of Cultures

There are two basic types of societies, each with its own set of merits and downfalls. The first is a society that emphasizes the individual—a society like ours in America. Because our fundamental belief is freedom for all, it makes perfect sense that we give priority to the uniqueness of each person. In an individualistic society, the priority is personal attainment rather than any particular goal of the group. Individual achievement, personal distinction, the sense of unique identity, personal satisfaction, and independence are heavily valued. Our kids receive positive reinforcement emphasizing these attributes from both their social world and their parents. From what we learned about social learning theory in Chapter 6, our kids are encouraged and reinforced to think of themselves and their needs. Generation Text kids take the "me" part of their development too far because of the power and frequency of cultural messages that emphasize narcissism and self-worth that's closely connected to what they have and what they do.

The second type of society is the group-oriented, collective society that places value on the group's mission, which is common in Asian countries. In a collective society, the individual's needs are often sacrificed for the good of the group. Individuals actually submit to the group's needs, giving up personal goals, values, and needs. Of course, there are many people in our society who do sacrifice their needs for the good of the group, but the overriding climate in American culture is not group oriented.

With these prototypes in mind, we can see that today's youth is on the receiving end of mixed messages. The mixed messages come from both parents and peers. Parents want their kids to be altruistic, generous, and considerate of others, yet they encourage winning, being the best, and getting high grades, and then they provide their kids with an excess of things—cars, state-of-the-art technology, vacations, clothing, etc. In other words, the juxtaposed messages are "think of others" and "get what you can, even if it is at the expense of others." This is confusing and causes anxiety and stress for kids.

The youth subculture is just as guilty of perpetuating confusion and pressure on kids with mixed messages. Our kids are torn between individualism and collectivism on a daily basis. On the one hand, they experience a substantial need for social acceptance among their peers and will do (or ask for) just about anything to fit in. On the other hand, they are taught, by their parents and the society at large, that they are unique individuals whose particular health and development is paramount above all else.

Today's Culture

One could argue today that cultural influence is more intense than ever before in history. Today's culture, with its embedded youth subculture, is so powerful that it has spilled over into how parents make judgments about what is acceptable or unacceptable for their children. The intense and constant pressure kids feel to accelerate socially leads parents to allow their children to engage in activities far beyond their maturity level. The social pressure stems from a narcissistic entitlement fostered by the culture of access and excess. There has been a trickle-down effect with the culture offering exposure to a world of plenty, causing kids to want more, putting pressure on parents to give more. By acquiescing to the cultural demands, parents have contributed to the concept of identity and self-worth being defined by material objects and social belonging. As a result, new norms for childhood experiences are being established.

What is not new are the culturally driven conflicts that people like Leigh and Hy Dayton experience. In fact, Hy's parents disapproved of their interfaith marriage. Other families of previous generations struggled with conflicts over homosexuality, interracial relationships, and even relationships that crossed socioeconomic lines. In other words, conflicts between the old and new values of different generations are nothing new. Every contemporary generation has challenged the social mores of their parents' generation and gradually changed basic social values. Aren't today's kids doing the same thing? In fact, what is happening today is markedly different from the rebellions of past generations.

The present culture clash between parents and their kids is spinning out of control. Today's kids are experiencing too much too soon. The cognitive and emotional limitations associated with the

various stages of development make it impossible for kids to manage all the objects and freedoms they receive when they receive
them. We can use one aspect of sexual behavior as an obvious example of how cultural influences are corrupting child development.

Oral sex has become a status symbol among kids as young as
eleven years old. The attitude toward oral sex has become so casual
that it is no longer associated with adult romantic relationships. It
is just a thing girls do to boys so that each obtains social status.
They don't even consider it sex (as was the view of a past U.S.
president). Twelve-year-olds are having oral sex parties. Boys line
up in what they call "trains" so that a girl performs oral sex when
their turn comes up. A Rainbow Party is where all the girls put on
different colored lipsticks to leave their mark on the boys who are
there to receive favors. And that is just oral sex. Your kids are faced
with so many contemporary cultural norms that challenge their developmental readiness—many of which have been identified
throughout this book. Social acceleration involving having and
doing things before kids are cognitively and emotionally ready negatively impacts development of their moral character, self-esteem,
and value system.

PARENTS AIDING AND ABETTING

Unwittingly, because of their own childhood experiences, Leigh
and Hy contribute to their kids' wanting questionable privileges
and possessions. As a child, Leigh had friends, but she was never
part of the popular crowd. Hy was a shy youngster who only began
to be socially active in college. As a result of their own personal
social insecurities, Leigh and Hy were both sensitive to situations
that potentially jeopardized their children's social status. While
their good parenting sense told them not to allow certain privileges,
their childhood memories often proved more powerful, convincing
them to give in to their kids' requests.

Although Leigh and Hy had the best of intentions by wanting
to spare their children any experiences of social awkwardness, they
essentially did themselves—and their kids—a disservice. It is loving
and noble to want to protect your children from experiencing your
own childhood wounds. But doing so may cause a different set of
problems for your kids. The consequences of being exposed to

things they are not equipped to handle can have very negative immediate consequences and long-term ramifications on their social and emotional development. The immediate consequences have to do with being placed in situations that could be emotionally or even physically hazardous. For example, allowing your fourteen-year-old daughter to ride in a car with older boys who drive has the potential for her to be manipulated emotionally, and it puts her physically at risk. Long-term social and emotional ramifications of being exposed to things they are not equipped to handle occur in terms of low self-esteem, depression and anxiety, and a lack of motivation and ambition. These maladies occur because when kids get things too early, they end up wanting more as they get older. Eventually, they reach a point where it is unreasonable not to get what they want.

Some parents are so enmeshed with their children that they can't separate their own needs from those of their offspring. If you believe that your child's social isolation is a reflection on you, or if you project your own childhood experiences onto him, you will soon compromise your parental objectivity. It is important to learn to separate your own needs and feelings from those of your children. For example, if you are a particularly competitive person, you may push your children to excel in sports beyond their natural abilities, damaging both your relationship with that child and his personal sense of self-esteem. Similarly, just because your parents once embarrassed you by not letting you go to an inappropriate event does not mean that you have to make up for that social wound when you become a parent.

In the Dayton family, this is most apparent with fifteen-year-old Lance, who has a tendency to take a mile when he's given an inch. For many kids, ambition surfaces in the form of wanting more and more as they shatter each age-determined barrier. If they get a TV in their room, they soon ask for digital cable with expanded channels. Once they get digital cable, they ask for HDTV service, and so on. Lance was once granted permission to go to his girlfriend's family lake house. A few weeks after that trip, Lance called from Cathy's year-round home, five minutes before his curfew, asking if he could stay the night, adding, "It's okay with Cathy's parents." When Leigh started to deny his request, Lance retorted, "But you let me stay at her lake house!" Leigh started to doubt her denial and began to weaken, eventually giving in after insisting on talking to Cathy's mother. Although Hy would have been prone to deny Lance this request, Leigh alone was unable to hold her parental ground in this situation, giving Lance fodder for future requests.

SOCIALLY DRIVEN PARENTS AND KIDS

Generation Text children like Lance have a distorted perception of what they should be allowed to do and have. This mistaken idea stems from a combination of exposure to options—all they have to do is look around at their friends, television, Internet, magazines, video games, music lyrics, and advertisements to see what's available—and the strong desire to fit in socially. In most cases, their need for social integration supersedes their own voice of reasoning. Their astonishing requests are motivated by this strong need for social acceptance and by feelings of jealousy, envy, and competitiveness.

Most of Lance, Nina, and Janet's requests are driven by participation in social activities with one or more friends. For Hy and Leigh, the fact that their friends' parents endorse these borderline social activities makes saying no even harder. Keeping your kids away from what has become the norm translates into social exclusion. Parents frequently struggle with the possibility that keeping their kids out of the social loop will result in complete isolation or at least the denial of key friendship-building experiences. The challenge then becomes how to keep your children socially affiliated while maintaining their safety and moral character.

When dealing with jealousy and envy, the discussion becomes murkier still. It becomes more and more difficult to discern between real wants and needs (today's teen going off to college really does need a laptop, rather than a desktop PC, because many schools require that you take notes or log onto the school's wireless network in the classroom) and pure jealousy (such as needing the latest and most expensive laptop because another friend has one). The technological evolution breeds a culture of "better and faster" that pervades our children, who will do almost anything to keep up with their friends.

Finally, there is the motivation of competition. Children are competitive in their own right, but today they want the newest video game, DVD release, *Harry Potter* book, or music download the day (and sometimes the minute) it is available. Today kids think nothing of asking their parents to prepay for movie tickets so that they can be one of the first to see it, or waiting in line at midnight with a tent and provisions so that they can be the first among their friends to own a newly released Wii video game system, iPhone, or Hannah Montana concert tickets.

DETERMINING WHAT IS OKAY

The word *normal* means conforming to a common standard. In that sense, normal is a statistical concept. Wanting to be normal—as in, "But Mom, *everyone* is going!"—is the primary rationalization kids use to appeal to their parents. The first message you need to drive home to your kids is what is right is not always popular and what is popular is not always right. Just because all of their friends are going to a party doesn't mean you *must* allow your child to go. At the same time, you must always be in touch with the cultural changes that have become the norm so that you can form an objective opinion about the appropriateness for your child. Saying no simply because it was not something you did as a child is no longer a valid argument.

Tony, a high school junior, is a perfect example. Tony pleaded with his parents to allow him to take a school trip organized to a state college he was interested in attending upon graduation. When I asked his parents to provide him a reason for their denying his request, they said that they never went to visit colleges in high school and they didn't think such a trip warranted missing a day of school. The fact is, however, that it has now become the norm for kids to visit several college campuses while they decide where to apply. Most of Tony's friends are college-bound and are planning to visit colleges both on school trips as well as with their parents. Tony's parents were preventing their son from attending an event that had significant benefit based solely on the fact that it was something they never did when they were in high school.

When facing these sorts of situations, the first question to pose to yourself is: "Even if it wasn't something I did when I was a child, will there be an appropriate educational, social, or personal benefit to letting my child experience it?" Considering the appropriateness of the present cultural norms is one way to help determine if your child's request is appropriate. But what if you are still not sure? It is easy to doubt yourself, erring on the side of conservatism at the expense of hurting your child. In that case, it is prudent to communicate with several other parents to get their thoughts. Consulting with your peers can shed light on your indecisiveness. More often than not, you will discover that other parents share the same sentiments regarding a specific request. Operating in isolation in a culture that you are vastly unfamiliar with can make it difficult to form an opinion. By discussing the issues with other parents whose children are involved, the decision often becomes clearer.

Strength in numbers is not just for kids. Just as peer pressure informs our kids' "needs," we as parents can stick together to provide a more unified front. Take, for example, Mr. and Mrs. Fernando, whose eleven-year-old daughter Cassie is the youngest child in her grade. Cassie's friends, who all turn twelve almost a full year ahead of her, are just beginning to express an interest in boys. Cassie told her parents that a boy in her class "likes" her, and that she wants to meet him along with two of her friends and their respective "boyfriends" at the local bowling alley. Cassie told her parents that the five other kids involved all had permission from their parents to go. The Fernandos argued with each other and with Cassie, unsure of how liberal they should be. It seemed that they were often the minority among other parents when they wanted to rebuff many of Cassie's requests.

The Fernandos asked me if I thought it was appropriate to allow their eleven-year-old daughter to go on a "date." I suggested that they call two of the other parents involved to discuss the matter. As it turns out, neither of those parents actually gave their kids permission for the bowling alley outing. One mother told her son she would think about it, and the other was hearing about it for the first time from the Fernandos.

Perhaps Cassie and her friends plotted to convince their respective parents that it was a normal thing to do by claiming that other parents had given permission. Or perhaps it was not quite so innocent. One youngster might tell another that she is allowed to do something for fear that she will be ridiculed if her friends know she is not allowed, or even just to look cool. Another possibility is that a child misinterprets a "maybe" or an "I'll think about it" as a "yes." By conferring with the other parents involved, you can assess the situation more objectively and accurately in an effort to determine its appropriateness, increasing your comfort level with granting your child permission or reinforcing your confidence in denying your child the privilege. In the case of the bowling alley group date, the parents banded together and agreed that it was premature to allow eleven- and twelve-year-olds to date. Cassie immediately dropped the issue with her parents once she learned her friends couldn't go either. In a subsequent conversation with her, I sensed that she was actually relieved, although she never admitted it.

Communicating with other parents and taking a unified approach to making these difficult decisions are good first steps. Keeping in mind that what motivates Generation Text kids is the need for social acceptance, jealousy, envy, and competitiveness, there are several other strategies to employ. Asking the following questions will assist you in establishing criteria for meeting your child's social needs while maintaining healthy development:

▶ *Is it safe?* When physical safety crops up as an issue, the decision is usually very clear. Nevertheless, there are times when parents might not see possibilities for danger clearly. Lance Dayton's request to go to New York City raises several safety issues, some of which may be less than obvious to certain parents. First of all, a big city like New York poses certain risks for a naive fifteen-year-old. Driving the relatively long distance with an inexperienced driver is another safety factor. The fact that the driver is someone the Daytons don't even know poses yet another threat. In this case, because his physical safety is in danger, it is easy for the Daytons to justify denying their son's request.

▶ *Does it contradict fundamental morals or values?* Nina Dayton wanted to see an R-rated movie on a school night by having her friend's father circumvent theater policy. Nina rationalized that she had no homework because it was the Monday before Thanksgiving. The Daytons happened to have seen the same movie the night before and didn't feel that its content was inappropriate for Nina, so it was consistent with their morals. However, they did not give consent because by doing so they would have gone against two fundamental values they try to teach their kids: the importance of education, and respect for authority and conformity to rules. If it is okay to evade the R-rated movie policy of no one under seventeen being admitted without an adult, is it then okay to break the law about not serving alcohol to minors?

▶ *Is it financially extravagant?* Janet Dayton wants her own cell phone. Lance wants access to the parents' credit card to purchase clothing. Nina wants a $600 Japanese hair straightening procedure. The Daytons are hardworking and live comfortably but cannot afford to be extravagant. The cost of purchasing a new cell phone for Janet and adding a monthly $40 service bill would be somewhat of a burden. Giving Lance carte blanche to buy clothes without regard for cost or quantity could be financially prohibitive. The extravagance of a semiannual $600 hair treatment is certainly not within their budget.

Parents cannot capitulate to their kids' desires when the monetary demand is discordant with their financial status. We already know that access and excess kids have a distorted view of what they can get because it is so available to them. They generally do not have a good sense of the value of money, so they keep asking. Janet had a hard time realizing how $40 a month could affect the total financial picture for her parents. Putting the cost into perspective for your children by discussing with them how it might affect the family finances is another way to explain your decisions. Here is where a weekly allowance can be very instructive in teaching your child about budgeting with his money. Let's say you give your child a fixed budget allowance of $30 per week. His allowance pays for school lunches costing $15 per week, and the rest is for his going-out money. You can now use his budget to help understand the impact of another monetary drain. He is getting $120 per month, half of which is spent on his school lunch bill. That leaves him $60 per month. Ask him if he would incur the $40 per month mobile phone bill. He certainly has enough to cover it—but what would it do to his going-out money?

▶ *Does it socially accelerate?* How can you possibly know if your child is the right age to engage in an activity or own something? Even after conferring with other parents, the number of variables involved in any one decision may cloud the issue for you and your youngster. Trying to determine whether something is age-appropriate for your child can be quite difficult. You must first ask the questions "Is it safe?" and "Is it legal?" When it comes to the issue of social acceleration, you must also answer the following series of questions to help guide you toward a decision:

▶ What are the risks in allowing your child to do or have what she is asking for?
▶ Is it consistent with your notion of moral behavior for a child her age?
▶ Is it consistent with the values you believe are important for a child her age?
▶ Can your child handle the responsibility?
▶ How will it contribute to your child's educational, social, or emotional growth?
▶ What is her track record? Does your child's general behavior, judgment, and ability to make decisions support giving her permission to do or have what she is asking for?

You need to consider each situation individually by exploring all of the issues prompted by these questions. In the end, if it is still unclear whether your child's request is socially accelerating or age-appropriate, you should not give your permission. If you have to grapple with it that much, it means you are uncomfortable enough with it to go with your gut and say no.

Using the Dayton family, again, as an example, we can explore this approach by looking at several situations they faced and the process of asking a question, analyzing the facts, and deciding on a verdict. As you read through each analysis, try to apply the same thought process to the situations you encounter with your kids.

Situation 1

Question: Should Lance have been allowed to go to his girlfriend's family lake house for the weekend?

Analysis: Lance is fifteen years old and has been dating Cathy for three months. Spending the weekend with Cathy and her family lends too much credibility to the seriousness of this new teenage relationship. Teenage relationships often terminate at the drop of a hat. How uncomfortable would it be for Lance if that happened on Saturday afternoon?

Safety is not the issue in this case because both of Cathy's parents were going to be present the entire weekend. The two issues really had to do with fundamental values and social acceleration. The Daytons realized that spending the weekend with a girlfriend at Lance's age was not consistent with the morals they were trying to teach their kids. Even though they were not sleeping in the same room, spending the weekend together all too closely resembled an adult tryst. The issue of social acceleration was considered by asking themselves the questions regarding the age-appropriateness of Lance's request. They concluded that Lance and Cathy are not emotionally ready to elevate their relationship to the level of spending the weekend together.

Verdict: As the Daytons discussed their thoughts and feelings they came to the conclusion that it was not a wise decision to have allowed Lance to go. They want their children to date a variety of people so that they can learn what they want in a partner and how to avoid or correct mistakes. Having relationship practice places their children in a better position of being able to maintain healthier long-term relationships with life partners as adults. They did not want to encourage a serious, committed relationship at Lance's young age.

Situation 2

Question: Should Nina's parents let her go to the Avril Lavigne concert?

Analysis: Between the two of them, the Daytons have attended about a dozen rock concerts. Neither of them saw a concert before the age of nineteen. Even though they thought Nina was too young to be attending rock concerts, they considered the fact that a parent they knew and trusted was accompanying the girls, and that the artist gives a relatively clean performance.

Verdict: Against their first inclination, based on their own childhood experience, the Daytons decided to allow Nina to go to the concert. Sometimes it is confusing and nerve-racking to go against your ingrained experiences. In this case, the Daytons felt comfortable going outside their comfort zone for several reasons: They knew Nina would be safe with the parent bringing her, for the most part the performance did not promote material that contradicted their morals or values, it wasn't financially extravagant, and they felt that Nina was mature enough to handle it. Sometimes it is difficult to negotiate your own childhood experiences with the norms that are acceptable for kids today. This is when you must leave your comfort zone and allow your kids to participate socially even if your childhood experience was different. Sometimes the change in social mores and norms are actually good for your kids. Using the criteria outlined above will guide you through a decision-making process to help you know when to leave a comfort zone that is based on the world in which you grew up.

Situation 3

Question: Should Janet be able to join her friends at the spa birthday party?

Analysis: The idea of a spa birthday party seemed incredulous to the Daytons (and admittedly, to me, too). This was a tough decision for them. On the one hand, they viewed this party as inappropriate for nine-year-olds. Facials, massages, manicures, and pedicures are luxuries reserved for adults. Were they going to serve champagne with the pizza and pretzels? Clearly, they wanted to say no. But all of Janet's friends were going, as confirmed by several of their parents, and denying her permission would mean that she would be the only one excluded.

Verdict: The Daytons finally came to the conclusion not to allow Janet to attend the party. Despite Janet's tears and pleas, they believed such a party was way out of whack for a girl her age. It was far too inconsistent with their values and socially inappropriate for a girl their daughter's age to allow her to attend. They used this conflict as an opportunity to teach Janet about the true meaning of friendship. Sure, she was missing out on something that all of her friends were doing, but good friends won't judge or shun her for it. Being liked, they explained, is not based on what you have or what you are allowed to do, but on how you treat others. Janet complained that she feels different because she doesn't get to do a lot of things her friends do. This expanded the discussion to the topic of being unique. Teaching Janet that being different doesn't necessarily mean that you are inferior is a key concept in battling negative peer pressure.

DO YOU KNOW YOUR CHILD?

Sometimes the deciding factor is based on having a good understanding of your child's particular strengths and weaknesses. Knowing your child enables you to individualize your decision making. Not only is it a myth that parents should treat each of their children the same way, but it is impossible and inappropriate. Sure, there are basic rules that apply to all of the children in a family, such as no hitting, no name calling, and doing your homework. However, it is difficult to impose the same expectations for your kids due to differences in age, intelligence, social and emotional needs, physical capacity, and personality characteristics.

Irwin and Lisa Brock, for example, have two children: Daniel is twenty and Abby is eighteen. Daniel attends a university far from home and Abby is in her freshman year at a college within two hours' driving distance from her family. Both Daniel and Abby received cars when they got their driver's license at seventeen years of age. The Brocks allowed Abby, the younger of the two children, to take her car to college while Daniel's car sits in their driveway. How can they give a privilege to the younger child and deny it to the older one?

Daniel is an extraordinarily bright, endearing young man. But he is the "absentminded professor" type. Daniel often loses things, doesn't manage his time well, and is poor at attending to the details of life. He is charming and well meaning, and his parents have learned to accept his weakness. Abby, on the other hand, is exceptionally responsible, conscientious, and organized. The Brocks were worried that Daniel, being so far from home, would ignore a mechanical need, forget to pay traffic or parking tickets, or simply not care for the car to optimally maintain its operation and value.

Irwin and Lisa explained the reason for their decision to Daniel. At first, he tried to negotiate with promises to be careful, but his objections were feeble because, as a twenty-year-old, he was able to realize his weakness. His inattention to detail was not a surprise to him. He even made a joke about parking the car somewhere and never being able to find it again. All things being equal with Daniel and Abby Brock, Abby gets the car at school and Daniel doesn't because of his difficulty with attention and responsibility.

Going through the blueprint of questions posed in this chapter to determine the appropriateness of your child's request is sometimes not enough. With each request, parents need to consider the child's readiness in terms of maturation and sense of responsibility. For example, when both Lance and Nina ask for consecutive overnights with their friends, Leigh and Hy decided to grant Lance's request to sleep at his friend's house two nights in a row but deny Nina's request. They did not base that decision on age, but on the fact that when Lance sleeps out, he tends to go to bed at a reasonable hour, comes home in a pleasant mood, and is able to attend to his chores and homework without issue. Nina, on the other hand, stays up to the wee hours of the morning talking, texting, IMing, and surfing the Web with her friends. She comes home in an irritable, grouchy mood induced by sleep deprivation. One sleepover is tolerable, but two in a row would disrupt the whole household.

When it came to sleepovers, Leigh and Hy made the right decision. But of course parents aren't perfect. When they granted Janet permission to have a television in her room a year or two before they had allowed their older children the privilege, the Daytons realized that they had made a mistake. Because Janet exemplifies self-discipline beyond her years, her parents thought she could handle having her own TV. Ironically, Janet started staying up later on school nights because she would secretly watch TV when she was supposed to be in bed with lights out. She kept the TV on while doing homework, so it started to take twice as long as usual. As it turns out, the Daytons misjudged her ability to cope with the privilege and had to remove the television from her room.

Not wanting Janet to feel badly about herself, or to view the removal of the television as a punishment, Hy and Leigh agreed to take the approach that it was their mistake—they were expecting too much from her, and they realized that it was too hard for her to avoid the temptation and distraction of the TV. They apologized to Janet and told her they would try it again in six months to see if she was ready then. Approximately six months later, Janet reminded them of their promise. This time, she made it work. Perhaps it was because she had matured in those six months, or perhaps she simply learned how to handle the mistakes from the first trial. Giving Janet a television was based on her parents' understanding of her capabilities. The decision was revoked when they saw that she really wasn't as ready as they had assumed, and they correctly took responsibility for the mistake.

Once she had the television, Janet wanted to watch certain shows with content that is questionable for her age. Most of her friends watch these shows and they are a frequent topic of discussion at school. Her parents were not crazy about the material, but they allowed her to watch specific shows because, as Hy stated,

"Janet has a good head on her shoulders." She is not impressionable, uses good judgment in social situations, and has a good sense of what is appropriate for her age. If you believe your child can successfully handle a sociocultural norm even though you are adverse to it, setting up contingencies can ensure success. In this case, the Daytons explained that if they felt Janet was being negatively affected by these shows, they would take away permission to watch them. That way, if it turns out that Janet is unable to handle watching these shows, her parents will have minimized the impact by removing the privilege quickly.

ENFORCEABLE PARAMETERS

In Lance Dayton's social circle, shopping for clothes without your mother or father is a rite of passage that most of his friends have reached within the past year. Leigh and Hy never dreamed of asking their parents for credit cards when they were teenagers. Faced with yet another new parenting challenge, they decided that there were several benefits to saying yes to Lance's request: It would communicate a message of confidence in his emerging maturity, help him appreciate the cost of clothing, give him an opportunity to experience an adult responsibility, and help him maintain his social status among his peer group.

Their apprehension had to do with the potential for Lance to lose or abuse the card or make poor decisions. To allay their anxiety, the Daytons gave Lance permission with some clear parameters. They imposed a ceiling on the total amount he could spend. They discussed the specific articles of clothing he could purchase based on need (for example, two shirts, one pair of shorts, and one pair of jeans). He had to keep the card in his wallet at all times and be careful to put it back immediately after each purchase. He could not give the card or the number to anyone other than the store clerk. He could not use the card for any other purchase whatsoever. If he had a question or wanted to deviate from these parameters, he had to call his parents to discuss it. If he was unable to contact them for any reason, he had to forgo his requisition.

Sometimes, as in the case of Lance and the credit card, your child's request has risk along with several benefits. If you can grant permission while maintaining specific limits and boundaries, you can optimize the potential for a safe and successful experience. These situations can even serve to promote healthiness in your kids by way of giving them a sense of responsibility, maturity, and self-esteem.

THE BIG PICTURE

The suggestions and questions outlined in this chapter will help you with the debate over how to balance the wants and needs of your children. Taking into consideration safety issues, morals and values, expense, and social acceleration will undoubtedly guide you to appropriate decisions. Considering the individual needs of your children and creating enforceable parameters once permission is granted will ensure a successful experience. Sometimes parents get bogged down in the dozens of decisions to be made and the minutia of daily living. Here is where you lose perspective, which can negatively affect your judgment to provide your child with an appropriate amount of things and privileges. Take a step back and look at the total picture of your child. Ask yourself the following questions about your son or daughter's overall functioning:

- ▶ Is he generally responsible?
- ▶ What is her level of maturity?
- ▶ Does he usually use good judgment?
- ▶ Is she honest?
- ▶ How does he cope with failure?
- ▶ Does she control her feelings well?
- ▶ What are his social skills like?
- ▶ Does she usually follow the rules?
- ▶ Is he a good judge of character?
- ▶ Do you approve of her friends?

Although the list of helpful questions to consider is virtually endless, the point is that if the general picture of your child is a positive one, you can lean toward broadening your comfort zone. If your perspective of your child leaves you with trepidation about his ability to handle specific situations, then err on the side of denying requests.

Using Lance as an example, his subsequent requests for video games, music downloads, and a trendy watch were all met with approval from his parents. The Daytons decided that their son appreciated and took good care of his things, was performing according to his potential in school, managed his time well, had a good work ethic, and usually followed their rules. It is for these reasons that the Daytons felt comfortable with providing Lance with certain luxuries.

By addressing the questions I've proposed, the doubt you sometimes feel in your own decision-making abilities will fade. Remember to provide your children with an explanation whenever you deny them a request. They need to understand that your motivation is to maintain their health, not to just treat them "like a baby" or to be mean and bossy.

Keeping up with the fads and social trends your kids experience helps you maintain perspective and balance. Use this knowledge to make informed, reasonable decisions, but be careful not to get caught up in a distorted social norm. On the other hand, be careful not to place your child at a social disadvantage because of your antiquated, stuck-in-another-decade mentality.

As your children grow up, you will find yourself taking calculated risks and frequently feeling uncomfortable with your decisions. This is normal and is to be expected. Breaking out of your comfort zone for the sake of socialization and mainstreaming your child may not be easy. As in all good parenting, monitor and evaluate your decisions based on outcome. Use successes and failures to help guide your next decision. Assess your child's friendships. If she is beginning to be excluded socially and is feeling lonely because of your restrictions, reevaluate your attitude toward her social activities. You may be too conservative and need to find a medial balance. On the contrary, if you find your child's behavior, attitude, or values changing in a negative way, you may need to adjust your level of permissiveness.

CHAPTER 9

How to Make Technology Work for You

....

"My brain just works better when I write on my laptop instead of paper."—Jared, age 15

"I was really mad at my parents for making me move. If it wasn't for my cell phone and IMing, I would lose all my friends back in Chicago."—Patty, age 13

"I take care of all of my Webkinz. It's like I'm their mommy."—Carol, age 8

"My kids call me the cool dad because I can help them with their iPods, talk about music, and watch YouTube videos they think are interesting or funny."—Norman, father of Layla, age 14, and Brandon, age 11

THERE IS NO DENYING IT: TECHNOLOGY HAS PERMEATED EVERY AS-pect of our society—from how we talk to one another, to the way we think, to our methods of obtaining knowledge. Kids growing up today simply consider technology an integral part of the cultural landscape. Our children take rapid changes and developments in stride, internalizing new gadgets as quickly as they are introduced.

We have already discussed how technology affects the psychosocial development of Generation Text and how parents can help mitigate the potential hazards they present. Never before did a parenting book have to dedicate so much text to the choice of toys for children. Sure, in the '60's and 70's we scrutinized the use of toy guns as a cause of aggression in children, and studied the psychological effects of excessive television viewing. But toy guns and television have been relatively easy for parents to control. As technology became the "toy" of choice for young children, parents quickly realized that it was more difficult to monitor and control. In this chapter, we'll face the fact that while unchecked technology can be dangerous to the well-being and mental health of your child, computers, cell phones, multimedia devices, telecommunications, and the Web are not just a fad and they are not going away. Trying to deny this reality, or avoiding it, or trying to insulate your kids from it, is useless. Instead, we need to find ways to emphasize the positive aspects of technology and use them to our advantage as we help our children navigate into adulthood. As the old saying goes, "If you can't beat 'em, join 'em."

Although our kids have seemingly limitless access to information at the touch of a button, no computer can ever replace your role as a parent. You are still the robust, primary teacher and role model for your children, and the wisdom of your lessons holds considerable sway over cyber-technology, telecommunications, and mass media. That said, with so much advanced technology at our fingertips, it only makes sense to use it to your advantage. Let the technology that is such an integral part of your kids' lives help you teach them crucial life lessons.

It is important to keep in mind the benefits technology presents. In the quotes above, Norman, the cool dad, has made a conscious decision to use the access and excess subculture as a means to connect with his two children. Jared's laptop helps him be a better, more creative writer. Patty is able to soften the resentment she feels when her parents move her to a new city by staying connected with her friends via the Internet and cell phone, which help her cope with her feelings of loss. Carol is able to express nurturing feelings in a caring relationship with her cyber-doll. These are just several examples of ways technology can be used for good and productive means.

THE IMPORTANCE OF TECHNOLOGY IN LEARNING

I once worked with a high school student who was severely learning disabled. Because of his significant disability, Antoine's IQ measured in the borderline mentally disabled range, even though his true intrinsic intellectual ability was much higher. The odds were stacked against Antoine achieving academic success, and when he entered high school, his guidance counselor began programming him in a non–college prep course of study. Antoine would have no part of that. He wanted to go to college. Antoine worked diligently to compensate for his learning deficiency, and he realized his goal. For Antoine, motivation was critical to success—without it, he might have accepted his guidance counselor's assessment and lived a less fulfilling life.

Antoine exemplifies the power of motivation in the learning process. Getting kids motivated is the key to successful growth. Most teachers and parents find it difficult to motivate kids when there is a lack of interest. When children are engaged in learning, their motivation increases and their learning curve improves dramatically. Electronic, high-tech gadgets are fantastic mechanisms that entertain, engage, and motivate kids. Generation Text is compelled to use any device that has buttons and a screen. They seem to have a natural attraction to the mesmerizing colors, flashy animations, and intriguing sounds emanating from that particular compilation of memory chips and processors. Since they are a completely captivated audience, why not use technology as an instrument of motivation to help our kids develop family values, positive self-esteem, and a decent work ethic, and to enhance their social, cognitive, and educational skills?

The first, very important step in using technological advancements to enrich our kids' lives is to believe that such a thing is possible. To create this mind-set, parents need to let go of their fear that all those electronic, Internet-connected gadgets only have the ability to harm and endanger their kids. Like most innovations and discoveries, technology has the potential to be a weapon or a tool, and a big part of how your children look at this subject has to do with your own attitude.

Many parents feel intimidated by technological advances—whether it is a new device or a new feature added to a familiar device. Your kids adapt instantly whereas you usually experience a learning curve until you feel comfortable with it. Until you reach that comfort level, anxiety is associated with the new technology, which could cause you to have a negative reaction to a potentially positive contribution to your child's growth. If you see computers,

PDAs, iPods, cell phones, or video game consoles only as toxic to your kids, their advantages will never be realized. They are not just word processing, mathematical calculating, high-tech entertainment toys. They are instruments to expand your kids' minds. Harnessing the power of what is available to your kids, and channeling it properly, may actually help these kids become the most informed, well-adjusted generation ever.

Chapter 2 discussed passive parenting (reacting to access and excess issues as your kids present them, rather than bringing them up ahead of time) and the negative impact it can have on identity formation. Making technology and the culture work for you requires active parenting. You must familiarize yourself with what is available to your kids and what the culture offers them if you want to minimize the negative effects of the generation crater. Yet another reason to stay on the cutting edge is that the more you understand, the more you will be able to help your child reap the benefits of technology. It is wise to not only maintain current knowledge of new technology and its applications, but to also stay on top of what your kids are doing on the Internet, whether it is the latest download craze or watching popular YouTube videos. It is not just about fighting off the evils. It is about facilitating your child's growth so that she becomes a happy, healthy adult.

CASE STUDY: DARA AND HER MOTHER

Although Kate kept both eyes on the newspaper she was only theoretically reading, both her ears were glued to her daughter's telephone conversation. Kate, the recently divorced mother of fifteen-year-old Dara, could not decide which was more astonishing: her daughter using the land line in the kitchen instead of her cell phone, or talking to her boyfriend within earshot of her mother. ". . . I can't—I have to get off the phone. I have homework to do. . . . I can't do it later. I have to watch this TV documentary on the migration of sea lions for bio, and it's coming on in a few minutes."

Dara's assignment was to watch a scheduled documentary on Stellar sea lions, write a two-page summary of the show, and then to make note cards and present the information to the class. The latter part of the assignment bothered Dara, because she did not feel comfortable standing up in front of people. With her daughter's self-consciousness in mind, Kate asked Dara if she would like to do a run-through with her once she was done. One hour after the broadcast, Dara surfaced from the family room with her report in one hand and note cards in the other. Kate listened to the presentation and then made some gentle suggestions based on the fact that Dara tended to stumble over her words and also needed more interesting information.

To find more detailed and comprehensive information about the social behavior and migration patterns of Stellar sea lions, Kate and Dara headed back to the computer in the family room and performed several Internet searches. They found an abundance of terrific articles on the migration patterns of sea lions but very little on their social behavior. Although Dara's usual inclination was to give up, Kate thought of different keywords to search, and they began to find the sort of information they'd been looking for. Once they started finding the right kind of information, Dara thought to try a different search engine, which also proved to be helpful.

At the end of their research time, Dara had collected material for a sophisticated written report and a comprehensive oral presentation. But there was still the issue of public speaking. Kate recalled a recent PowerPoint presentation Dara did for her U.S. history class. Because she did so well on that assignment, Kate suggested that she do something similar for this project instead of using note cards. Dara took her mother's idea and ran with it, embedding an audio recording she made into each slide in the presentation. If she didn't like the way each WAV file sounded, she simply rerecorded it until she got it right. Each slide containing a prerecorded explanation would reduce Dara's oral presentation to interjections and additions. When the PowerPoint presentation was complete, she rehearsed again with her mother, this time simply running the program and providing minimal ad lib interjections. Her confidence, enthusiasm, and knowledge of the material had clearly brought the quality of the assignment and presentation to the next level. Dara, with the help of her mother and technology, turned a mediocre performance into a stellar report worthy of the Stellar sea lion.

This story illustrates several general strategies you can use to capitalize on the benefits of the access and excess available to your children.

1. The first thing Kate did was to *make technology available* to her daughter. Making technology available enables kids to use the positive power it has to offer. In Dara's case, the family computer is located in an easily accessible, easily monitored room, and it is properly set up with hardware and software that are conducive for educational purposes (specifically, a word processing program, a multimedia presentation program, and an audio mixer with an external microphone).

2. Not only did Kate make this technology available, but she was able to *demonstrate appropriate use of the technology available* (in this case, for effective problem solving and acquisition of useful information).

3. Beyond having the technology readily available for positive use, Kate made the effort to astutely *observe and listen* to Dara. Without glaringly eavesdropping on her phone conversation, Kate was nonetheless tuned into her daughter so that she was aware of the assignment and was able to assist her in getting the most out of it. Obviously, it's hard to be involved in your children's activities when you don't actually know what they are doing. When you do become aware of activities, through careful listening and noninvasive involvement, you can provide your child with the wisdom of your life experience and advice.

4. Kate took advantage of an opportunity to *seize the moment* with Dara. Many parents feel that they are too tired at the end of the day to spend a few hours helping a child with a homework assignment. Because Dara has been less than receptive to her assistance in recent times, Kate could have easily chosen to leave Dara alone and focus on the many other things she needed to get done around the house before going to bed. But Kate pushed herself to offer assistance to Dara instead, with great results.

5. Because Kate demonstrated she could *master the technology* herself, it not only impressed Dara—a teenager who might easily consider her parents clueless—but it gave Kate credibility. Working as a team, they pooled their tech skills and research strategies and created a cohesive, productive experience. In turn, Dara was able to resist distractions and learn more about her topic. Kate's working knowledge of technology and encouragement to *investigate and explore* provided Dara with valuable academic help; it also enhanced

their relationship in another way, giving Dara much needed emotional support at a time when she is struggling with her parents' divorce. Each moment a parent has to demonstrate support and positive attention brings the relationship that much closer.

6. By choosing to *capitalize on the full power of the technology,* Kate addressed an issue she has with her daughter. Dara often has mediocre expectations for herself. Consequently, she tends to be satisfied with efforts she considers "good enough." Kate was able to motivate Dara to take an average piece of work and bring it to the next level by using technology to create a spark in her daughter, energizing and motivating her to improve her paper and presentation. As a result of the excellent grade and positive feedback she received on the project, her self-esteem improved greatly.

7. Finally, Kate had a good understanding of her daughter's needs and was able to *use technology to compensate for weakness.* Understanding Dara's anxiety about oral presentations, Kate suggested the use of PowerPoint. Most technological innovations help make life easier for people. They can also help kids compensate for the skills they lack. Kids who have fine motor problems can learn efficient keyboarding so that their written work is printed. Shy kids can make easier social contacts using text messaging, instant messaging, and e-mail. Skillful gamers can display their prowess to other kids when they are not particularly athletically inclined.

To summarize, in one single interaction between Dara and her mother, we learn several ways parents can harness the power of available technology to improve their lives and the lives of their children:

- ► Make technology available and demonstrate its appropriate use.
- ► Listen to and observe your child.
- ► Seize the moment to offer help to your child.
- ► Develop a working knowledge or even mastery of technology.
- ► Investigate and explore ideas with your child.
- ► Capitalize on the full power of technology.
- ► Use technology as a means to compensate for your child's weaknesses.

TAKING CONTROL OF TECHNOLOGY

To use the power of technology to enhance your child's life, you must maintain an up-to-date working knowledge of technology and maintain control of it. Constantly changing technology makes it easy to lose control over your child's exposure to the inappropriate aspects of access and excess.

Would you buy a Rukamat for your kitchen? How about a Systream Balting to attach to your shower nozzle? Do you even know what these products are? If not, chances are you wouldn't buy them until you had a better understanding of what they were and how you could benefit from them. Buying software for your children is no different. Although many parents buy computer and video game software based on their child's desire to have them and nothing else, selecting software for your kids necessitates scrutiny. Understanding the content and moral messages of any given game or program will help you assess the age-appropriateness of the software so you can choose software that will entertain them without introducing unsuitable messages.

There are many ways to become educated about appropriate software that will help your child grow cognitively and socially. First, ask around. Ask your child's teacher what is being used in the classroom. Talk to other parents who have children of the same age to see what they buy and allow in their homes. Find a competent tech person in a local computer or gaming store to rely on for software descriptions. Read reviews written by professionals and other parents on websites such as Superkids.com and Geocities.com, and consult educational organizations that critique computer and gaming software.

Next, always check the Entertainment Software Rating Board (ESRB) rating on the packaging. The various ratings include:

EC	Early Childhood
E	Everyone
E10+	Everyone 10 and over
T	Teens
M	Mature
AO	Adults Only (18+)
RP	"Rating Pending"

In addition to the actual rating, a description of why the game received the rating can be helpful. For example, a game rated "T" (Teens) may have earned its rating due to language as opposed to sex or violence, influencing your decision about the game's acceptability. Video game ratings and content descriptors can be found at the ESRB website (www.esrb.org/ratings/ratings_guide.jsp).

Be aware that the rating alone may not make the software appropriate for your child, and so it must not be used as your sole judging criteria. Your values and moral criteria may not be commensurate with the ESRB. Reading the back of the package will give you more information about the software, and additional information can be obtained from ESRB.org, but the best thing you can do is to preview the software yourself. Just like you might watch a DVD before showing it to your kids, you can make sure that various software programs are appropriate by experiencing them firsthand.

Software needs to be continually evaluated for its usefulness and appropriateness. Children often master the program to the point where it becomes mindless play for them, defeating the purpose of the software. Even when it is purely entertainment, if they are playing the game repetitively it has an aimlessly mesmerizing effect on them. Parents also need to continually evaluate the manner in which their children are using software. Generation Text kids have a way of taking an educational game and reducing it to a level of inappropriateness. Eight-year-old Sammie plays a shopping game that helps reinforce basic math computation and money concepts. The game involves dressing up a model, and she often dresses the model in a seductive manner. Matthew plays a word game to increase vocabulary and fiendishly inserts inappropriate words to be defined.

Scrutinizing video game purchases is needed for all children and teenagers, but it is especially important for younger kids, or those thirteen years old and under. The "cool" games tend to be the most inappropriate for this age group. When selecting computer or video game software for young children, consider the following criteria:

▶ *Open-Ended Play.* You want games that will facilitate your child's experimentation with thoughts and problem solving. When a game challenges your child to use cognitive skills such as analytical thinking and deductive reasoning, it can be mind-expanding. Solving mysteries and figuring things out is not only fun, but it builds strategy skills needed for academic success. Games that involve shooting the enemy, fighting, and overcoming obstacles to advance to the next level simply reinforce the instant gratification button and do not enhance thinking skills.

▶ *Ability to Control the Cadence of the Game and Level of Difficulty.* Particularly for younger children, make sure the game is within their cognitive and visual and motor skill capabilities if you want to avoid frustration. Many games allow the user to proceed at their own pace as opposed to constantly trying to keep pace with the game.

▶ *Immediate Feedback and the Ability to Keep Your Child's Attention.* Although you don't want to reinforce the immediate gratification button too much, young kids especially cannot realistically wait too long before the game provides them with feedback regarding their actions. They will become bored and will then want to play action-packed games, such as shooter games, that are inappropriate for their age.

▶ *Emphasis on Values Consistent with Your Own.* By reading game reviews, determining the ESRB rating, talking to other parents, watching demos, and examining the back of the box, you can determine if the messages in the game are contrary to the values you are trying to instill in your child. For example, look for how women are treated and if laws are broken. Does the game involve indiscriminate aggression? Does the game involve trickery and deception?

▶ *Promotion of Appropriate Socialization.* Try to find games that allow two or more players to enhance social interaction. Some games involve cooperative teamwork with your kids playing against the computer as opposed to against each other.

▶ *Sensitivity to Cultural, Racial, Gender, and Individual Diversity.* Be careful not to purchase games that stereotype women or ethnic and racial minorities.

▶ *Verbal or Visual Directions.* Most games designed for young children do not require the child to read written directions. If the game does not have verbal or visual directions, it may not be appropriate for your child's age group.

▶ *Attractive Video and Audio Elements.* Most recently released entertainment games are able to entice kids with state-of-the-art graphics. Making sure the graphics are attractive is more important when presenting your kids with educational games.

▶ *Positive Reinforcement.* Whether educational or purely for fun, video game play is an activity that can contribute or diminish your child's self-esteem. Make sure the game incorporates feedback that strokes your child's ego and helps your child feel empowered to learn. Some games simply inform the players when they fail or make an error. You want your child playing a game that actually communicates or even celebrates accomplishments. This translates into increased motivation to learn new things.

▶ *Quality Entertainment That Invites the Use of Imagination, Sense of Humor, and Exploration.* Young children enjoy fantasy and laughter. When a video game facilitates the use of their imagination and makes them laugh, it can be both entertaining and mind-expanding.

Obviously, teenagers will want to pick out their own games instead of having you choose them. Still, you need to scrutinize teen-directed games as well for open-ended play, values consistent with your own, and sensitivity to cultural, gender, racial, and ethnic diversity. The need for attention to the violence, stereotyping, and lack of respect for authority (and people in general) is particularly important whether the game is for younger children or teenagers.

Technology provides an opportunity to promote the development of many important areas in your child's life, including family relationships, self-esteem, personal growth, work ethic, social relationships, cognitive development, and education. In the following sections, we will discuss how to maximize your relationship to technology so that you can take advantage of these positive associations.

FAMILY RELATIONSHIPS

Friends, boyfriends and girlfriends, coworkers, and sometimes even spouses come and go, but for better or for worse, family is forever. You will always be someone's child, sibling, parent, or grandparent. The quality of those primary relationships varies, but their status is such that they always remain as the most intrinsic, automatic, and important relationships you have in your life. And parents must work hard at solidifying the family connections, despite their emotional nature.

There is a great fear among mental health professionals that today's cyber-kids will develop into isolated and socially inept adults because of their excessive contact with machines and lack of face-to-face human interactions. The technological explosion catapulted by the public availability of the Internet in the mid-1990s, the pervasive use of cell phones and cable and satellite television, and the video game craze, all have the potential to create disconnection for society at large but also among family members. For Generation Text, this means that parents and children can be separated by many layers of technological "insulation." Excessive amounts of time spent texting, IMing, surfing the Internet, watching television, and playing video games can easily begin to replace time spent with family members. In some ways, technology facilitates contact among family members when they are away from one another, but it is far too easy for kids to maintain a private life away from family members.

The good news is that these same technologies can also be used to facilitate family connections. If you wanted to have a conversation with your child, but she was in her bedroom with the door closed, what would you do? Presumably, you would knock on the door—an obvious barrier to a productive conversation—and then enter the room. Technology, like the bedroom door, can be a barrier between parents and their children. But like a door, removing technology would not be realistic or even smart. You have to enter the world of technology, just as you would enter through the bedroom door, to connect with your child. Connecting with kids using their preferred means to communicate, such as calling or texting them on their cell phone, will open the door of communication. Doing so allows you to speak their language and enter their comfort zone, a key means of getting through to them when they are experiencing the most egocentric developmental period of their lives. As with most things, children are more receptive to your involvement when you enter their world, as opposed to being asked to join yours.

The Smith family learned this lesson when it came to resolving a case of sibling rivalry. Adam, six, loves his new Nintendo Wii video game system. He is not as crazy about his four-year-old sister, Brooke, who he tends to bully, annoy, and tease at every opportunity. The Smiths have made many attempts to help Adam overcome his feelings of displacement and competition with his sister, but nothing seemed to work. When I met Adam, he presented as a charming, sweet youngster. His parents report that he is well liked by his peers and is very sensitive to the feelings of other people. But despite his natural capacity for kindness, Adam refused to direct such positive attention to Brooke. Finally, Mr. Smith came up with the idea of using Adam's video game skills to help him overcome his sibling rivalry.

Brooke, who looks up to her big brother, wants to emulate him and play the Wii. She observes Adam making all sorts of quirky arm motions and having fun as he plays, and she imitates him with the controllers when he is not around. The Smiths decided to present Adam with the idea for a new game. While Brooke played with an unconnected set of Wii controllers on the couch, he could hide behind the couch and use the set that was actually connected to the game, controlling the characters. Young Brooke, of course, would have fun no matter what, but especially as she began to think that she was actually "playing" the game. At first, Adam reveled in the cunning deviousness of this game, as if he was tricking his sister. But after a short while of experiencing Brooke's smiles and giggles, he quickly realized how much fun she was having as a direct result of his actions. This led to some of Adam's first expressions of positive feelings toward Brooke and loving interactions with her.

SOCIAL RELATIONSHIPS

Virtually any object or situation a child encounters can be used to practice social skills. Technology is no exception, and for Generation Text kids it is the optimum medium for developing and honing interpersonal skills from the time they are very young. Our children willingly use computers and video games in their play with peers because they enjoy playing and working with the technology so much. Social interactions, even if they happen in front of a computer or television screen, are a valuable way to facilitate friendships, to learn how to deal with issues of competition, negotiation, sharing, taking turns, cooperation, and talking to one another. Just as sports may have been the primary vehicle of social exchange for ten-year-olds in the past, video game play is a genuine play activity in the new millennium and should only be discouraged when it is used to avoid other activities such as homework and chores.

Similarly, the Internet, when monitored properly, provides a world of social connections for Generation Text kids, who are able to meet all kinds of peers online without fear of rejection. Message boards, buddy lists, chat rooms, and themed special interest groups are available even once you install safety and security controls. Kids can take advantage of these forums to expand their social networks and practice interpersonal skills. Unlike face-to-face interactions, cyber-relationships allow children to carefully express their thoughts in words and edit them as necessary before the other child receives them. In this way, they can experiment with different ways to greet people, ask questions, assert themselves, and respond to others pensively with the ability to reflect before sending.

Social networking sites such as MySpace.com and Facebook .com are only growing in popularity and will continue to be a major interest for teens in particular. On these sites, kids can keep up with the latest events, get invited to parties, and maintain relationships. For many children, spending time on these sites has replaced the need to hang out in malls, pizza parlors, and pool halls. Spending a few hours on Facebook may actually be safer than those old-fashioned activities—namely because it means your children are at home where you can supervise them and keep them safe from unwanted contacts.

Beyond social networking sites, other websites and computer software such as The Coolien Challenge and SocialImpactGames .com promote a more meaningful dialogue between kids. The Coolien Challenge is a computer game that engages kids using all kinds of multimedia visual, audio, animation, and user interactive bells and whistles, while promoting nonviolence and social conflict resolution. The game glamorizes harmonious and peaceful attitudes as "cool" and prestigious. SocialImpactGames.com is a website that identifies hundreds of "serious" games. In gamer language, serious games promote social consciousness, values clarification, and mores instead of simply entertaining kids. Several websites, such as FreeArcade.com, AddictingGames.com, and Braingle.com host a slew of games that when played with peers promote cooperation and group problem solving. When you see your children accessing these kinds of games and websites, it is important to guide them as to how they can use the technology to play cooperatively with siblings and peers. Sit down with your child and discuss the particular site or events occurring in the software, and how that may help him learn to consider other people's feelings and the impact he has on others. Eventually, you want your child to be internally guided by a solid moral code and an empathetic orientation to others in social situations even when you are not present. Using technology is just another means of accomplishing that goal.

SELF-ESTEEM AND PERSONAL GROWTH

As parents, we place our child-rearing efforts on promoting positive self-esteem and personal growth. When used properly, technology can be a helpful tool for enhancing your child's feelings about himself, while also opening him up to areas of development to which he might not otherwise be exposed. Many computer programs provide immediate and positive feedback to children. Characters in educational and serious computer games (and some entertainment games) don't communicate mistakes in tones of annoyance, condescension, or anger. Instead, they acknowledge errors in a pleasant, couched manner that protects the child's sense of self-worth. Of course, when the child gives a correct answer or excels in the game, the software's programmed response is more dramatic and enthusiastic, but no matter how they perform, children obtain constant positive feedback throughout these games.

The concept of "levels" in video games is another tremendous pedagogic tool. As they move from one level to the next, children can readily relate to their progress. The kids in my office are frequently announcing with a sense of pride: *"I'm on the fifth level of Mario Cart!"* or *"I beat the boss in Spider-Man!"* or *"I went from novice to expert in one week!"* This approach not only strokes their budding egos, building their sense of competence, but it gives them status among their peers. I once worked with a seventeen-year-old who had difficulty connecting with peers until he became the first documented individual to beat a popular video game. His name appeared in a major gaming magazine and he has had friends ever since. As parents, it is important to recognize what these games mean to your child and to find ways to praise their efforts when they announce their accomplishments to you. Just as you would proudly clip a newspaper article about an award your child won or a goal he scored in the school soccer game, make an effort to

Google your child's name to see, for example, if your son or daughter has been featured in an online posting of the school honor's roll, or as a participant in a school charity or sporting event or spelling bee contest, or as a poetry reader in a school event.

Technology can also be used to facilitate identity formation in Generation Text kids and to foster their self-expression and creativity. Virtual magazine sites such as Kaneva.com, which are often free, accessible, and interactive, enable kids to contribute their own thoughts and ideas to the site. These sites are structured as a forum for preteens and teens dealing with youth issues, interests, and information. They provide opportunities for self-expression in an emotionally safe environment. There are also countless websites that cultivate the particular interest of a child whether it be reptiles, music, drama, sports, or dinosaurs.

Independence is yet another skill that can be practiced through technology. Being able to initiate and complete a task without adult assistance contributes to a child's sense of autonomy, and this certainly happens with great frequency in the world of access and excess. I remember that when my son was very young, he needed my help to solve each quest in the (now ancient) educational computer game called *Where in the World Is Carmen Sandiego?* One evening when I returned home from work I found a note left on my desk:

Dear Dad,
      Good news. I don't need your help with Carmen anymore. I was able to figure it out by myself.

                                             Love, Dan

Once I recovered from the blow to my own ego—my son didn't need me anymore!—I was able to recognize that his newfound independence was a big step for Dan, who was gaining self-confidence every time he played this game.

CULTURAL DIVERSITY

As discussed before, computers and the Internet have certainly made the global community much smaller and more accessible today than it ever has been before. This is apt because today's generation of children, more than any other past generation, needs to be sensitized to cultural diversities in our ever-expanding global community.

Before you can use technology to help expand your children's exposure to various cultures, you must instill in them an acceptance of people from other countries and other ethnic, racial, or religious backgrounds. Next, when choosing various software programs and games, make sure that they include many different kinds of characters and avoid stereotypes and negative connotations. Additionally, these programs need to reflect the real world as we want it to be, free of gender and racial bias and representing people of varying competencies as well as alternative family constellations. Unfortunately, the majority of popular games and programs do not reflect these important social messages. The idea is to make sure you incorporate as many of the ones that do into your child's library of software and games.

Another new way to enhance a child's exposure to cultural diversity is to have them take cyber field trips. Under your direction, let your child explore websites based in different countries to gain exposure to a variety of languages, cultural rituals, dress, and cuisine. Assuming your child responds well to these field trips, encourage her to meet and correspond with "pen pals" from around the world. Virtual pen pals, offered by sites such as Kids.com, create relationships between children from every corner of the earth. Over time, these relationships will result in a vast pool of knowledge about different cultures and life experiences.

WORK ETHIC

We have already discussed how technological advancements have made it easier for kids to get what they want without much effort. However, being able to get what you want doesn't automatically create a sense of entitlement. Take, for example, the children of Donald and Ivana Trump, who certainly never wanted for anything in their lives, but still worked conscientiously in high school, got into some of the most competitive colleges, and then earned respect by working diligently in the Trump companies. Work ethic, as the saying goes, is "not getting what you want, it's wanting what you've got."

Your children's cherished devices and gadgets can be used as a means of learning how to care for their possessions, promoting a sense of appreciation for belongings and a willingness to work to maintain those belongings. Posting a sign next to the family computer reminding kids not to bring food, drinks, or magnets nearby is one way to teach kids how to care for their things, as is asking them to clean the keyboard and screen properly and regularly.

When it comes to cell phones and video game controllers, you can teach valuable lessons about responsibility by refusing to replace lost items unconditionally. Mrs. Cortez, for example, complains about her daughter Anna's lack of work ethic in school. Meanwhile, Anna has had two cell phones end up in the laundry and has broken three PlayStation 3 controllers in the past year, all of which her parents have replaced. Although the Cortezes can easily afford to buy new phones and controllers, they are cheating their daughter of the opportunity to learn about taking care of her belongings. Ideally, Anna should have been told that in order to replace the cell phones and controllers, she would have to earn the money to pay for them by doing chores, saving her allowance, or working a part-time job. Surely, if she had to put in that kind of effort to raise the money, she would be more careful about washing her phones along with her jeans.

Having a good work ethic involves budgeting time and understanding monetary limitations. Cell phones are excellent tools to use in teaching both these skills. Many kids regularly go over their monthly allotment of minutes talking to and texting their friends. Oftentimes, the parent delivers nothing more than a verbal reprimand and a request to be more careful the next month. Still more often, parents grit their teeth and pay the bill, accepting the additional cost silently. Still others call the service provider and change their plan so that they are allotted more minutes per month, increasing the monthly fee. Rather than accept or encourage this behavior, ask your children to find a way to pay for the overage charges, or simply take away the phone when they have used up the number of minutes allowed.

Taking this concept one step further, simulation software such as the Sim City series, Karma Tycoon, and Roller Coaster Tycoon requires users to adhere to good business practices and a positive work ethic. These programs have kids building and running roller coasters, amusement parks, a variety of businesses, and even whole cities. The games help kids practice decision making, budgeting of time and money, marketing strategies, attention to detail, and the concept that hard work reaps rewards.

Finally, technology offers an avenue for the entrepreneurial child to put her ideas into action. Generation Text kids have the advantage of knowing how to use the computer and Internet to institute their ideas and make them a reality using programming skills, Web design talent, and virtually anything wireless technology has to offer. Four very ambitious university students are the perfect example. Justin Goldman, Chris Jeffrey, David Laiderman, and Jason Kwicien saw the need to create a fast-food ordering service for all of the local town eateries college kids frequent. The result was Lionsmenu.com, a website that allows their fellow Penn State students to order from their favorite restaurants using online menus and have it delivered right to their dorm. My own son, along with a close college friend, recently started Ignighter.com, a website that combines social networking with in-person group dating.

COGNITIVE DEVELOPMENT

Cognition relates to thoughts—conceptual, ideational, and analytical—and acquisition of knowledge, and it is a key to your child's academic success. Cognitive functioning also relates to the learning processes, also known as *perceptual functioning*. Children use auditory and visual perception skills as their primary learning channels. They learn by hearing information and by viewing visual stimuli.

The Generation Text child lives in a world so stimulating that it cannot help but contribute to cognitive development. Almost anywhere you turn there is a button or a gadget or a technological device that challenges the child cognitively; the potential for this generation to be great thinkers correlates directly to this technology. As technology continues to evolve at a rapid pace, so will our children's ability to keep pace with it and understand its workings. As parents, we need to provide our kids with the materials and guidance they need to use their cognitive abilities to the fullest potential.

Some cognitive development occurs naturally as children perform daily, routine interactions with the machines in their lives. For this reason, I advocate the use of computer and video games that stimulate both the visual and auditory perceptual learning modalities. As your child responds to the sights and sounds that jump off the screen, she has to receive, process, and respond to them—in a split second. Video games allow your child to be contemplative and to practice skills such as planning, analyzing information, predicting, understanding cause-and-effect relationships, using flexible thinking, long-term memory, short-term memory, fluidity of thought, and reading. Interestingly, IQ tests judge how children perform at those very same skills to assess a child's innate intelligence. Even the Air Force and Navy train their fighter pilots using simulators that are essentially expensive, complicated video games.

Most educational computer software teaches kids to use their investigative skills; role-playing and challenge games in particular require the use of analytical thinking and problem-solving skills and the ability to formulate conclusions. The games also teach them to organize complex material, to consider what it might mean, and to recognize conceptual patterns. Development of hand-eye coordination and attention span are further benefits of providing your kids with appropriate games and software.

Multitasking has become a necessary skill in our complex, fast-paced society, and Generation Text excels in this area. Their ability to operate and coordinate the sensory input from multiple devices at the same time is uncanny. I can barely walk and talk on my cell phone at the same time, whereas kids tend to thrive on doing three or four things at once.

Some kids, like thirteen-year-old Jessica, manage to do their homework while watching television, listening to their iPod, and instant messaging on their laptop. Although Jessica's parents were dismayed by this behavior and tried many times to take away at least some of the distractions, Jessica argued that she actually worked better when she had the TV, the iPod, and the laptop turned on. To her, they are not distractions, but ways to stay on task. For example, she finds that she is better able to focus when there is some background noise in the room. Although it goes against logic and traditional educational principles, it makes sense for Generation Text. Because she has grown up with constant multisensory input, a lack of stimulation is disorienting and distracting. With music or television playing in the background, Jessica is able to focus on her work without daydreaming.

Parents who bring home premature babies often experience something similar: After several weeks of living in the neonatal intensive car unit, with the constant beeping of monitors, nurses bustling about, bright florescent lights overhead, and dozens of other babies crying, these newborns often have difficulty sleeping in a quiet, dark nursery at home. Their parents find that it is better to leave a television on for the baby, or simply to put the baby to sleep in the living room in the middle of the family's action.

EDUCATIONAL ADVANTAGES

Nowadays, a computer is as common in the American classroom as blackboards, chalk, and bookcases have been for decades. Although computers were once used as supplemental instructional aids, they are now central to our children's education. Many private schools and some public schools even provide their students with laptops for the duration of the school year. Classrooms are now being equipped with Smart Boards, an interactive instructional aid that combines computer and digital projection technology. In addition, the Internet has all but replaced the reference section of the school library. Because the Internet-connected computer has become so integral to the learning process, it behooves you to expound on its use as an educational tool at home.

The Internet is filled with educational sites and games that invite kids to learn. Your child, more than likely, will be able to show you how to access these sites. I encourage parents to sit down and let their children demonstrate how to use these sites and play the games. For example, on Elementeo.com, you can play a child-oriented chemistry game that was developed by a thirteen-year-old.

When learning to use the Internet as an educational tool, one of the most important things to remember is that Generation Text kids are great at learning passively, and they are used to being entertained. Your job as a parent is to transform them into active learners who seek out thought-provoking and interesting information on the Internet. Encouraging your kids to take control over their learning will help them develop a passion for particular subjects, a skill that will certainly help them in the age of specialization. Once your child knows what she is passionate about, help her find relevant newsgroups and appropriate message boards on the subject and encourage her to make her own contributions to the discussion. Often, you can spark this kind of passion just by discussing the games and software your children use on a daily basis. Kids love to talk about technology, so if a particular game makes use of an historic or current political or world issue, encourage your child to engage in an intellectual, high-level discussion on the subject. For example, the *Medal of Honor* video game series (rated T) closely follows the events of major international conflicts such as WWII. *Viking: The Battle for Asgard* (rated T) is also a first-person shooter game with violence, but it is rooted in Norse mythology.

Once you begin to see how well your child responds to this technology, you can find ways to combat one of the most divisive family issues around: incomplete homework. Parents are often frustrated when they learn how often their kids do only part of their homework assignment or forget the assignment altogether. Poor organizational skills are usually the culprit in these cases: Kids forget to write the assignment down, are unclear about the requirements, don't bring home the necessary books or papers, and can't remember if the assignment is due the next day or by Friday. Technology has rescued many a student from this dilemma. Appealing handheld schedulers and planners encourage kids to enter the information they need to complete their homework properly. Most modern cell phones have features like voice memo, alarms, reminders, calendars, and scheduling capacity. Encourage your child to use these features and to develop a system of organization using their phones, PDAs, and computers. Next, remind kids that fax machines, image scanners, and e-mail can also be used to send a missing document from one child's home to another, preventing an incomplete assignment. Although it may be hard to believe, some teachers also make themselves available to their students via e-mail, so that kids can contact them with questions while they do their homework.

Not only will technology help your children, but it will also enable you to stay involved in their education. School websites that post important dates and events, and systems that give parents usernames and passwords in order to access their child's school records, are making your job of overseeing education easier every day.

TECHNOLOGY AND MEDIA: PARENTS' HELPERS

Although it is by nature passive, watching television together is a valid family activity. Maximize that opportunity by choosing to watch appropriate family programming together and then discussing with your kids the moral themes those shows present. Without preaching, ask your kids what they think about the behavior of the show's characters or the storyline presented. When the program presents mature themes such as sexual overtones, violence, and illegal activities, it is not only important to discuss them openly, but to brainstorm about alternative ways to deal with these issues. You can prompt similar discussions about inappropriate messages in commercials, Internet pop-up ads, magazine advertising, and billboards. These discussions should reinforce your family values, as well as make your children better consumers, once you explain to them how commercial packaging and emotional appeal can interfere with good judgment. It is amazing how many moral and character-building issues one can find in a single TV commercial. Try watching them with your child, looking for messages about honesty, integrity, individuality, uniqueness of identity, and work ethic. Chances are, you will have great opportunities to emphasize the importance of these character-building traits. Be on the lookout, too, for advertisements communicating material that needs further explanation from you, such as prescription psychotropic and erectile dysfunction medicines.

Beyond television and other forms of mass media, video games can also aid in developing parenting skills. In the case of Adam and Brooke, their parents used a video game to facilitate a positive sibling relationship by elevating Adam's status as an adept Wii player to help his little sister feel good about herself.

You can help build stronger family connections in general by purchasing and using games that the whole family can play together, such as versions of TV game shows or sports-related games. Teaming parents with kids fosters companionship, and it is also a way to open up discussions of competition, winning, losing, and playing just for fun. For fifteen-year-old Billel, a video game enabled him to develop a relationship with his first cousin who lives in faraway Singapore. Both boys love the same particular game, and despite the time difference in their home countries, they tend to play together online every week, talking via the software they have both installed. In this way, the cousins have formed an extremely close relationship even though they live halfway around the world from one another.

When Mara, the nanny who cared for seven-year-old Joey since he was a baby, needed to return to Ecuador to care for her aging mother, Joey experienced serious feelings of loss. Despondent about her absence, Joey moped around the house and looked at pictures of Mara. His mother, Lena, decided to send Mara a webcam so that she and Joey could speak over the Internet and actually see one another in real time. Once Joey was able to communicate with Mara in Ecuador, he was better able to deal with the separation.

Other parents have confirmed that helping their kids facilitate a sense of connectedness with family members via technology has done wonders for their relationships. Not only can cell phones and online messaging minimize the physical distance between two people, but they can also help to foster various relationships. For example, don't use your child's cell phone exclusively as a way to tell her to come home or to check up on her whereabouts when she is out. It is just as important to call her just to say hello, having a light and chatty conversation. Family social networking groups are another wonderful way to maintain a sense of belonging when family members live far away. On these sites, family events, individual accomplishments, and even hardships can be shared despite geographic distance.

It is a good idea to let your children teach you about the different programs and sites they are using. Find out how they use the computer, which applications they find helpful, and which ones they think will help you. Let them show you how they log onto the Internet and where they go to access their favorite sites. This accomplishes several things simultaneously: It allows the child to feel that he has something valuable to share with you, enhancing his self-esteem; it conveys the message that you support his activities and are interested in them; and it also helps you monitor his online activities in a nonthreatening way. When you spend the time connecting with your child via the computer, you send the message that technology is not a closed door to your relationship. Rather than letting the computer become a barrier leading to familial isolation and emotional disconnection, use the computer to communicate with your child.

Undoubtedly, you will be amazed at how adept your child is at navigating through cyberspace—so don't miss the opportunity to praise her skills and bolster her self-confidence. Rather than simply letting your child program your new cell phone (since she does it so much faster than you ever will, and without reading the instruction manual), ask her to teach you how to do it. The idea is that technology can be used to create opportunities to communicate and bond with your child.

Of course, you can and should also use technology to help you when the time comes for punishment. Parents have taken away television privileges as a punishment for their kids for decades. Computers, video games, and cell phones, all meaningful privileges to Generation Text kids, can be used in the same manner today, just as effectively. However, when removing cell phone, computer, or video game privileges, be careful not to punish yourself in the process. When your parents took away television, they were removing a simple leisure-time activity. Now that technology permeates virtually every aspect of life, kids need it to do basic tasks such as completing their homework and staying in touch with their parents. For that reason, it is important to decipher which kinds of technology can or should be taken away in order to effectively teach the child a lesson, while allowing modern life to continue unhindered.

PARENTS AS GATEKEEPERS

During my years of clinical training, I was fortunate to have had a mentor who was at the top of his field. Of all of the valuable lessons he taught me, though, the one I remember most often is: "Don't let your practice run you. Make sure you run your practice." The same advice applies to parents and technology. Don't let technology run you. Make sure you always run the technology. If you recognize and heed this warning, you will be better able to stay in control of the technology that is at your child's fingertips. Remember, as a parent, you are the gatekeeper and you decide what enters your home and what stays out. Parents alone should determine how technology is integrated into family life.

For example, it has always been a good idea to know where your kids are going, and with whom, and how they are getting there. With the advent of Global Positioning Systems (GPS), parents can now literally track their kids if they choose to. When remote parenting is a necessity, GPS helps ease parental concern by allowing you to determine the exact location of your child, either via a website or an alert transmitted to your office or cell phone. Of course, using

GPS to keep tabs on your kids is controversial in terms of privacy issues. Should you really be able to know where your child is at every moment? Until what age is that appropriate? Despite those questions, the fact remains that if your kids are being honest about their whereabouts, they have no reason to worry about being tracked. Even our cars have GPS-based tracking devices in case of emergency or theft. When my kids were in college I got a sense of how they were spending their time by glancing at the date and time stamping of their monthly cell phone and automated toll bills. My daughter was surprised when I asked her why she was talking on the phone at 2:00 A.M. on a night before a 9:00 A.M. class. Today, as the technology has advanced, our abilities as long-distance parents have increased.

The bottom line is that with all technology has to offer, it would be difficult for Generation Text kids not to constantly assimilate new information, make better social connections, or learn more about themselves and the world. No matter how involved you choose to be in these matters, your children will be expanding their knowledge and experiencing personal growth from incidental use of various technologies. With your intervention and concentrated effort, your kids will be better prepared to realize the magnitude of technology's power and to use that power in a productive way, and you will learn valuable lessons about the world they live in along the way. As much as Generation Text kids live and thrive while being bombarded with magical, multisensory electronic input, nothing replaces the influence of a parent.

CHAPTER 10

Integrating the Old and New

··

Regaining Control

REMEMBER BOBBY AND JAKE, THE TWO TEENAGERS FROM TWO DIF-
ferent eras in Chapter 1? By now, we have discussed many of the
ways in which Bobby's world of the 1960s differs from Jake's contemporary world. We've also come to realize that both boys are
more alike than we might at first assume. Although they face different circumstances and challenges, Bobby and Jake are at heart two
boys with similar goals, feelings, and adolescent experiences.

Today we tend to idolize childhoods like Bobby's and to assume
that something is missing or lost for kids like Jake, who are growing
up as part of Generation Text. Two things are wrong with this assumption. First, we cannot make sweeping generalizations about
entire generations. Not all kids who grew up in the 1960s experienced wholesome family values, had great work ethics, and became
adults with exemplary social skills. Not all Generation Text kids
have distorted identities, gratification issues, poor work ethics, and
negligible relationship skills. Second, returning to the values and
culture of the "good old days" at this juncture is neither possible
nor prudent. We may need to work on reviving some of those old-
fashioned values and ethics, but we shouldn't discard the rich cultural advantages that our high-tech age offers. Instead, our goal
should be to integrate elements of both traditional and contemporary culture to the best of our ability.

My hope is that this book has given you new ways to cope with
the constant wave of inventions and concepts that the ever-changing
techno-social culture throws at you. By integrating the parenting
tips discussed throughout this book into your own family, you will
doubtless discover your own personal ideas about how to manage

and capitalize on the power of technology and the unbelievable cultural opportunities available to your children. One thing is certain—standing by your old parenting styles exclusively will result in losing out to the hazards of access and excess.

Since both traditional and contemporary culture (and the values associated with them) have healthy offerings, we should encourage our children to engage in both. This may be difficult for Generation Text kids, due to the powerful influence of the culture and peer pressure. Most children and teenagers are not secure enough with themselves to resist the pressure of pop culture and risk social rejection by rebuffing the latest fad. In the following essay, seventeen-year-old Margot Kotler discusses her conflicts as she struggles to integrate her appreciation for classical culture and pop culture:

The Renaissance Child

By Margot Kotler (age 17)

"This is the strangest mix of pop and classical music I have ever seen," a friend once commented while browsing through my iTunes library. "It is so weird." It must have surprised her that I had both Mozart and Kanye West on the same playlist, or that I even listened to Mozart. However, I believe that my cultural milieu, characterized by a bizarre compromise between two separate worlds, is a consequence of living in a society where there is such a heavy emphasis on popular culture.

The culture that I experience regularly is based on a series of contradictions; I exist in two radically different worlds. I sometimes read Brontë, Woolf, and Nietzsche in my spare time because I have a passion for literature and philosophy, but I also have popular culture interests. I find myself watching *Access Hollywood, My Super Sweet Sixteen,* and *The Fabulous Life of Paris Hilton* more often than I would like to admit. These interests are all part of my cultural environment, and they should therefore be treated equally—right? Who is to say that one should prefer George Eliot to Missy Elliott, Nietzsche's Superman to our comic book hero, and Jane Eyre to her modern counterpart, Ugly Betty? Even if these two distinct realms are not equal, if one is art and one is not, I do not have to choose between the two. Susan Sontag once wrote, "If I had to choose between the Doors and Dostoyevsky, then—of course—I'd choose Dostoyevsky. But do I have to choose?" I merely see simultaneity in my experiences of pleasure;

I think it is possible to have many kinds of experiences and maintain a hierarchical sense of values.

. . . [O]ne cannot resist the allure of the media; if I do not hear about Lindsay Lohan's latest stay in rehab on television, I will see it on the computer. I think that we must accept a balance between the two extremes if we are to function in our society.

The struggle Margot experiences between the old and the new is very apparent. She feels a tug, perhaps even tremendous pressure that pop culture places on her to remain in today's enticing cultural environment and ignore the offerings of a previous era. Margot embraces the best of previous cultural offerings, whereas most Generation Text kids don't even notice them because they are too wrapped up in the hottest new whatever or whomever. Margot's conflict between the old and new is not limited to literature, media, and pop culture. The notion expands to the clash between old and new norms for social behavior, values, and attitudes. The point is that in order to help your kids to grow up well adjusted, you need to restore and emphasize the positive core values from previous generations while taking advantage of the positive aspects of today's culture. Margot poignantly surmises that integrating the old and new in a healthy balance is the best solution.

Margot's insightful perspective continues in her essay, addressing the excess she experiences in her life:

My family owns six televisions and four computers, even though there are only four of us; I have no choice but to be exposed to the media—it surrounds me constantly. For people who have only one television, or only watch television to see the news, succumbing to the media is still inevitable. Anyone who does not know who Brad, Angelina, Nick, Jessica, Paris, and Nicole are, without the last names, is either lying or does not own a television. My parents have a friend who does not own a television; he claims that watching one is like "sitting in a room with a screaming five-year-old." I understand the basis of his rationale, but it is unrealistic to not own a television. Also, it is futile because popular culture already has an iron grip on us, whether we own a television or not.

Again, Margot feels the "iron grip" of the cultural demands and offerings. It is inescapable for her, as it is for your kids. You cannot ignore the pervasive impact of technological access and cultural excess that your kids experience every waking moment of every day. It is all your kids know. It behooves you to make sure they are exposed to educational, social, and moral information beyond their passive ingestion of Internet, media, and peer messages. Margot writes:

> Living in today's society, where it is more difficult to find educational entertainment than mindless amusement, and by being part of my generation, I am obliged to watch television and use the computer. While my only option may be to accept popular culture, I can have other interests as well, even if I cannot shield myself from perpetual exposure to the media. However, this is quite depressing, to know that popular culture is a constant, unavoidable part of my life, which I must pay attention to, whether I want to or not. From my bleak outlook, the media is everywhere, and I know that I cannot escape—it is on the news, on the computer, on the radio, and in the newspaper. I can only hope that my environment, where, despite my compulsory attraction to popular culture, I am edging toward complacency and bordering on cultural malaise, does not begin to resemble 1984.

Margot is on the right track with her desires to have an appreciation for the old and new.

Many parents I know wish their kids felt more like Margot; that is, they wish their teenagers desired to connect with anything outside of pop culture. Parents of Generation Text kids often feel like their children are slowly but surely slipping away from their control and influence. The television and computer seem like an extra set of parents, and time spent on cell phones and the Internet threaten to replace family time altogether.

But, as Margot points out, exposure to pop culture is inevitable, and it has a powerful pull on Generation Text. Without making any concerted effort, they see what is out there and available. More often than not, when they ask or demand to have the newest things, their parents acquiesce. When this happens, it becomes difficult to know who is shaping whose behavior, because today's kids have the ability and power to control their own environment more than ever before.

When dealing with the significant issues facing your Generation Text son or daughter, the first thing you must do is to accept that technology can enhance your child's growth in positive ways. Next, realize that only if you take back control of your child's environment—including the distractions, machines, and cultural forces that neutralize and contradict your values and philosophy—will you be able to effectively combat the negative aspects of those same technologies. To find this balance and integrate traditional values with contemporary opportunities, I suggest following what I call "the Ten Commandments of contemporary parenting."

RULE 1. EMPHASIZE THE IMPORTANCE OF FAMILY

People are social animals. We long to belong, and belonging to a family unit is the most powerful connection your children will ever feel. The family provides us with a sense of belonging that overshadows our seeming need to join athletic teams, social groups, political parties, or Internet cliques. Perpetually working on developing a strong, cohesive sense of family—an unbridled connection and love for one another—will eventually eclipse any external force that challenges your fundamental values.

Most of us can recall going through phases of closeness and alienation in our families. The good news is that while most adolescents tend to stray from their families at some point in time, that phase is usually temporary. No matter how far removed your child may seem to be from you, if his sense of belonging to the family is thoroughly ingrained, he will inevitably return. I tell parents all the time that the evidence of their good parenting will not be apparent until much later in a child's life than they might like. Kids don't automatically become adults when they turn eighteen or twenty-one; only when they finally move out of your home after high school or college and enter the real world do they start sounding like you. When your son starts a family of his own and remarks that when he opens his mouth he swears he hears you talking, then you will know that your job has been done well. When that happens, you can be assured that your family's values and morals have been ingrained to such an extent that they are being passed on to the next generation. When that happens, you will realize that they were actually listening all those years.

RULE 2. DEMONSTRATE UNCONDITIONAL LOVE AND BALANCE

It is important to create a climate of unconditional love, protection, honesty, and respect within your family. Your children need to feel loved, respected, and accepted regardless of their behavior or expression of identity. Don't confuse respect and acceptance with permission to act or dress as they please. Let them know that you always love them, even if you are angry, disappointed, or disapproving of their behavior. If they experience unconditional love and acceptance for who they are, your children are more likely to come to you in time of need. Combine this climate of unconditional love and acceptance with balance and the family bond will strengthen.

You need to achieve balance in a number of areas. There's the balance between time spent as a family, with your spouse, at work, with each child, with your friends, and with yourself. Attending to all these pieces of the pie will contribute to healthy family relationships in which no one feels suffocated or detached.

You want to seek a balance between being a child-centered family and a parent-focused family. The concept of the child-centered family can be an effective way to boost your child's sense of importance and self-esteem. To avoid giving too much empowerment to your kids, however, be sure to create a balance between the amount of energy and money you spend on them and how much you spend on yourselves as parents. Balancing your decision making so that it meets the needs of all family members will help your child cope with delay and denial of need gratification.

Balance also applies to developing a well-rounded child. Help your child develop competence in all areas of life by promoting social, intellectual, academic, artistic, athletic, and musical endeavors.

Teach respect. Communicate and demonstrate the priority of treating others with respect, including respect for bodies, feelings, time, and possessions. Valuing *who* people are instead of *what* they have will suppress your child's superficial, materialistic temptations.

RULE 3. CONSCIOUSLY DEFINE FUNDAMENTAL VALUES

Consciously define the fundamental values a child needs in order to grow into a healthy adult. Never assume that your kids are "getting it" when it comes to the basic values you want them to learn. Actively teach them by pointing out and explaining behaviors and interactions, using teachable moments with yourself, your child, and others as examples. For example, if your twelve-year-old dishes off a pass to his teammate on a fast brake in his basketball game instead of taking the shot himself, let him know that it was a very unselfish thing to do. Saying, "Good pass!" is not enough. Or, if your daughter sticks up for a close friend, let her know that her loyalty and commitment to that friendship is admirable. Those values will guide you and your family through the ups and downs of the high-tech, culturally demanding world. Emphasizing and never letting go of your basic values enables your kids to take full advantage of the power of technology and all that today's culture offers, without losing sight of the bigger picture.

RULE 4. CONSTANTLY REEVALUATE NORMALCY

Parenting is a conscious, contemplative endeavor. It means not giving in to the same pressures your kids face, and being careful about what you allow to become "normal" in your family. Every once in a while, find a way to step back and gain the perspective you need to stay calm and maintain objectivity, creating your own idea of normalcy for *your* family. Know yourself, being careful not to make parenting decisions based on inadequacies or voids in your own childhood, and know your kids and their specific needs and vulnerabilities. Finally, never be afraid to discuss any topic with your children, even the most embarrassing and sensitive ones.

It is quite easy to be swept up in cultural normalcy. Once a lot of kids start doing something, it becomes the thing to do. There is an underlying feeling that it is okay to go along with something simply because most people are doing it. Once something is commonplace, it becomes what is expected. Try to remain objective and make sure that what your kid's friends are doing is commensurate with what you deem as appropriate for your child.

RULE 5. PRACTICE ACTIVE PARENTING

The need for active parenting was discussed at the very beginning of this book. It is very easy to become wrapped up in the trials and tribulations of daily life. Many parents who are trying to keep their heads above water, juggling time and money, become passive in their parenting. These parents are loving and provide everything their kids need and want. But they are not actively and proactively involved in helping their kids navigate through the access and excess issues that kids face every day. Typically, passive parenting results in damage control instead of prevention of negative situations.

The more you are available to your children, the more likely you will be able to take advantage of teachable moments. Your strong presence avows your love and attention and helps you meet your children's emotional needs and thwart the power of negative external influences within the techno-social culture. An active parental presence puts you in the position of stimulating emergent creative talents and moral development. Sitting down to discuss what your child is doing on the Internet or watching on television or in movies should become as common as tossing a ball back and forth in the yard.

RULE 6. MODEL BEHAVIOR CONSISTENT WITH MORAL CHARACTER

"Do as I do" is a credo that will have a great deal of power and influence in developing well-adjusted kids with high moral character. The model you present to your kids should demonstrate that you adhere to the same moral traits you preach to your kids. As your children get older it becomes very evident that they emulate many of your mannerisms, facial expressions, voice intonations, and certainly your values, attitudes, and morals. They will surprise you because even when you think they are not paying attention, you discover that they really are picking up even your most subtle traits. It is for this reason that you not only have to pay close attention to your kids' behavior, but you must monitor your own behavior as well. This entails having an awareness of how you portray yourself to your children and others, including your personality traits, your strengths and weaknesses, and your limitations.

If your credo is "Do as I say, not as I do," your kids will become wise to it sooner than you think. So it is best to exhibit a model of moral character from the time they are toddlers. Remember, behavior communicates messages far more fervently than words.

RULE 7. KEEP PACE WITH THE TECHNOLOGY AND YOUTH CULTURE

Remember *The Jetsons*? George, Jane, Judy, and Elroy, and of course their robot housekeeper Rosie and dog Astro. They dominated children's cartoons in the 1960s and then again in the 1980s. They lived far in the future, driving flying saucers and living in homes suspended high in the air and running with incredible efficiency. Rosie could do just about anything in a matter of seconds, and the refrigerator and oven, among other appliances, were easily manipulated with voice-activated commands. I can remember watching this cartoon with my children and wondering if a life like this might actually one day be possible.

Today, we sometimes seem to be closer to the Jetsons lifestyle than ever before. The technological evolution is unfolding at such a rapid pace that nothing seems completely out of the realm of possibility. And although most scientists are limited to thinking no further than three to five years into the future, those of us who experience the benefits of their inventions can certainly dream up endless future possibilities. As science and technology become increasingly complex and available, the best we can do is to try to anticipate general trends and stay alert, both as consumers and as parents of future consumers. Keeping pace with "whatever they think of next" will help you maintain your edge over machines when it comes to influencing your children. Keeping up with technology will also help you get a bead on changes within the youth subculture because it often dictates the new norm for your kids.

Being complacent about the impact technology and culture have on your kids is risky and dangerous. After all, your kids readily adapt to what is new and popular, inculcating it into their lives with ease. Just when you think you have a handle on what they are up to, they are discarding it for the new "in" gadget, hairstyle, video game, or Web adventure. If you are lagging behind in the discussion, you are sure to fall behind in your parenting as well. What happened to Robert, father of sixteen-year-old Hayley, can be rather typical of parents who feel like they are always behind the "technological eight ball."

Robert and Hayley frequently go jogging together. Robert found their time together to be important in maintaining their relationship as well as promoting good health and fitness, and he wanted to spend those hours talking with Hayley about her life. Hayley, however, always brought her iPod on the run and preferred listening to music to talking with her dad. When Robert asked her not to bring the iPod, Hayley objected, stating that she needed music to run and preferred not to talk. Besides, she argued, just spending the time together was enough.

At my suggestion, Robert adopted the "if you can't beat 'em, join 'em" strategy. He started to fiddle with Hayley's iPod, with the goal of learning how to use the gadget before buying one for himself, because then he could use music and technology as a way to connect with Hayley on their runs. Eventually, Robert proudly mastered the iPod, learning how to download songs from the Internet, place them on the MP3 player, and arrange them in playlists. But just when he was about to buy his own iPod, he noticed that Hayley stopped bringing hers on their runs, grabbing her cell phone instead. Annoyed, Robert assumed that Hayley was now planning to talk to her friends while they ran together, but Hayley explained that her new cell phone had a music feature that allowed her to listen to her songs on it. She offered to give him her old iPod, since she no longer needed it.

Robert found this experience to be understandably frustrating. He had spent time and effort learning how to use the iPod, only to be one-upped by the pace of technological inventions. He was certainly on the right track, even though cell phone technology outpaced him. While it may be frustrating, the reality for parents like Robert is that it is no longer enough to rely on your present knowledge and previous experiences. Today's parents need to re-tool continuously when it comes to understanding new technology and cultural fads if they are to have any hope of keeping up with their kids.

For Robert, identifying and preparing for possible new trends will become part of his proactive parenting. Keeping one step ahead of the technological and cultural demands, instead of always playing catch-up, will help him realize the potential for growth and usefulness inherent in new technologies.

Keeping pace with what is new in technology and what your kids are into will undoubtedly increase your chances of raising kids who are physically safe and emotionally healthy. Because technology is constantly providing more ways for kids to display their personal lives for all to see, and because kids sometimes engage in questionable behavior, it also falls on your shoulders to maintain knowledge of potential legal issues associated with the technology your child uses. To stay informed, you must have discussions with other parents; regularly access news reports provided by broadcast, Internet, and literary media; periodically check free information websites such as www.TechnologyLawUpdate.com and www.soft warefreedom.org (the Software Freedom Law Center); and attend seminars offered by local police departments (usually sponsored by your local school system).

RULE 8. ESTABLISH AND MAINTAIN APPROPRIATE LIMITS

Your children need limits and boundaries. Without them, the world becomes a scary and unsafe place for them. It is disconcerting to realize that Generation Text kids have the ability for limitless access to the world. It is also worrisome that the fast-paced, competitive, socially accelerated culture constantly pushes appropriate parameters for your kids. Considering the technological and cultural strain on boundaries for Generation Text kids, it is even more imperative that parents establish and maintain limits.

In Chapter 6, and throughout most of the book, I strongly advocate the establishment of limits as early as possible for your children. Habituation and normalcy will work for your kids in a positive way if they get used to having parameters imposed on them. Once they understand that there are definitive limits to what they are allowed to do and have, there will be less of a chance that they will wander off into risky places. You will also decrease the chance that they will ask for things excessively. Establishing and maintaining limits eventually transforms into your kids having self-discipline, positive self-esteem, a good work ethic, and respect for themselves and authority.

RULE 9. WORK TOWARD A HEALTHY BALANCE

There is no doubt that your kids are growing up in a world of plenty. The more they see, the more they want. They experience social pressure to engage in activities that you would never even dream of doing. This can all lead up to distorted values, poor attitudes, and a lack of healthy perspective. If you want to avert raising a self-entitled, high-risk, "you can't tell me what to do, I want it now" child that the access and excess culture begs to breed, then you must consistently create a healthy balance in your child's life.

Working toward a healthy balance means constantly evaluating what and how much you are providing for your child. Maintaining a healthy balance entails distinguishing the difference between wants and needs. It requires an examination of social expectations and an assessment of your child's readiness to meet them. Strike a balance between what you permit your children to do, and what things and privileges you deny them. Staying on an even keel and maintaining a healthy balance will help your child see the world with a healthy perspective.

RULE 10. USE THE GENERATION TEXT CULTURE TO BENEFIT YOUR CHILD

I have repeatedly warned of the deleterious effects the culture of technological access and material excess can have on your children. By now, you have certainly realized that by following the numerous suggestions and strategies outlined in this book, you have a good chance of mitigating the perils of growing up in today's high-tech age. Managing the culture is not enough to raise well-adjusted kids. You must take advantage of all it has to offer in terms of intellectual and psychological growth. You can even transform potentially negative exposure to Internet, media, or peer influence into a positive growth experience for your child. In other words, even if your kids are bombarded with messages contrary to the values you are trying to promote, by following my guidelines you can use these inappropriate messages to teach your kids a better way.

The information age is there for the taking. Providing your kids with supervised access to unbelievable amounts of important information will help Generation Text become a very well-informed generation. Being careful not to promote excess and wasteful consumerism, you need to keep your kids equipped with enough technology to keep them socially mainstreamed and educationally advantaged.

Fifteen-year-old Rebecca is a perfect example of how antiquated technological access creates a social and academic abyss between the haves and the have-nots. Rebecca tragically lost both of her parents at a very young age. She lives with her grandmother, who is on a fixed-income budget. Rebecca is an extremely bright and diligent student. She also works part time in a local pharmacy. Rebecca spends her money judiciously on clothing, trying to blend in as best she can with her middle-class peers. Her technological "arsenal," which consists of a four-year-old cell phone with a basic service plan, a six-year-old computer without Internet access, and a first-generation generic brand MP3 player, is a far cry from what her fully equipped, state-of-the-art peers have at their disposal.

Rebecca often has homework assignments requiring Internet access. Fortunately, she lives downtown and in walking distance to the public library. However, Rebecca also has to use her Internet access judiciously due to time limitations. Unlike her peers, she doesn't have the luxury of routinely surfing the Net and expanding her horizons. Her limited Internet access has an immediate impact on specific assignments and a long-term impact on her cognitive growth. Rebecca is at a disadvantage because of the limited amount of time and attention she is able to put into completing academic assignments. She cannot leisurely surf the Web and access mind-expanding information, but she is also hampered socially. Rebecca is not a member of a social networking site and doesn't have an e-mail address. She experiences obvious social disadvantages because of her economic status, missing out on the highly active cyber-social life occurring through e-mail, instant messaging, and texting. Her cell phone has text capabilities (a primary means of communication among Generation Text), but she cannot use the feature because her plan charges extra for it. She even has to closely monitor her cell phone minutes in fear of exceeding her plan limits. Her ability to keep up with the latest music, clothing, and rumor mills is close to impossible due to her lack of technological access. Rebecca is hindered, and will continue to be socially and educationally impaired, because of her inability to keep pace with technology. Because Rebecca has a tremendous work ethic and drive to achieve, she will probably be able to attain moderate social and vocational success. However, she runs the risk of not reaching her social or academic potential due to her limited ability to take advantage of the rich culture that is just beyond her reach.

Rebecca is unique in that she has limited economic and parental resources due to the loss of both her parents. However, she is an illustration of how difficult it is for your children, too, if they can't keep pace with their peers. You must enable your kids to take full, appropriate advantage of all Generation Text culture has to offer. To that end, it is important that you keep your kids wired with the technology that will enable them to grow cognitively, educationally, and personally, to the extent that you can afford to do so. This doesn't mean that to be a good parent you must buy your child every new gadget that is displayed in your local electronics store. Instead, try to provide your children with the right kind of innovations so that they are not placed at a disadvantage.

TAKE BACK THE POWER

The overriding feeling from the parents with whom I work is that they are losing control of their children. Just as Alice in Wonderland was drawn into the looking glass, Generation Text kids are immersed in their cell phones, Internet, television, and video games. And they are enamored by the sociocultural temptations of the day. By now, you have realized that you cannot stop technological evolution and you aren't going to change what is available in your kids' social world. Sex, drugs, and the plethora of inappropriate messages that challenge your idea of what is appropriate for your children will be there for the offering—whether you like it or not. But the flip side is that this same world that harbors hazards to your children's healthy development also provides them the richest access to information and social experiences that may yield a generation of the most resplendent thinkers with the most robust emotional experiences. For this to occur, you, as Generation Text parents, must collectively and consciously regain control of the access and excess culture and corral it. Using all the strategies outlined in this book, reel it in so that your kids can integrate solid, old-world values and behavioral conduct with all the positive aspects the new world of access has to offer, while taking full advantage of the tremendous social activities available to your kids. Use the excess that is available to help them grow socially and emotionally in a way that they become more humane and experience healthy, fulfilling relationships.

Taking the power back means not allowing yourself or your children to slip into a debilitating dependence on technology or succumb to negative cultural influence. Ultimately, though, your power and influence over your children is limited. The best you can do is to teach and show them as much as you can while you can, and then trust that they will make sound decisions as they embark on their own. If you work to take back the power from the hazards of the high-tech, instant-everything world, you will equip your kids with the tools they need to take what it offers them and become part of what may be the most talented generation ever.

FINAL THOUGHTS: YOU CAN MAKE THEM GREAT

The possibilities for the future are literally endless. We have already seen such remarkable progress in the last twenty years that it is easy to picture the seemingly impossible becoming realities. No matter what shape or form it takes, the future of technology will certainly continue to affect the values, attitudes, behavior, and psychological development of our children and grandchildren. Always remember that you are the most powerful source of psychological impact on your child. Maintaining a loving, communicative relationship is quintessential to parenting a new generation that has unbridled access to the world. Your active presence and guidance will equip your child with the potential to thwart the perils and capitalize on the assets. It usually takes a long time to observe the evidence of your good parenting, but by heeding my advice, you will see that your role in your children's life will eventually dwarf the negative influence of technology and culture. This will happen if you keep a pulse on the inevitably changing technology and cultural variables.

Because of this inevitability, preparing for the future of parenting is imperative despite the difficulties it presents. Maintaining control and balance over new technology while being careful not to stifle its benefits to your children is in order. Present and future parenting means keeping an open mind, staying abreast, and embracing newfangled innovations. Try to be one step ahead of your kids, or at least walk side-by-side with them.

Scientists will continue to influence our culture and its impact on the psychological development of our children. The technology race is so fiercely competitive that it has the potential to be reckless. Whether scientists are motivated by good intentions to benefit humankind or by fame and greed, they hold the power to influence vulnerable children, and so the release of new technology needs to be executed responsibly. Parents must be diligent in scrutinizing new inventions in order to protect and maintain the values that are important to their families.

Maintaining control and making sound decisions about what technological innovations your child owns, how her technology use is monitored, and the social privileges granted will prevent your family from becoming victims of whatever comes next. By taking the time to understand the function and broad capabilities of new technology, you will be commanders of the new age, rather than its casualties. No matter how a product is marketed, it is always up to you as the parent to filter how and when it is used by your kids, or whether it should be used at all. At the end of the day, parents who understand how to meet the emotional needs of their children will always override the influence of machines and the compelling attractions of the child's social world.

You have the ability to help your child grow up to be a remarkable adult. Being a parent is the most important job anyone can undertake. As proud as I am to have helped countless families in my work as a psychologist, my biggest joy derives from my job as a parent to my three children. With all my formal degrees, my phenomenal training by the most talented mentors, and thirty-plus years of experience working in mental health, my most valuable training has been provided by my own children. That is my final message to you, as a parent. Using your children as teachers and as a purpose, learn how to express love and caring for one another. Be respectful and honest in your relationships. Always act with integrity and humility. Accept your children and others for who they are, not what they achieve or own. Allow your children to elevate you to a higher standard so that they can do the same for themselves and, in turn, their children. Do these things and you will transform Generation Text into Generation Best.

Index